3"02

בס"ד

There is no such thing as coincidence...

and other stories of Divine Providence

BARUCH LEV

HAMODIA PUBLISHING

FELDHEIM PUBLISHERS
JERUSALEM · NEW YORK

The stories were edited for this publication by Deena Nataf

First published 2003

Copyright © 2003 by Baruch Lev

ISBN 1-58330-615-3

FELDHEIM PUBLISHERS
POB 35002 / Jerusalem, Israel

208 Airport Executive Park
Nanuet, NY 10954

www.feldheim.com

Printed in Israel

Introduction

The Holy One, Blessed is He, said, "Who will inform (*modia*) My children of these miracles?"...The well flowed down into the valley...and Israel saw, and sang a song [of thanksgiving].

(RASHI, BEMIDBAR 21:16)

THANK YOU, HASHEM, for the skill You have afforded, for the gift of writing You have granted, and for the ideas You have planted, in the head of one of the lowly members of Your Chosen People.

Thank You, Hashem, for the power You have placed in our mouths so that we may tell Your wonders and recount Your miracles every hour of every day, in every situation.

Thank You, Hashem, for the enormous response these stories generated, and for the readers who have transmitted the message of faith borne by these stories to their children and students and others, with the purpose of augmenting the glory of Heaven.

Thank You, Hashem, for opening our eyes to see the goodness concealed in Your world. Where we once saw distress, we will now see consolation, and it is this consolation that will afford Your children the strength to go about their daily lives.

I thank You, Hashem, for You are the Father of all ideas, Father of skills and abilities, Performer of wonders. Everything stems from You.

Thank You, Hashem, for the prayer you have placed in our mouths. Please take these prayers, accept them, and answer them. Do not conceal Your Face from us, for You are our God, there is no other like You, and our existence depends upon You.

Let us raise our eyes heavenward and be aware that we are fortunate! We, the children of Hashem, know that He is good and merciful. Let us try to really feel that, so that we may leave the world of

xi

darkness and pain — the world of *galus*, and enter a world of faith and great wonders — the world of *geulah*.

Let us thank Him and glorify Him and repeat His wonders forever and ever.

Thank You, Hashem!!

The author would like to thank the many people who have sent the stories featured in this book.

To the entire staff at the Hebrew and English *Hamodia* newspapers who have invested so much effort in publicizing the material — may Hashem amply repay you.

To R' Yaakov Feldheim and the editorial, design, and production staff of Feldheim Publishers, Jerusalem — thank you for all your great efforts in bringing this book to light.

To my parents, R' and Mrs. Dovid Lev, and to my in-laws, R' and Mrs. Nachman Kepler, and to their families — may Hashem bless you with long lives of happiness and health and everything good.

Baruch Lev

Preface

THE WEEKLY *Nifla'osav Livnei Adam* column, skillfully presented by ha-Rav Baruch Lev in the Hebrew-language *Hamodia* newspaper for the past few years, has *baruch Hashem* succeeded in strengthening readers' *emunah* — faith, and *bitachon* — trust, in ha-Kadosh Baruch Hu and His Divine supervision.

When the English-language *Hamodia* was launched five years ago, it was clear that this popular column would be translated in order to offer the same inspiration to English-readers across the globe. The continuous flood of letters to *Hamodia* testifies to the success of the column in uplifting its readers to higher levels of faith and fear of Heaven.

Now the time has come for a collection of these stories to be printed in book form, which we hope and pray will delight and inspire readers as much as the collections published in two Hebrew books already have.

Hamodia — both the English- and Hebrew-language editions — was founded with the blessings and encouragement of *gedolei Yisrael* (Torah leaders) with the goal of serving Torah Jewry. The paper serves the dual purpose of publicizing the Torah viewpoint on every issue affecting our community and presenting the news in a professional manner through a Torah lens so that Torah Jews are protected from alien influences. In addition, the paper strives to enrich its readers' spiritual world and to enhance the honor of Heaven.

Columns such as *Nifla'osav Livnei Adam* help *Hamodia* realize its lofty goal by disseminating Torah and spreading faith among Jews wherever they may be.

This book is unique since it is the first to be jointly published by *Hamodia* and the well-respected Feldheim Publishers.

We would like to express our gratitude to the author of the column, to our staff, and to Feldheim Publishers — all of whom helped bring this book to fruition.

We are deeply grateful to *Hashem Yisbarach* for the kindness He has showered upon us up until now, and we pray that He will grant us the merit of continuing to play an instrumental role in increasing love and admiration for the Name of Heaven throughout the world until we all merit the Final Redemption, speedily in our days, amen.

3"02

A Reason for Everything

Just as you do not know
the way of the wind...
so you can never know
the work of God Who makes all.
(Koheles 11:5)

Neighbors

REB EPHRAIM WAS an unusual person. Quiet and reserved, he fulfilled his task in this world without making a splash or a fuss. He quietly earned his living through the labor of his hands, with some difficulty, and lived in a small apartment along with his wife and thirteen children.

One day Reb Ephraim decided that the family really needed more room than their small apartment afforded. Since they lived on the ground floor, he hoped they could build an extra room extending into the yard. He worked hard to get the permits, to find ways to finance the projected great expenditure, and to do whatever was needed to earn the blessing of an extra room.

Reb Ephraim spoke to contractors and sought the advice of friends who had built additions to their own apartments. Soon he was ready to begin. A contractor arrived to look over the site, and he spoke to Reb Ephraim at length. The family gathered around to listen in. The children were all excited at the prospect of more room, new beds, a big closet, maybe even a desk.

The next morning, after the workers had arrived, Mr. Klein, the neighbor from the building next door, came knocking on the door. "Did I see workers?" he asked. "What's going on? Are you going to build?"

The children answered in excited chorus, telling him about the additional room and the extra space they would soon have. Their mother explained the plans more exactly.

Mr. Klein, whose window was going to be directly opposite the new addition, shifted uneasily from foot to foot. Finally he announced, "Madam, I am sorry to tell you that a new room will not be built here." The word *Not* shook the warm, pleasant walls with cold force.

"But what about the permits we got, and the contract we signed

3

with the contractor, and the deposit we gave? And we're so crowded with thirteen children, *b'li ayin ha-ra*.... We've made the plans, and we're so happy about it. We promise we won't disturb you," she concluded. But Mr. Klein stood firm.

"It will block the light, the sun, and the view. I'll call my lawyer. I'll get a restraining order. I simply won't allow it," he declared.

Mr. Klein walked out, slamming the door and leaving the whole family thoroughly dismayed.

In her usual good-hearted way, Reb Ephraim's wife tried to figure out what was really bothering Mr. Klein, but she failed. Still, she had taught her children that in unpleasant moments such as these one must not speak against another person. They could not judge Mr. Klein; everything was from Heaven.

Late that evening, when Reb Ephraim had come home from an exhausting day at work and had just barely begun to eat his supper, his wife told him the events of the day. He always ate supper in the living room, since two children slept on mattresses in the kitchen.

"*Nu*," Reb Ephraim said tiredly, "so we won't build, that's all. We don't get into arguments with neighbors."

Though the children protested in shock and disappointment, it was clear to everyone that their father's word would be accepted. "We'll cancel everything and drop the plans. We'll continue to manage the way we are, *b'ezras Hashem*. We won't get into a fight with people." He even managed to call Mr. Klein and tell him that he would have his view and his light and everything would be fine.

Neither of the parents was an educator or a psychologist — just simple parents, working people. But their children were extremely well brought up. And what they learned that evening was stored deep within them to be put to good use during the course of their lives.

Two weeks later, their eldest, married son burst into the apartment, surprising Reb Ephraim.

"Abba! Have you heard the news? The government has announced a new program to help large families and is giving out a limited number of permits to build or buy low-cost apartments on very easy financial terms!"

Reb Ephraim was cautious. "What does this have to do with us?"

"Abba," the children cried out together, "the apartment opposite ours is for sale. We can buy the apartment with a government loan and join it to ours, and we'll have a beautiful, big apartment!"

And so they did. Within a few months the work was completed and to this day Reb Ephraim and his family live happily in the combined apartments. Reb Ephraim always used to say, "'A pleasant home expands a person's mind' — but it is supposed to expand it, not destroy it."

The family was amazed to hear that the government aid program expired soon afterward and was never offered again. It seemed as though ha-Kadosh Baruch Hu had arranged matters just to reward Reb Ephraim for his insistence on keeping the peace with his neighbors.

A Strange Promissory Note

FOR MANY YEARS, I managed a *gemach*, a free-loan fund called Keren Yisrael, which grants interest-free loans to fellow Jews for a period of up to twelve months. As is the custom with such funds, borrowers left twelve postdated checks with me when they received the money.

Once a woman came to me and requested a loan of six thousand shekels. She wanted to repay the loan in twelve installments of five hundred shekels each, but she had neither a bank account nor a checkbook. She promised, however, to come to my office every Rosh Chodesh with five hundred shekels in cash.

I felt I had to refuse her. A properly run loan fund may never deviate from the rules. Experience had taught me that such loans often end up as gifts, and the fund loses out. I refused to grant the loan without the usual arrangement of postdated checks.

Deeply distressed, the woman appealed to Mrs. Chayah Weissblum, *a"h*, a noted *ba'alas chessed* in our community who was famous for her great efforts on behalf of the poor and needy. The woman described her predicament, and Mrs. Weissblum promised to help. She accompanied the woman to my home and told me she was willing to act as guarantor that the woman would come to pay each month. She firmly declared that she was willing to sign a note to that effect.

Naturally, I agreed to Mrs. Weissblum's proposition, and I immediately prepared the following loan document:

> I, Mrs. X, borrowed the sum of 6,000 shekels on Rosh Chodesh Cheshvan. I will return the loan in 12 installments of 500 shekels each.
>
> Date of first payment: Rosh Chodesh Kislev, 500 shekels
> Date of second payment: Rosh Chodesh Teves, 500 shekels
> Date of third payment: Rosh Chodesh Shevat, 500 shekels
> Date of fourth payment: Rosh Chodesh Adar, 500 shekels
> Date of fifth payment: Rosh Chodesh Nisan, 500 shekels
> Date of sixth payment: Rosh Chodesh Iyar, 500 shekels
> Date of seventh payment: Rosh Chodesh Sivan, 500 shekels
> Date of eighth payment: Rosh Chodesh Tammuz, 500 shekels
> Date of ninth payment: Rosh Chodesh Av, 500 shekels

The woman signed the note, and Mrs. Weissblum added her signature as guarantor.

At the time, I didn't notice that I had neglected to list the dates of the tenth, eleventh, and twelfth payments. Somehow none of us realized that three payments — a total of 1,500 shekels — were not listed on the document. There is no way I can explain this oversight.

On 20 Av, ten days before the date of the tenth payment that I had inadvertently omitted from the list, the borrower arrived with 1,500 shekels. "I unexpectedly earned a larger sum of money than usual this month," she said, "and I want to pay off the rest of the loan." I pulled out the card with the woman's payments checked off and marked it "Repaid." I had by then forgotten about the promissory note, which was in a different file.

The following day, on 21 Av, I heard the sad news of Mrs. Weissblum's passing. I remembered that she had signed as guarantor for someone's loan from the *gemach*, but I couldn't recall the name of the borrower.

It was then that I found the promissory note on which she had guaranteed the woman's loan. I was astonished to discover that I had neglected to list the last three months of payment. Even more amazing was that the entire loan had been paid off just before Mrs. Weissblum's passing.

The Holy One, Blessed is He, had protected Mrs. Weissblum's pure and holy soul by sending the borrower of the loan a "large sum of money" just in time, so that she could pass away with a clean slate — the entire debt she had guaranteed had been repaid.

I pray that the publication of this story may lead to the strengthening of people's emunah in hashgachah pratis, and may it serve as a merit for Mrs. Chayah Weissblum's soul.

A Long Ride Home

otti the van driver reached exhaustedly for his cellphone for the umpteenth time that day. On the line was a family from Jerusalem who wanted to go to Bnei Brak. He had just let off passengers at a town on the outskirts of Jerusalem, and he really didn't want another job.

It had been a long, hard day. Motti had spent the greater part of it transporting passengers in his white ten-seater van, and all he could think of at the moment was getting home to Bnei Brak as soon as possible, taking a much-needed rest, and then going to his nightly *shiur* at shul.

The man on the other end of the line apologized for calling on such short notice. He had arranged for another driver to take him and his family to Bnei Brak, but the man had not shown up. Now they were left with no way of reaching their destination on time.

"All right," Motti conceded reluctantly. He hated to see people stranded. "I'll be there in, say, twenty minutes."

"Great! We'll send one of the children downstairs to let us know when you arrive."

Though traffic was heavy at the entrance to the city, it moved freely after that. Motti arrived at the appointed address and pulled up. A little girl wearing a small backpack skipped smilingly up to the van, opened the door, and hopped in. She made straight for the back seat, next to the window, and sat there quietly.

A minute later the family came down and took their places in the van. The father sat down next to Motti, the mother sat with the older children in the middle seat, and the younger children scrambled into the rear seat next to the little girl.

As they drove off, Motti and the father began a lively conversation, which helped alleviate Motti's weariness and made the traffic more bearable. In due course the van stopped in front of a wedding hall in Bnei Brak. The father thanked Motti, paid him and stepped down, helping the rest of his family descend onto the sidewalk.

Less than five minutes later Motti parked the vehicle in front of his own apartment building. No sooner had he turned off the headlights and locked the door than his cellphone came to life. Motti reluctantly looked at the screen before answering. It was his wife. After a perfunctory exchange of greetings, Motti explained that he was already in front of their building and would be right up.

"Terrific!" was his wife's enthusiastic response. "Don't bother coming up. I was just on my way to a fundraising event for Ezer Mitzion. I need you to take me there."

There was silence on the line. Motti's wife felt her husband's hesitation. "Oh, come on, Motti. It'll only take a few minutes. Everybody's waiting for me and I'm running late. Please. There aren't any taxis; it's the height of the wedding season. Please, Motti, I should have been there already. You'll see, it won't take longer than five minutes."

Motti mumbled his acquiescence and shuffled back to the van. He was too tired to argue. He had been hoping not to have to look at the steering wheel until the next morning. As soon as the motor came to life, Motti's wife came down and hurried over to the van. She quickly opened the rear door to deposit her things on the seat when she emitted a startled cry.

"Who's this? Motti! Who is this little girl?"

Motti turned around to look. At first he did not see anything, but on closer inspection he could make out the sleeping form of a child with a backpack lying on the back seat.

"Oh, no," he groaned in horror. "The family I brought to Bnei Brak must have forgotten one of their children. How irresponsible can people be? And they haven't even called me to check! What a miracle you needed me to drive you and we opened up the van again. I don't even want to think about what could have happened..."

Their excited chatter soon awakened the little girl. Frightened by her strange surroundings, she began to cry. His earlier fatigue forgotten, Motti anxiously tried to think of what to do. While his wife climbed into the back of the van and tried to soothe the girl, Motti quickly sped to the wedding hall where he had dropped the family off not long before.

Motti's brakes screeched as he parked in front of the hall. He ran inside the hall and searched for the father of the little girl, whom he quickly found. "Hey, Mister! Don't you know you left a child in my van? Didn't you even notice? Do you realize what might have happened if I hadn't gone back into the van, *chas ve-shalom*?" Motti, greatly agitated, struggled to catch his breath. He stared wild-eyed at the father, who perplexedly went to find his wife.

"Whom did we leave behind?" he asked his wife in confusion. "Brachale? Sarale?" His wife didn't understand what he was saying. "Brachale? Sarale? Here they are, both with me. What's the problem?"

"Listen, lady," Motti began shouting. "You left one of your children behind. She's crying right now in my van. Come and get her!"

As they followed Motti out of the hall, the mother said, "But we didn't forget anyone! I have four daughters, and they are all here with me!"

"Well, you must be mistaken," Motti said as they approached the van. The side door was open, and inside they could see a woman with a sobbing little girl. "There! You see?" Motti said.

"I'm sorry," the father turned to Motti. "This isn't our child. We don't know her."

Motti couldn't believe his ears. "But she entered the van with you!"

"Not really," the mother said. "When we came downstairs she was already sitting in the back seat next to the window. We thought she was your daughter. She fell asleep as soon as we left Jerusalem."

There was a bewildered silence. Whose child could it be?

Motti remembered that the little girl with the backpack had boarded as soon as he arrived at the Jerusalem address, before the rest of the passengers. He had had no doubt that she was a member of the family, especially since they had said that they would send down one of the children to wait for him. This child has been in the van for more than an hour and a half, Motti thought to himself. Her parents must be frantic.

Motti's wife opened the backpack to see if there was any identification and found a music book. On the inside front cover was written: Tzipporah Yerushalmi, 16 Rimon Street, Jerusalem, and a telephone number.

"Hello, is this the Yerushalmi family? Your daughter...mmm... we think we have your daughter with us."

"Where is she? Is she all right? What happened? Who is this?" Mrs. Yerushalmi pelted him with questions and hardly gave him a chance to answer.

"She's in Bnei Brak. She's fine, *baruch Hashem,* and we're taking good care of her. You see, this is what happened..."

The little girl's father arrived within the hour to take her home. It seems his daughter took music lessons once a week at the address where Motti made his pickup. Ordinarily, the father would call for the little girl when the lesson was over, but that day he was not able to make it. He had arranged for a friend to pick her up and had told Tzipporah to wait out front for someone driving a white van.

The eight-year old had dutifully waited for her lift, and as soon as she saw a white van stop in front of the house she got in. The ride home had seemed longer than usual, she said, but she was tired and soon fell asleep. When Mr. Yerushalmi's friend came by and did not see the child, he immediately called the Yerushalmi home. They had all passed a terrifying two hours until Motti called them.

How fortunate that Motti's wife had to go to a fundraising event that evening, and what a blessing that he allowed himself to be persuaded to be kind to his wife and drive her there! A coincidence? Somehow, we don't think so.

The Missing Carryall

ALL OUR SUITCASES were packed and standing ready near the door. We were traveling abroad for a family wedding, and our flight was scheduled to depart in the early morning hours. We had already ordered a taxi to take us from our home in Bnei Brak to the airport, and the taxi company promised to have a car waiting downstairs for us at 2:30 A.M. The babysitter who would be staying with our children was already in residence, and we had kissed the kids goodbye before they went to sleep.

The taxi arrived at the appointed time, and we piled our suitcases in the trunk and set off for the airport. The children slept on peacefully in the now darkened apartment.

After a while I realized that I had only my purse on my lap; the carryall with my husband's tefillin and other items we thought we might need during the flight was not there. I asked my husband if he remembered placing the carryall in the trunk, and he said he was positive that he hadn't seen it at all. We would have to return home to get the carryall; we couldn't possibly travel without it. It seemed strange that it had been left behind. All our luggage had been standing next to the front door. How had we forgotten such an obvious item?

Neither one of us became flustered or angry, because we always try to meet such situations with the calm and certainty of our reliance on the One Who plans every event. We try not to forget that there is a reason things happen, and that we are not the ones in control of events. Neither did we try to fix the blame on each other for "forgetting."

Obviously, we were meant to return home now, whether we understood the reason or not. This was what had been planned for us from Above, and no amount of human intervention or prevention could have changed the plan in the slightest. If this was the plan, we thought, it would make more sense to accept it happily than to agonize over it.

The driver, understandably, was reluctant to turn back. However, we insisted, and soon were headed back to Bnei Brak.

As we pulled up in front of the house, we saw a large van backed up at an angle underneath the balcony of our first-floor apartment. The two doors to its back compartment were wide open, and as we pulled up, two men with hoods over their heads quickly closed the doors and the van drove off. It was all very suspicious.

We found our carryall right by the door. We quickly checked the rest of the house and found everything as it should be. Apparently we had interrupted an attempted burglary in the small hours of the morning. We speculated that the robbers were looking for easy pickings, and had somehow seen us loading luggage into the taxi and assumed the apartment was empty. We had interrupted them before they were able to break in.

We awakened the babysitter quietly, and told her what had happened. We asked her to notify the police the next morning. Since we hadn't noticed the license number of the truck, there was nothing to be done that night, and we did not want to miss our plane. As we left, we asked her to please leave lights on at night while we were gone so that the apartment would not appear to be deserted.

The building was quiet; the residents slept on soundly. The Guardian of Israel, however, neither slumbers nor sleeps. He made us inexplicably leave behind our carryall, the most essential part of our luggage. It was hard to imagine what Hashem's kindness had spared us.

On our way to the airport once again, we called our neighbors on our cellphone to let them know what had happened. We thought it was forgivable to wake them up under the circumstances. *Baruch Hashem*, the rest of the journey passed smoothly, and we gradually calmed down. We realized that we had been granted the privilege of witnessing firsthand an awesome manifestation of *hashgachah pratis*.

A Heartfelt Mission

Rabbi Akiva said, "Whoever does not visit the sick is considered to have committed bloodshed" (Nedarim 40a). It goes without saying, then, that those who do visit the sick have the merit of strengthening and reviving both the sick person and his dependents.

I LIVE IN BNEI BRAK, Israel, and part of my job is working for the benefit of patients in various Israeli medical institutions. My work for the sake of the ill and their families has often brought me face to face with Hashem's incredible *hashgachah*. On one occasion this *hashgachah pratis* was responsible for saving my own life and improving the quality of life for many others, even though at first glance it seemed that I was the victim of an evil decree. This amazing miracle that happened to me is a firsthand account of Hashem's greatness and His boundless compassion.

In 1986 I organized a medical fundraising mission composed of a group of Israeli doctors, including two well-known specialists. Our destination was Antwerp, Belgium. The money we hoped to raise on this particular mission would be used to purchase new, state-of-the-art medical apparatuses for the Ichilov Medical Center in Tel Aviv.

Our mission was very successful, and we were blessed with much *siyata diShmaya*. These busy, skilled medical men took time off from their important work in the hospitals and medical centers of Eretz Yisrael and spoke to lay audiences in Europe with such heartfelt sincerity that we received substantial pledges from many well-to-do patrons. The doctors returned to Israel as soon as their speaking tour ended, while I remained behind to collect the pledges and purchase the new equipment.

Improbable as it may sound, precisely at the height of this important mission I suffered a massive heart attack. I have lived with a heart condition for years, since 1977, when I suffered my first attack. I have had minor attacks since then, but am able to keep my condition under control with medication, exercise, and a strict diet. My cardiologist, having consulted with other professionals, advised me some time ago not to undergo open-heart surgery. This limited me in many ways, but I managed to live with it.

Now, in the midst of the largest fundraising mission I had ever undertaken, I found myself hospitalized with no one at my side — a stranger in a strange land.

At moments like these a person realizes the extent of his nothingness and utter dependence on Hashem. If I had not been absolutely and unstintingly reliant on ha-Kadosh Baruch Hu's unerring wisdom in all things, I might have resented the apparent injustice and irony of becoming ill just when I was involved in a project to alleviate the suffering of the sick in Eretz Yisrael. My staunch *emunah* notwithstanding, however, I must confess that it was hard to accept. Alone and sick in a foreign country, I did not even have the comfort of doctors who were familiar with my case.

But Hashem, in His great mercy, let me see with my own eyes that everything He does is truly for the best. After my attack, the doctors who treated me understood that my condition was a complicated one, and they sent me without delay to a nearby medical center, which happens to have one of the best cardiology departments in the world.

The chief cardiologist was called in and, after checking me, recommended that I undergo a particularly complicated heart operation immediately. Despite my weak condition, I had the presence of mind to explain to the doctors that my Israeli cardiologist had unequivocally proscribed open-heart surgery.

The specialist listened carefully, checked me thoroughly once again, consulted with his colleagues, and reaffirmed his original opinion. He thought the operation was possible in spite of the danger involved because they would be using a new technique they themselves had developed. He even spoke to my cardiologist at home and, describing the new technique in detail, assured my doctor that he would take special precautionary measures during the operation. At this point I sent a message to my Rebbe in Eretz Yisrael and received his blessing to go ahead with the surgery.

I was, of course, nervous before the impending operation, but the Rebbe's blessing had convinced me that all would be well. And I could not ignore the clear *hashgachah pratis* that had brought me to that particular medical center. Had I suffered the attack in Eretz Yisrael, it is doubtful that I would have undergone surgery at all, and my health most likely would have deteriorated. No one at home would have thought of searching for a doctor abroad who might have a different opinion, and who might have developed a new technique and would be willing and capable of performing such delicate surgery. But Divine Providence had brought me straight to Hashem's emissary.

Meanwhile, in the few hours at my disposal while I was awaiting my turn in the operating room, I would not remain idle. From my hospital bed I phoned the people who had pledged to donate money to the Ichilov Hospital fundraising campaign and, in a voice weak from fasting, told them where and how to send the money. I had opened a special bank account for this fund.

The doctors and nurses who were preparing me for the operation tried to get me to rest, but I felt that any efforts I could make to assure the success of the mission would count in my favor Above. A few minutes before they wheeled me into the operating room, I made one last call. One of the largest donors, a wealthy man whose hand was always open to Torah and *chessed* projects, realized my voice was faltering and asked me if anything was wrong. I astonished him by saying, "I am about to undergo heart surgery." I told him my name and my mother's name, and asked him to daven for me.

The man was taken aback. "Rabbi," he said, "one month ago I

gave a large sum of money to a young couple, both orphans, who did not have the wherewithal to make a wedding and buy an apartment. I wish to transfer the merit of this mitzvah to you so that you will have a complete recovery! I renounce all connection to this mitzvah — it's all yours."

Baruch Hashem, the operation was successful. I felt better than I had felt in a long time. The doctor had performed, with Hashem's help, a sextuple bypass operation, using an extraordinarily difficult and previously untried technique. Not only was I the recipient of Hashem's wondrous miracles, but as a result of the success of my operation, this technique was soon instituted in hospitals in Eretz Yisrael, and many other Jews were able to benefit from it.

We know that we cannot always fathom Hashem's ways, but it is enough to know that even things that appear negative result in good one way or another. How much more grateful must we be then when we see the good with our own eyes!

A Minyan in Tel Aviv

IT WAS A RAINY winter's day. I needed to travel to an office in the center of Tel Aviv to have an important document signed. Having braved the rain and cold, I arrived at the reception desk and asked to see a particular government official. The reception clerk told me that I had arrived too early — the official was not expected for another half hour.

"No problem," I said. "I will leave my document with you. You can have it signed for me when the official comes in, and I will return in half an hour to pick it up." I left the papers with the clerk and went out in search of a *beis midrash* where I could sit and study for the next half hour.

I walked for a block or two until I saw a building with a small sign bearing the name of a *kollel*. I walked in, shook the water off my umbrella, hung up my raincoat, drew a glass of water from the cooler, and entered the *beis midrash.*

No sooner had I settled myself on a bench in the corner with a *sefer* than I noticed the men were getting ready to daven *Minchah*. I glanced at my watch. It could just barely be considered afternoon. It surprised me to see that they were going to daven so early; it was the earliest permissible time for afternoon prayers. By the time we finished davening, I realized it was time to return to the office to pick up my papers, which I did.

That evening I met a friend I had not seen for some time. In the course of our conversation, he told me he had a problem but doubted that I would be able to solve it for him. He had just started commuting from the small settlement where he lived to the center of Tel Aviv, where he was teaching in the mornings. When he left Tel Aviv each day, it was still too early to find a minyan for *Minchah*. By the time he got home after the long ride, however, it was usually too late for him to find a minyan. He had always been particular about davening with a minyan, and he did not know what to do.

"You are not going to believe this," I said. "Just today I was in the center of Tel Aviv, and I was not even thinking of davening *Minchah*. But I practically stumbled into the earliest *Minchah* minyan I have ever seen."

I think I must have been sent to central Tel Aviv half an hour early that day especially to help out a fine Jew who would not forgo praying with a minyan.

A Burst Pipe

I WAS A NEW DRIVER when I took my family up to the north of Israel for a trip we'll never forget, and my inexperience showed. I didn't even have a map in the glove compartment of our new car, since I naively assumed that road signs along the highway would be enough to guide me. So when we reached a junction at the foot of Rosh Hanikra and I turned left onto a quiet side street, it didn't faze me.

Neither did the attention-grabbing signs lining the road — "Stop, border ahead!" — give me pause.

They should have.

I drove on, and as we reached the end of the road I felt the car slow down. Minutes later, I was forced to stop and see what was wrong.

The gas tank was empty. It turned out that the needle in the gas gauge had been stuck on full, giving me a false reading. I chided myself for not noticing that the level hadn't changed for hours.

There we were, out of gas, stranded in some remote spot near the Lebanese border, with not a soul in sight. Boy, was I nervous. My wife and kids were sitting in the car, trusting me to get us out of this mess, but I didn't have a clue what to do.

How could I have been so unthinking? My conscience worked overtime as I berated myself for my lack of responsibility in leaving home without a map and without a spare can of gas, and for not paying attention to the stuck gas gauge. We were in a tight spot.

I looked up. Before me were towering mountains — from where would my help come?

The silence was broken by the sound of an engine in the distance. As it came closer, I was relieved to see that it was an army patrol jeep. It stopped right next to us, and a few soldiers jumped off and sauntered toward me.

"What's the matter with you? What do you think you're doing stopping here?" they demanded gruffly. "Can't you see you're at the border? Right over there" — the soldier pointed to the mountain opposite us — "sit Lebanese snipers, who are liable to fire at you at any moment."

I sheepishly explained to them what had happened, but my tale of woe didn't make much of an impression.

"If you value your life, take your family and get into the jeep. We'll drive you to a nearby army base. You can't stay here." But despite the danger, I didn't want to abandon our brand new car out there where it could be stolen. My mind raced to come up with an alternative solution.

"Look," I said, "the only problem is that I ran out of gas. Is there some way I could get some?" I was hoping they'd offer to siphon some from their jeep.

"No go," said one of the men. "Your car is a Ford. Our jeep uses diesel fuel."

"So maybe I'll wait for another car to drive by," I suggested.

From the soldiers' impatience, the sense of immediate danger became more of a reality for me.

"Listen," one of them said curtly, "you need three miracles. One, that a car will pass by; two, that he'll have extra gas with him; and three, that the gas will be the same type your car uses. If all three miracles happen, then you're all right. But I wouldn't count on it if I were you. Days can pass without a single car driving along this dangerous road. The chance that one will come right now is almost nonexistent."

While I was toying with the idea of walking to the main road to try to flag down a car, the soldier interrupted me. "Mister," he reminded me, "you have kids with you. Think about them; climb up and let's go."

At that moment, a white car suddenly appeared on the horizon. To me right then it looked like an angel sent from Heaven, like Eliyahu on a white donkey. My car and the jeep were blocking the road, so the white car was forced to stop.

That was the first miracle.

The driver of the car opened his door and got out. After being told what the problem was, he turned back to his car, opened the trunk, and pulled out a jerry can of gas he kept in reserve. Miracle number two. I thought I was dreaming. The soldier's jaw dropped.

But if his gas wasn't the kind my car used, what good would it be?

"Hold it a minute," I said. "Are you sure the gas is the right kind for this car?"

"Yup," came the laconic reply. "I carry all kinds."

Why would he do that, I wondered.

Soon enough my gas tank was filled and I was able to start the engine. Three for three, I thought. Before we drove off, however, I had to satisfy my curiosity.

"Why on earth do you carry so many different kinds of gas?" I asked my benefactor.

"You're not the first to ask," he grinned.

"I work for Mekorot, you know, the water company. I spend a lot of time on the road, and the company requires me to carry an assortment of gas types, so that I if come across a car that is in need of gas, I can help him out."

I was astonished. What *hashgachah*!

The soldiers were fairly amazed themselves. "What made you travel this route? And why right now?"

"Well, I'll tell you. A water pipe burst in one of the nearby settlements. It's pretty much of an emergency, and I thought I'd save time on the side road where there's no traffic. Better be on my way."

One of the soldiers moved the jeep to the side of the road, and the man in the white car drove off.

The soldiers suddenly remembered that we had all been standing around in this dangerous spot far too long, and left. As for me, I turned the car around as fast as I could toward the holy sites in Tiberias to thank Hashem for bursting a pipe in a certain settlement, in order to help get me and my family out of that dangerous spot.

As I drove, I thought about the sequence of events. The people with the burst pipe were probably annoyed and frustrated. They had no idea that at that moment a certain Jew from Bnei Brak was speeding along the highway thanking Hashem for the burst pipe.

I did not know what other parts there were to the puzzle; I had only seen the parts that involved me. I wondered if I would be able to use the lesson when I was on the other side, when I was the one feeling annoyed and frustrated. Would I then remember that God alone can see the whole puzzle?

I hope so.

How Wondrous
Are Your Ways

(Tehillim 104:24)

Random Doodling

ONE MORNING, somebody who owed me three thousand dollars came to my home to return it in the form of thirty crisp one-hundred-dollar bills. I was speaking on the phone at the time, so he placed the stack of bills on my desk and left.

As is my habit, I had been doodling on some scrap paper while conducting my phone conversation. Without even realizing what I was doing, I began to copy down the serial numbers of the bills. I don't remember ever having done this in the past; I generally just scrawl odd shapes and figures.

When I concluded my conversation, I did not throw out the scrap of paper I'd been doodling on, for there were a few telephone numbers and other bits of important information I needed also scrawled on the paper. I got up and placed the bills in an old book on a shelf of my bookcase and went about my business. I actually forgot all about the sum of money.

One day, quite some time later, I was asked to donate some old books to the local library. I collected a number of them that I thought suitable, took them over to the library in a shopping bag, and piled them on the librarian's desk. The librarian was busy looking at the titles printed on the covers of the books, while I was checking the bag to make sure it was empty. We were both astonished to suddenly see hundred-dollar bills scattered all over the floor.

We stared at each other. What was going on? After a moment the librarian bent down and collected the scattered bills. He

23

counted exactly thirty one-hundred-dollar bills — three thousand dollars in all. I never carry around such large sums of money, so I was certain the bills could not have fallen from my pocket or briefcase. "The money must have been lying on one of the upper shelves, and was shaken loose by the wind from my fan," said the librarian, placing the bills in an envelope in his drawer.

It was only after I returned home and saw the empty places on my bookshelves that I suddenly recalled the money I had placed in a book some time previously, and realized that the shower of money in the library belonged to me. I immediately phoned the librarian and told him that I had suddenly remembered that I had once placed precisely three thousand dollars in one-hundred-dollar denominations in one of the books I'd brought him. The money had obviously dropped out when I'd taken the book out of my bag. The librarian was polite but skeptical. "With all due respect, sir," he said, "I find it strange that you recalled nothing of the incident here at the library, yet everything came flooding back to you as soon as you returned home."

I understood the librarian completely. There really was no reason for him to believe me. On the other hand, I was now convinced that the money was mine, and I wanted desperately to prove it.

Two days passed. I still do not know what prodded my memory at that exact moment, but suddenly I recalled that I had "coincidentally" scribbled down the serial numbers of the bills on my doodling pages. Yes, they were still there.

I returned to the library once more, this time with the serial numbers of the hundred-dollar bills. The startled librarian gave me the money after checking to see that the serial numbers, in fact, matched.

I learned that there is no such thing as "coincidence."

A Minyan on the Mount of Olives

*D*ANIEL BOARDED A BUS going to the Kosel. He wanted to pray for a relative who was gravely ill. That day also happened to be the yahrtzeit of the Rashash, who is buried on the Mount of Olives, only a stone's throw away from the Kosel. Many of the passengers on the bus were planning to get off the bus before it reached the Western Wall and walk the rest of the distance to the grave. Daniel knew that Hashem hears every prayer, no matter where it is said, but saying a prayer at the graves of holy *tzaddikim* has a special power to open the gates of prayer and carry the entreaties Heavenward. Daniel made a quick decision to join the crowds that were walking toward the grave of the Rashash to pray.

Daniel poured out his pleas at the *tzaddik's* grave. Since his grandfather's grave is also on the Mount of Olives, Daniel wanted to visit it before leaving the cemetery. Not knowing his way around there too well, he climbed a bit higher on the mountain and turned in what he thought was the direction of the section where his grandfather was buried. He threaded his way through the gravestones, until at length he realized that he was getting farther away from his destination instead of closer. He could clearly see Arab houses at the edge of the nearest section, and he began to feel afraid.

As he turned back and headed down, a sudden gust of wind blew his hat off, carrying it up the hill, where it finally landed between two tombstones in one of the higher sections.

Chasing his hat frantically, Daniel ran up the incline. Near the landing place of the hat, he saw with astonishment several black-hatted men clustered around a gravestone. The men called him over.

"Here he is!" Daniel heard them say. "The *tzenter*, the tenth man for our minyan."

They explained to Daniel that they came to say Kaddish at the grave of a well-known Jerusalem personage, and had been waiting for a tenth man for some time. A few of the men had not wanted to wait around, given the precarious security situation, but others reminded them of the dictum that when nine men are present, a tenth is sure to appear.

"You can imagine how amazed we were to see a hat come sailing by and land almost at our feet — and you in its wake," the man said.

And I had not even planned to be on the Mount of Olives today, Daniel thought in wonder. Not only that, but I surely would not have come up this high by myself. And now I have the merit of completing a minyan.

"*Yisgadal ve-yiskadash Shemei rabba.*" Indeed, He was the One Who arranged for Daniel to be there. "May His Name be glorified and sanctified forever and ever."

After they recited the Kaddish, Daniel asked those worthy Jews if they would recite some chapters of *Tehillim* for his relative, who was in need of Heavenly assistance, and the men happily obliged. They even offered a special *Mi shebeirach* on his behalf.

Daniel's relative recovered, *baruch Hashem*, shortly after that. Daniel's heart tells him, although no one can understand these things, that it was the prayers of a minyan of Jerusalemites, whose fear of Heaven was apparent on their faces, standing at the grave of a righteous person, that reached the Heavenly Throne.

Travel Plans

AS PART OF MY JOB as the director of an institution in Jerusalem, I often travel overseas to meet with philanthropists and potential donors. Throughout my many long years at the job, I have often merited to clearly see the Hand of Hashem and feel His personal supervision. I feel an inner sense of peace and trust, knowing that Hashem is with me wherever I go.

People visiting a foreign country for the first time often feel somewhat apprehensive and disoriented. Even self-assured business executives feel a bit uneasy in a noisy, bustling metropolis where everyone speaks a language they cannot understand, much less converse in. He who is fortunate enough to live with trust in Hashem, however, feels no more discomfort or apprehension in a strange place than he does at home. A man of faith is fully aware that he is wholly dependent upon *siyata diShmaya* even when he sits in a comfortable chair in his own office, surrounded by familiar co-workers. He has peace of mind in the knowledge that ha-Kadosh Baruch Hu is watching over him, protecting him from all harm. He therefore feels the same sense of trust and reliance when he arrives in a foreign city. He may not have the faintest idea how he is going to find the address he needs, but that doesn't discourage him. In the end, ha-Kadosh Baruch Hu will lead him there safely.

I hope my story will serve as a way to publicly acknowledge Hashem for having so clearly shown me His Divine supervision on so many occasions. From repeated instances such as the ones enumerated below, I gained more than just the blessing of His help at the moment I needed it; I acquired a deep-seated sense of *bitachon* that accompanies me always.

A man who trusts in Hashem is never alone. He has ever-present help — a hotline always available and always with him. A powerful Bodyguard walks before him wherever he goes, leveling mountains and raising valleys. He is indeed fortunate.

Heaven has taught me to open my eyes wide and see how every aspect of my daily life is Divinely orchestrated.

Once I traveled from Israel to Switzerland by air and then by train from the Hauptbahnhof, the central station in Zurich, to the central station in Milan, Italy. Huge signs had clearly marked the way until this point in my journey. But this was the first time I was in Milan, it was already dark outside, and I was not sure how to proceed from the central train station. I took my suitcase up to the main hall and stood there for a few minutes amidst a babble of voices speaking foreign tongues, while I tried to get my bearings.

Suddenly I heard a voice behind me say, "Shalom Aleichem." Surprised, I turned around to see a smiling, obviously Jewish young man who asked if I needed help. He told me in Hebrew that he was from Petach Tikvah in Israel, and was studying at the medical school in Milan. I told him I had come to see Rabbi Belsky, who lived on the Via Grazia.

"Well, it is certainly *min ha-Shamayim* that I spoke to you," said the young man. "You might have been wandering around Milan at night for hours trying to find Rabbi Belsky. I know the rabbi, and he no longer lives on the Via Grazia. He moved to a new apartment on the Via Sardinia last week."

Baruch ha-meichin mitz'adei gaver! Had I not met this young man, I would have endured a most frustrating evening.

(Come to think of it, though, I know beyond the shadow of a doubt that had I not met the young man, Heaven would have helped me in a different manner. A Jew is never alone.)

On another occasion, I was planning to travel first to England, then to Toronto. When my business in England was finished, I wanted to make arrangements to fly directly to Toronto, but discovered that a direct flight was very costly. The travel agent explained that there was a special reduction on tickets from London to New York, and there were constant shuttle flights from New York to Toronto. The total cost would be lower than a direct flight, and he said I would not lose too much time. Therefore, I asked him to make reservations for me on both flights.

When the travel agent delivered the tickets to me at my lodging, I was distressed to see that he had made out only one ticket from England to New York. "It's not a good idea to reserve a place on the flight from New York to Toronto from this end," he explained. "Trust me. I have experience in these things. If, for any reason, the flight from England is delayed, you may miss the Toronto flight. In my opinion it is wiser to purchase a ticket to Toronto at the counter in New York."

"But what will I do if there is no flight scheduled for Toronto when I get to New York?" I asked worriedly. "And what if it's full?" I had an appointment in Toronto to meet with the renowned Jewish philanthropist, Joseph Tannenbaum, *z"l*. I did not want to keep Mr. Tannenbaum waiting, much less miss out on seeing him. He had often contributed generously to my institution, but I knew he was a very busy man. I might be stranded in New York with no way to get to Toronto on time, and he might not have time for me later.

The travel agent assured me there was no need to be concerned. "Getting from New York to Toronto is no more complicated than traveling from Jerusalem to Tel Aviv," he said. "There are flights all the time, and they are usually half empty."

The travel agent was, after all, more experienced than I, and I conceded. I would fly to New York, and from there I would catch a flight to Toronto, God willing. He Who had brought me that far would lead me farther.

Contrary to the travel agent's predictions, I left England exactly on time and arrived in New York twenty minutes ahead of schedule. I immediately made my way to the ticket counter to reserve a seat on the next flight to Toronto, expecting matters to progress quickly and smoothly. After all, it was supposed to be like "traveling from Jerusalem to Tel Aviv." It soon became clear, however, that I would not be setting out to Toronto that day.

"There are no seats available," the clerk blandly announced.

"What do you mean? How can that be?" I asked. "I was told that there are flights leaving to Toronto every few minutes; there must be one seat available on one of them."

"Whoever told you that was right," the clerk said politely. "That is the case — ordinarily. However, there is a big sporting event taking place in Toronto today, and plane tickets are all sold out."

I was greatly distressed. I should have insisted the travel agent book me through to Toronto. I felt very foolish for having listened to him. I should have... If I had only....

It seems I had no choice. I would have to make a reservation for the following day, and spend the night with relatives in Brooklyn. It did no good to rant and complain.

As I rode to Brooklyn, I had time to think about what had happened. You silly man, I lectured myself. Do you really think you were the one that "allowed" this to happen? There is but One Who allows things to happen in this world. It was He Who caused the travel agent to urge you to do what you did, and it was He Who moved you to agree to it.

I leaned back in my seat in the taxi and relaxed. So now I was traveling through the streets of Brooklyn instead of flying above the clouds. I had no idea what the next day would bring, but I knew one thing: The One Who had planned that day's events would do so again the following day.

The next morning I boarded the plane for Toronto. I made my way to my seat where, to my utter astonishment, I saw a familiar figure in the next seat. Was I dreaming? At first I certainly thought so. Sitting next to me was none other than Mr. Joseph Tannenbaum himself, the philanthropist I was supposed to have met in Toronto the evening before!

"Reb Yosef!" I exclaimed. "Reb Yosef, I am on my way to meet with you!" I told him.

"Yes," Mr. Tannenbaum said. "I know we had an appointment last night in Toronto, but I was unavoidably detained in New York, and there was no way to let you know."

During the flight, I would be able to talk with him at length without feeling I was imposing on him or taking up his time. What could be better?

Greatly uplifted, I fastened my seatbelt. I knew I would never look at annoying delays the same way again.

Lift Up Your Eyes

OST PEOPLE COULD tell you stories similar to the one I'm about to tell. It's an everyday story, but personally experiencing it brought home the point again that we cannot understand the meaning behind events. Hashem constantly sets in motion a series of chain reactions, sometimes without us even knowing how we are affecting the life of another person — and all this may be for the sake of yet another person. This is what happened to me.

We were a group of teachers who carpooled every morning from our suburban community to the nearby city. Once, after oversleeping, I missed the van and found myself waiting resignedly for a bus at the bus stop. You can imagine the small grin of satisfaction I allowed myself when after a few minutes I spotted a colleague, apparently another deep sleeper, coming to join me at the stop. Our amusement became an outright chuckle when a short time later a third member of our carpool also turned up at the bus stop. What a coincidence!

The bus was delayed, probably stuck in some traffic jam. Now our whole day would be thrown off schedule. Our impatience mounted, knowing as we did that in thirty minutes three delighted classes and one annoyed principal would be waiting for us at the school.

While we were waiting, a taxi pulled up at the curb and announced, "Hop in for the price of a bus ride." Quick as flash, almost before the words were out of his mouth, we had all jumped in. What a stroke of good luck! In our sleepy suburb, it is quite unusual for a taxi to drive by, especially along the regular bus routes.

But our relief was premature. The driver refused to budge until he had a fourth passenger. Why should he forgo a quarter of his profit on the ride?

If we could have physically grabbed the wheel from him and stepped on the gas pedal we would have. Every passing minute made us more late, while he sat there calmly waiting for a passenger as if he had all the time in the world. Now we appreciated the fact that we were a group of three, for therefore the driver only needed one more passenger and that upped our chances of getting to school on time.

But the mere oversleeping of three people on one morning was not the only remarkable thing we were about to witness that day. After a few moments the driver's cellphone rang. It was his uncle on the line saying he needed a ride to the city urgently for a medical appointment.

Now, there's nothing unusual about an elderly gentleman having an appointment in town. And if his nephew is a taxi driver, it's

only natural that he ask him to drive him in. But when three teachers sitting tensely hoping to get to school on time breathe a collec-
tive sigh of relief when the uncle calls, you know it could only be
hashgachah.

During the ride, our driver told his uncle that at that particular
time of the day he was usually in the city, where there are more customers and he can make more money. "I don't usually waste my
time looking for passengers out here where most people organize
carpools or have monthly passes for public transportation."

So what happened that day? "I just happened to be out here because I don't have my own taxi license number yet."

"What does that have to do with it?" one of us asked.

"It costs a lot of money, so until I can swing it, I'm renting a
friend's number for five hundred dollars a month."

"So?" we asked. "What's the connection?"

"Well, today I had to pay the fee on his taxi number in this
neighborhood, and that's why I'm here. You're in luck," he smiled
back at us in the rear-view mirror.

We were tempted to explain to him that while he may have
thought he had driven out to the suburbs to pay his license fee, we
had a sneaking suspicion that he had been sent to drive his uncle to
the doctor and to release us from our wait at the bus stop.

We made it to school on time that morning. Instead of annoy-
ance, however, we were greeted with amazement by fellow staff
members, who wondered how we had gotten there so fast.

"We made it in time because of a taxi driver who had four seats
in his car, and who decided he couldn't afford to buy a new taxi license number but would instead rent an old number from a retired
driver."

"What's the connection?" wondered our fellow teachers.

"The connection is," we said, "that today is the day the driver
decided to pay the fee. On his way back, he drove by to pick us up."

"Not bad, not bad at all."

"And how was the taxi filled up?"

We told everyone about the driver's uncle, who had an urgent
appointment in town.

"This is a story to tell in class," said one teacher, "to show how Hashem sets events in motion one after the other."

"With your permission," interrupted another teacher, "let me keep the ball rolling with another connection. While listening to your story I remembered that I happen to need that information on taxi licenses because only yesterday someone asked me about it."

A discussion ensued as to what exactly was the main purpose of the morning's incident. Who was the main beneficiary? Was the taxi driver's paying his fee that day for the benefit of the three latecomers or for his uncle? Was his uncle's needing treatment for the benefit of the three latecomers — or did they come late for his benefit?

"Maybe," suggested one of us, "all three incidents combined were predestined to happen only for the purpose of the latecomers' hearing the details about acquiring a taxi license number and repeating it in the staff room for the benefit of a certain Jew who needed just this information."

We can only assume that everything happened for everyone. Only Hashem knows exactly what, when, and how to trigger a chain of events — just as He is doing at this very moment while you are reading these lines. Perhaps you too are part of another intricate combination of factors without being aware of it, just like the driver was unaware of all that lay behind the paying of his license rental fee.

Let us take a closer look at what lies behind all these commonplace, everyday occurrences, and realize Who orchestrates them. As *tzaddikim* are wont to say, "Lift up your eyes" — elevate yourself spiritually, raise your gaze up high — "and see Who created this." Then you will clearly see the Hand of the Creator coordinating each and every event.

THE "BIG" THINGS

In the Merit of Rabbi Shimon

XACTLY TWO YEARS ago on Lag ba-Omer, I traveled to Meron. As I stood in the midst of the immense crowd, one lone Jew among thousands of sisters and brothers, my heart was frozen with pain. Immersed in my small *sefer Tehillim*, I sobbed the ancient holy words, "See my pain and hardship..." I couldn't say any more. The words stuck in my throat.

Pandemonium surrounded me; the multitude raised their voices in prayer all around me, but I was oblivious to it all. I beseeched Hashem on behalf of my wife and myself to look down and see our pain and anguish, and bless us with a child.

We had been to many doctors but they could not help us, and our only hope was mercy from Heaven. I did not feel that we personally were worthy of a miracle, yet I pinned my hopes on the intervention of the saintly Rabbi Shimon on our behalf, in the merit of coming to pray at his burial place.

I prayed and promised that when, *b'ezras Hashem*, our salvation would come, I would distribute a quantity of wine equivalent to eighteen *rotel* here at the grave site of the saintly Rabbi Shimon, thereby spreading word of the wondrous greatness of Hashem throughout the land.

A feeling of faith and hope permeated my being for the first time since our many disappointing sessions with medical specialists. As I stood before Rabbi Shimon's grave, my heart danced and rejoiced with *emunah. With the help of Hashem, in the merit of Rabbi Shimon,* I thought, *we will yet hold a child of our own in our arms.*

The joyous feeling that accompanied me as I left the grave was like nothing I had ever experienced in my life. As *sefer Bnei Yissachar* asserts, the joyousness that is prevalent in Meron on Lag ba-Omer transcends nature.

And God was indeed good to us.

Less than a year later, my wife and I stood next to our son's crib. Anguish overrode our joy in receiving this miracle from Heaven, however, because we had to stand by helplessly and watch the tiny baby scream and writhe in pain. Dark red blotches covered his face, and his skin was peeling and raw.

"What else can we do?" my wife cried. "Is there something we haven't tried?"

An enormous array of creams, powders, and ointments stood on the baby's dressing table. We had spared neither money nor effort to find the remedy that would relieve his pain. We had even sought medical advice from overseas. We had tried everything, but nothing helped.

Naturally, we could not sleep from worry. In desperation, I decided to travel to Meron. The grave of the holy Rabbi Shimon seemed to call out to me to come and pour out my prayers there once again, though it was not yet Lag ba-Omer. I needed another injection of hope and faith, and I knew that I would definitely get it there.

Yet when I reached the grave of the holy *tzaddik*, I did not feel the immediate uplift I had expected. I began to say *Tehillim*, saying each word slowly, as if savoring the sweet taste in my mouth. The words joined into sentences, and I concentrated intensely on the meaning of the holy prayers. Soon I was oblivious to my surroundings and praying with fervor. Slowly, the sweetness of prayer penetrated my heart and warmed my soul.

Using King David's words, I begged,"*Hateh Hashem oznecha*, Bend Your listening ear, Hashem, and answer me, for I am destitute and poor." I begged forgiveness for my past sins, and entreated ha-Kadosh Baruch Hu with all my heart to accept my sincere remorse.

I took the burden I was carrying in my heart and placed it in the Hands of He Whose strength is infinite and Whose mercy is everlasting.

I arrived home, tired and weary, yet somewhat relieved. I talked to my wife at length, and we decided to put aside all the ointments, remedies, and salves. From that day onward we would place all our hope and faith in the trustworthy Hands of our merciful Father in Heaven.

This conversation took place after midnight, immediately upon my return from Meron. A few hours later, I was awakened by my wife's excited cries.

"Elimelech, come here right away!" she called from the baby's room. I jumped quickly out of bed in alarm and hurried into the adjoining room.

We stood there transfixed. There was a definite improvement in the baby's appearance. His skin was no longer dark red but pink, and the blotches had faded. And he smiled up at us. We both knew that our son still had a long way to go, but, *baruch Hashem,* that was the beginning of his complete recovery.

Believe it! Hashem's salvation comes in the blink of an eye, especially in the merit of Rabbi Shimon bar Yochai.

There Is No Such Thing as Coincidence

Ashdod, 1996 — Lag ba-Omer night

*W*E WERE A GROUP of *kollel* students, gathered together on the yahrtzeit of Rabbi Shimon bar Yochai to rejoice. Caught up in the holy spirit of the day, we began to recount all of the miraculous stories about Rabbi Shimon bar Yochai, in his own days and throughout the generations.

The discussion came around to the *segulah* for childless couples recorded in *Sefer Ta'amei ha-Minhagim.* It says that on Lag ba-Omer, you should daven at Rabbi Shimon bar Yochai's grave for those needing a *yeshuah,* and promise that if Ploni ben Plonis is blessed with a child within the coming year, you will bring eighteen *rotel* of drink to Meron on Lag ba-Omer of the following year to distribute among those who come to daven there.

During the discussion, one of the group mentioned that the previous year at a Lag ba-Omer *seudah*, a friend of his had promised to bring eighteen *rotel* of grape juice to Meron on behalf of a certain person who had been childless for years, and that person had indeed been blessed with a child. "Tomorrow," our friend concluded, "he intends to fulfill his promise and bring all those bottles of grape juice to Meron to serve to the thousands of people there!"

On hearing this story, I was reminded of a close friend who also had been waiting for a child after six years of marriage. Enthusiastically, I stood up and announced, "I take upon myself, *b'li neder*, to bring eighteen *rotel* of grape juice to Meron next Lag ba-Omer, 1997, if my friend Ploni ben Plonis has a child." Another one in our group also jumped up and promised to bring the same amount on behalf of another childless *kollel* student.

We drank a *L'chaim* and wished each other Mazal tov with high hopes of hearing good news. We had great hope that our friends too would be blessed through the merit of Rabbi Shimon bar Yochai.

The following day at the grave of Rabbi Shimon bar Yochai in Meron, we each repeated our promise to bring the eighteen *rotel* the following year if our friends would merit having children.

A month before Lag ba-Omer 1997, the friend I had davened for made a *bris* for his newborn son, after seven years of childlessness. The couple that my other friend had davened for also merited a child two weeks later. We made joyful plans to fulfill our promises and bring thirty-six *rotel* of grape juice — about 108 liters — to Meron on Lag ba-Omer. It would total six very large cases.

The rest of my story is about how those 108 liters finally got to Meron, ending with the amazing "coincidence" that happened the next year, in Tammuz 1998, and which demonstrated once again that nothing happens by chance and that everything is planned Above, right down to the last detail.

We live in Ashdod, and every year buses are chartered directly from Ashdod to Meron for Lag ba-Omer. We planned to go to Meron on one of those buses to bring the six cases of grape juice, as we had promised. The simplest thing would have been to buy the grape juice at one of the discount supermarkets in our neighborhood and put the six cases in the baggage compartment of the bus.

But we decided to buy the bottles in Bnei Brak instead because there is a *chessed* organization there that voluntarily transports people's *segulah* wine to Meron every year and distributes it for them. We didn't want to take any chances of not getting the grape juice there, so we were willing to spend the extra money to buy it in Bnei Brak at a regular store in order to have the distribution done by professionals.

About a week before Lag ba-Omer, we made a special trip to Bnei Brak, bought the six large cases of grape juice, higher price and all, and lugged them to the place the *gemach* had indicated — from where they were to collect it and take it to their warehouse. Later that day, we called and confirmed that the grape juice had indeed made it to the warehouse, and that it would be taken to Meron that very day.

Our second follow-up call, though, brought us the disappointing news that the cases had been left behind in Bnei Brak by mistake. But, they said, we shouldn't worry, because the *gemach* was making another trip to Meron the following day and they promised to take the cases then.

Such was not to be our luck, however. The following day, either the deliveryman misunderstood the instructions or couldn't find our cases, because they were again left behind. Another day passed and another, and for some unexplained reason, our cases refused to make the trip to Meron. Finally, on Lag ba-Omer morning, we called the otherwise perfectly reliable *gemach* and found that they still had our cases of grape juice safely tucked away in their warehouse, in…Bnei Brak.

My friend and I discussed our options and decided that we would take the grape juice to Meron ourselves. However, we wanted to go with our group of friends from Ashdod on a specially chartered bus — and we needed their help to *shlep* all those cases up Mount Meron's steep hill. That meant that we would have to travel to Bnei Brak, collect our grape juice, and get on the 12:10 bus back to

Ashdod in order to make the 2:00 bus to Meron.

It was a ridiculous situation. We had made a special trip north to Bnei Brak a week before to buy bottles of grape juice for more money than we would have spent otherwise, in order to make another trip on Lag ba-Omer itself to bring them back south to Ashdod, in order to take them north again to Meron! But what could we do? A promise is a promise.

We got to Bnei Brak, borrowed some pushcarts, and made it to the warehouse and back to the bus stop with ten minutes to spare. It was just enough time for my friend to run back and return the carts while I stayed and watched the cases. I began to feel more than a little foolish. Why were we running so hard? Wouldn't it have made more sense to spend some money on a private taxi and be done with the whole deal? What were we doing sweating it out in the heat of the day in Bnei Brak on Lag ba-Omer? Why was this happening to us?

Just then, my thoughts were interrupted by the arrival of the bus to Ashdod. It had come at 12:05, five minutes early — and my friend was still not back. As the passengers boarded the bus, I strained to see if I could see him running down the street toward me. No such luck. What was I going to do with the cases? The line of passengers was nearing its end and still my friend was nowhere in sight. I kept stalling, hoping to see him. I couldn't decide what to do. Should I start loading the grape juice onto the bus or not?

Suddenly I saw a figure sauntering slowly down the street. I waved my arms frantically, trying to catch his attention and make him realize that the bus had come early and he should run — but in another second I realized that it was someone else altogether. The heat did nothing to help my disappointment.

By now really anxious, I turned back to the driver to ask him to please wait just a minute longer — only to watch helplessly as the doors of the bus closed in my face. The bus drove off, leaving me standing there like a fool, with six cases of grape juice at my feet.

The whole situation seemed unreal. "What," I wondered in exasperation, "is going on today?" I was still standing there in a daze when, less than a minute later, my friend came running. Seeing his questioning look, I broke into peals of laughter. It was the only thing to do. When I finally managed to explain what had happened, he almost didn't believe me.

There are people who are always late for everything, who are used to being left in the lurch like that, but my friend and I are not among them. I told my friend my feeling that there must be a reason why we were facing so many obstacles. Nonetheless, we had a mission to accomplish, no matter what, because those cases of grape juice simply had to get to Meron.

We started discussing our options once again. The chances of catching one of the intercity taxis to Ashdod were nil, since they usually never came by bus stops right after the scheduled buses left. We considered taking a private taxi to Ashdod after all, despite the cost, but we didn't have the cash for it, so that ruled out that plan. We were thinking about taking a shared cab (*sheirut*) directly from Bnei Brak to Meron, when all of a sudden a van pulled up right in front of us out of nowhere, its driver calling out, "Ashdod! Ashdod!"

We ran over excitedly, repeating incredulously, "To Ashdod?" We hung onto the door of the van, almost as if we were afraid that it would vanish into thin air.

The driver got out and helped us load the cases, after which we fell into our seats with a mixture of exhaustion and disbelief.

"Since when does a *sheirut* come around at such an hour?" we asked our driver.

"I don't know myself," came the answer. "It just worked out for me to leave for Ashdod right now."

We began to think that we did know why, though, we had been sent a *sheirut* straight from Heaven. How wrong we were.

As we neared Ashdod, we began to haggle over the price of the ride with our driver. We wanted to pay eight shekels each, the regular fare, but the driver wanted to take a hefty surcharge for the grape juice.

In the course of the discussion, I somehow mentioned what the bottles were for. I explained the *segulah* of promising at the grave of Rabbi Shimon bar Yochai on Lag ba-Omer to bring fifty-four liters of drink to Meron the next Lag ba-Omer if the person you daven for is blessed with a child. We told the driver the whole story of how we had davened for our friends the year before, and shared with him the happy news that both couples had been blessed. Now, we told him, we were on our way to fulfill our promises.

The driver, who appeared to be secular, was so strongly affected by the story that his hands gripping the steering wheel began shaking. In an emotional voice he said, "We also have this anguish in our family. My sister and brother-in-law have been married for twelve years, but their home is still empty. We have no peace because of it; my parents are in despair. It is a tragedy, a terrible tragedy."

I was overcome. Could this whole strange story of ours have come about just so that we could meet up with this driver and tell him about Rabbi Shimon bar Yochai's *segulah*? Maybe, if he davened for his sister, too, and she merited a child, it would influence his whole family for the good. After all, stranger things had been known to happen.

The driver, whose name was Rafi, wasted no time on speculations. "I'm giving you the 'shipping' for free," he announced, "but I want you to do this thing for my sister. When you go up to Meron, mention my sister and brother-in-law's names and promise fifty-four liters of wine for them if they have a baby. I'll worry about bringing the wine next year, God-willing." His face shone, reflecting the *pintele Yid* within, and his eyes filled with tears. If Hashem would only help...

We arrived in Ashdod and Rafi helped my friend and me load the cases of grape juice onto the Meron bus. "We'll be in touch," he told us happily as we parted. We felt that the whole roundabout trip of ours had been worth it, just in order to bring a *yeshuah* to another Jewish family.

We finished our job with the same elation we had felt the year before, when we had undertaken this project. We had fulfilled our promises and our friends had merited families of their own. We had handed out our grape juice to hundreds of people and had gone to Rabbi Shimon bar Yochai's grave to thank Hashem for our friends' *yeshuos.* We made sure to mention Rafi's sister and her husband, declaring in Rafi's name a promise to bring wine the following year should his sister be blessed. We felt that among the thousands of situations needing Divine salvation that had been brought to Meron that year, ours was somehow unique. We davened that Hashem should show mercy to Rafi's family in order to sanctify His Name to yet another family of Jews in Eretz Yisrael. Maybe this would be the turning point that would start them on the road to stonger Torah observance...

Lag ba-Omer 1997 came to a close. The sun set, and among the millions of prayers that had risen heavenward that day was one belonging to Rafi of Ashdod on behalf of his sister. I called him that night to tell him that we had davened for her at Rabbi Shimon bar Yochai's grave. He told us that his whole family, simple, believing Jews, were waiting for Hashem's salvation with all their hearts. They had all davened, too.

Life goes on, and the whole event receded into a corner of my memory. Days, weeks, and months passed. Now and then I wondered briefly about what had happened after the end of our comedy of errors; that is, what had become of our driver and his family, but having misplaced his number, I supposed that this would be one more mystery that would remain unsolved.

Tammuz 1998

My family set out from Ashdod to celebrate a *bris* in Bnei Brak. Since the mother and baby were coming in our van, we ordered one early and made sure it was clean, new, and comfortable. We headed out of the H Quarter of Ashdod as scheduled, but we had only gotten as far as the G Quarter when the car ground to a halt. After checking under the hood, the driver reported in incredulity that the battery seemed to be dead. He found it hard to believe. After all, the van was brand new. But after further investigating, he was forced to admit that the battery was gone. He told us he would only be able to drive a few more yards at the most.

We knew nothing about batteries — dead or alive. All we knew was that we would have to switch vans as soon as possible because it was getting late and the entire extended family was waiting for us in Bnei Brak. The driver offered to order us another van, but I suggested instead that he try to drive us to the nearby office of the Galgalei Darom taxi company so we could switch vans immediately.

As our van rolled to a stop, we were pleasantly surprised to find a free van there at the taxi stand. We all piled out, mother, baby and all, got into the second van, and set off on our way. As we were getting into the new van, I noticed the driver giving me strange looks, but until we were settled, which took quite some time, I didn't have time to think about it.

Once we got on our way, the driver began to share with us some happy news. That very morning, he said, at 3:00 A.M., his sister and brother-in-law had been blessed with a baby girl — after thirteen years of marriage. Everyone was dancing with joy for the happy parents, he told us, thrilled that the long years of unbearable suffering had finally come to an end. They felt blessed, he said. All of us in the van were delighted with his story and shared in his joy as well.

Suddenly, it hit me. Could this be Rafi from Lag ba-Omer of the previous year?

I was embarrassed to ask in case I was wrong, so I took a good look around me for some clue. The van wasn't the same — yet the situation sounded exactly the same: thirteen years without children, a sister and a brother-in-law... Ribbono shel Olam, could this be the same couple we davened for in Meron?!

Then, while I was still wracking my brains for a reliable indication, the driver turned to me with an embarrassed smile and asked, "Excuse me, but you look familiar. Have you ridden with me before?"

Startled and confused, I looked back at him. There was no doubt about it — it was Rafi! I was speechless. I barely managed to get out that I was the passenger from Lag ba-Omer a year ago. We were both stunned. Rafi started to sob and I began to cry with him, and with a shaky hold on the wheel, he filled us in on the details of the past fourteen months.

"And then, this morning," he concluded, "this very morning, at 3:00 A.M., when they told me the wonderful news, I thought to myself, 'How can I get ahold of my good friends and benefactors to tell them that their prayers were accepted?'

"I just can't believe it! That your van should break down for no good reason, exactly next to our taxi stand — it has to be from Hashem. Just so that I could tell you the good news."

He wiped his eyes. "Thirteen years, thirteen years! Who can understand what is happening here..."

I was too overcome to answer, so I began reciting *tefillas ha-derech* instead. Rafi took out a *kippah* and put it on.

"I have to do this," he explained. "I am coming closer to *Yiddishkeit*. This incident has really strengthened me."

I couldn't stop thinking about the astonishing *hashgachah pratis*. If the battery had died just a few minutes earlier or later, we would have switched to a van arranged by our first driver, or gone with some passing van. But Heaven decreed that the "mishap" would happen exactly in the area of Rafi's taxi company and nowhere else. The functioning of every part of that battery had been directed straight from Heaven, with nothing left to chance, just in order to "bring the hearts of the fathers back to the sons..." (*Malachi* 3:24). I had the privilege of seeing the strengthening of *Yiddishkeit* in a whole extended family who had been given the *zechus* to see Hashem's *chessed* and wonders, and who were turning their hearts to Hashem with thanks, in the merit of Rabbi Shimon bar Yochai.

All of a sudden I had a flash of insight, and the whole sequence of events from the year before fell into perspective. Apparently, those bottles of ours had been fated to stay behind in Bnei Brak, in spite of all our efforts, and that bus to Ashdod had been fated to arrive five minutes early, all so that I should meet Rafi — and not just to help his sister finally have a child. Now I understood what our first driver had been unable to understand, "how the battery of a brand-new car could die at the very beginning of a trip." It can happen, at the exact time and in the exact place that Heaven has appointed it to happen. True, not all "mishaps" have such a dramatic ending, at least not one that we can see. But I learned yet again that there is no such thing as "coincidence." And we could only hope that when we went up to Meron the next Lag ba-Omer, in 1999, we would see a very happy family — one that had grown much closer to *Yiddishkeit* — singing praises to Hashem Yisbarach and handing out a very large amount of wine to the thousands of people there.

And we knew that we would be struck once again by the awesomeness of Hashem's special *hashgachah*, and would declare with renewed conviction that "there is no such thing as a 'mishap' in life!"

The Segulah of Giving Drinks in Meron

According to *Sefer Ta'amei ha-Minhagim* (p. 263), the Bobover Rebbe, ha-Rav Bentzion Halberstam, *Hy"d, zy"a*, wrote a letter to Reb Yaakov Yisrael Shmerler of Jerusalem, father of the Rosh Yeshiva of Sanz, in 1932, asking him to distribute eighteen *rotel* (fifty-four liters; approximately fifty-seven quarts) of drinks at the grave of Rabbi Shimon bar Yochai in Meron on Lag ba-Omer. He asked to have this done for one of his chassidim, who heard from Jerusalem Jews that this is a *segulah* to be blessed with children.

Rabbi Shraga Shnitzer of Agudas Ohel ha-Rashbi in Meron has many amazing stories to tell of singles who have found their spouses, and of patients who have recovered after their doctors had lost hope, after they, or someone in their name, had given eighteen *rotel* of drinks to distribute to the worshipers in Meron.

For example, a man whose daughter was in critical condition from an inflammation of the brain completely recovered after her father donated eighteen *rotel* of drinks twice over a three-month period.

Similarly, just a week before Lag ba-Omer one year, a religious couple were told by doctors that they would never have children. The husband, though distraught by the doctors' "prophecy," invoked the *segulah* and had drinks distributed on Lag ba-Omer. That same year, the couple rejoiced with the birth of their first son.

In another story that Rabbi Shnitzer tells, a man did the *segulah* in order to find a shidduch for his not-so-young son. The father reported that just one month after drinks were distributed, his son became engaged.

All's Sweet That Ends Sweet

MY GRANDDAUGHTER SURI suffers from diabetes and her parents must be constantly alert to see that her blood sugar level stays within the normal range. Yet after all is said and done, a little girl is a little girl, and it's hard to watch her constantly. Children crave treats, even more so when they know they can't have them.

The hardships incurred in handling this complex issue are a story in themselves. Of course, as believing Jews it is easier for us to face the challenge, for we firmly believe that Hashem is behind it and that everything is for our ultimate good.

One day Suri didn't come home from school at the usual time. Her mother's concern grew with each passing minute. Finally, she left the house to check with friends and neighbors to see if they knew where Suri was.

As the mother of a child with diabetes, Suri's mother lived in constant fear of Suri's falling into a coma. Constantly on her lips was a prayer to Hashem that the girl's condition cause her neither to lose consciousness nor to lapse into a coma. Now as she looked for Suri, this thought was uppermost in her mind. "Hashem," she silently pleaded as she looked for her daughter, "help her wherever she may be."

A couple of inquiries revealed that Suri had last been seen at the local grocery store. *Oh no!* thought her mother. *I hope she didn't give in to temptation and buy something sweet.*

"Hello, Mrs. Schwartz," the cashier greeted the distraught

mother with a smile. "Your daughter was just here with her friends."

"Where are they now?" asked my daughter anxiously.

"They're out in back, on the bench. They were so helpful, you can be proud. They were on their way home from school when they spotted me organizing the shelves — our worker called in sick today — and they came in to help. I couldn't help but show my appreciation by buying them each a chocolate bar."

That was all my daughter needed to hear. Her heart pounding like a sledgehammer, she hurried out back.

Yes, there was Suri sitting with her friends, a partially eaten chocolate bar in her hand.

"Why, Hashem, out of all the girls for whom chocolate is harmless, did Suri have to be the one to get rewarded with a whole bar of it?" thought my daughter.

Suri saw her mother and came over. "What could I do?" she apologized, in answer to her mother's unspoken question. "Everyone else was eating it and you know how much I like chocolate."

"But, Suri," her mother said with real concern, "you know chocolate and candy can make you sick. It's fine for your friends but for you it's poison." Her heart went out to the child, but she knew she had to make the point strongly.

Suri didn't answer. Silently, they started to walk home.

As soon as they entered the house, Suri sank down on the sofa. "Ma," she whispered, "I don't feel good."

My daughter prayed to Hashem that He might help her stabilize the situation, whatever it may be. She quickly took out the glucose checker, placed a special strip into it, pricked Suri's finger, and put some of her blood on the strip. My daughter waited with increasing fear, dreading to see the machine's digital display showing a high glucose level.

Yet, to her amazement, as she watched the display arrive at the final reading, it showed a lower-than-normal number. It took a few moments for the full implication to sink in: the glucose level in Suri's blood was low, not high — way too low.

A shiver ran down my daughter's spine as she realized that if not for the chocolate bar Suri had eaten, her blood sugar would have been at a dangerously low level.

Tears of gratitude and relief filled her eyes. What *hashgachah*!

Hashem protects children as He does all of us. Hashem protects a person even when he is unaware of the need to protect himself. Behold, the Guardian of Israel neither slumbers nor sleeps.

In an emotional phone call to the cashier at the supermarket, Suri's mother told her how she had been a messenger of good to save her daughter. "You don't know what a great merit you have," she said emotionally. "You have a share in saving a Jewish life. If not for the chocolate you gave my Suri, her dangerously low blood sugar level might have sent her into a coma, and she might now have been lying somewhere unknown to us. It was your chocolate that saved her."

A Chanukah Miracle

T WAS THE AFTERNOON of the seventh day of Chanukah. We had just been to the grave of my father-in-law, as it was his yahrtzeit. I planned to travel by bus from Bnei Brak to Jerusalem to participate in the Rebbe's (the Pnei Menachem, *zy"a*) lighting of the eighth light of Chanukah.

The afternoon was waning, but still I hoped not to be too late. I hoped a bus would come soon so I could make it there in good time.

I had been standing at a bus stop on the Geha Highway when my friend Reb Peretz ha-Kohen drove by. He pulled over to the curb alongside me and offered me a lift with him to Jerusalem. I gave thanks to Hashem for the *hashgachah pratis* — now I would almost certainly make it to the Rebbe on time.

The drive went smoothly. Neither of us had davened *Minchah*, and we hoped that we'd reach Jerusalem before sunset in time to daven there. But heavy traffic was slowing us down. Our anxious glances out the window showed the sun sinking on the horizon, and we were still making our way up the incline near the Kastel Junction. We decided to pull off the road to daven at the first opportunity.

A few minutes later, we drove into the courtyard of the Motza Inn and got out of the car.

I am sure that among the hundreds of thousands of Jews who pass this place, very few stop to daven in this particular courtyard. We prayed with deep emotion, thanking Hashem *al ha-nissim,* for the wonders He wrought for our ancestors in those days at this time — and perhaps also at this very place.

But at those moments we did not yet know with what depth of feeling and intensity we should have been thanking Hashem for the miracle and wonders He did for us on that day, at that time.

We finished davening by sundown. In Jewish homes everywhere preparations were being made to light all eight Chanukah lights, but we were still traveling. We got back into the car in a rush to get to Jerusalem. My friend turned the key in the ignition and started to drive. Then he stopped, shut the engine, and got out of the car. Something didn't sit well with him. Something about the brakes just didn't seem right.

He lifted the hood and checked the brake fluid.

Empty.

All the brake fluid had drained out due to an invisible leak.

I asked Peretz what exactly this meant. He explained to me with some emotion that without the brake fluid, the brakes are totally useless. He voice trembled as he said, "You can't brake. You can't stop the car."

My breath caught. You can't stop the car? What a miracle! My heart wanted to shout, "Ribbono shel Olam! Your *chessed* has no limits!"

I was shaking as I thought of what could have happened. If the fluid had completely drained out just a couple of minutes earlier, we would have been driving down a hill with no brakes. And if the brakes had given out a few minutes after we had stopped to daven *Minchah,* it would have caught us on the long ascent to the city. In the slow-moving traffic, where one foot is always on the brakes, we would have slid right back into the traffic behind us, causing a serious accident, God forbid.

I realized that if not for the miracle we had just experienced, these lines would not have been written by me. How much pain, sorrow, and anguish Hashem prevented in His great mercy and kindness.

My thoughts turned to a verse in II *Shmuel* (14:6): "For there is no stopping of Hashem's salvation, big or small." At this time of "no stopping," Hashem's salvation was big indeed!

My heart skipped a beat as I remembered that this was what we say every day in the blessing of *Modim*: "For our lives which are given over into Your hands, for our soul that we entrusted to You." And it suddenly hit me — what incredible depth of meaning lies in these words!

We come and go, the brake fluid doesn't leak — it's a miracle that is "with us each day."

Yes, a great miracle had happened there. We arranged for a tow truck to take the car, and continued on our way to Jerusalem by bus.

Later when I thought about what had happened, I was struck by the memory of another incident involving my friend Peretz, myself, and a car.

It had happened two years previously, when my father-in-law's health took a turn for the worse and he needed professional nursing care at home. Among other things, we had to provide him with a special bed, like those used in the hospitals. I went to a medical equipment *gemach*, where I was given the needed bed. Given its size, however, I wondered how I would get it into my father-in-law's home.

While I was pondering my predicament, I met my friend Reb Peretz ha-Kohen. No sooner had he heard the problem than he offered the use of his car. I was doubtful of his car's ability to transport such a heavy load, especially since it wasn't that big a model, and had other items in it already.

"*B'ezras Hashem*, we'll manage; don't worry," he reassured me.

I knew that my friend was a busy man and I hated to impose on him, but he was adamant. He called home to tell them he would be delayed. I was uncomfortable about putting him to the trouble, but his smile and good-natured banter convinced me that he felt no inconvenience.

We set to work taking apart the bed, and he helped me carry the pieces out to the car. It was only while struggling to load them into the car that we realized how heavy they were.

We drove off and reached my father-in-law's home, where we were faced with a new hurdle: carrying everything up to the second floor, maneuvering the tricky twists and turns of the staircase. This too we managed, and the bed was soon installed in place.

The sweat of exertion trickled down the face of my friend. I tried to express some words of thanks, but Peretz was already racing down the stairs. My father-in-law, may he rest in peace, benefited from this bed for a long time, until his passing later that year on the seventh day of Chanukah.

Days pass and events in the present obscure those of the past. Although I never forgot the *chessed* Peretz did for me then, I can't honestly say it was at the forefront of my memory. Yet the One Who dwells in the Heavens, before Whose Throne there is no forgetting, had observed the effort of Reb Peretz ha-Kohen and the great favor he had done for my father-in-law, and recorded them in the Book of Remembrance.

Two years had elapsed until, on the exact same day as the yahrtzeit of my father-in-law — the one who had benefited from Peretz's *chessed* — *hashgachah* once again arranged a meeting between Reb Peretz and me, in that very same vehicle of *chessed*. In the very same car, on the very yahrtzeit of the beneficiary of the *chessed*, Hashem had wrought this marvelous miracle to the two who had performed the *chessed*!

How are we to know? Was it the merit of Peretz's *chessed* that helped us in our hour of need? Was it the merit of the act of *chessed* that was done with the car that protected us and saved us in that very same vehicle? Or perhaps it was the one whose yahrtzeit it was — he, whose family had stood at his grave just two hours before, beseeching that he be an advocate for us — who had pleaded our cause before the Heavenly Throne at the crucial time.

The Power of a Jewish Soul

THIS STORY GIVES food for thought on the power of a Jewish soul in the Heavenly realms on the day of his passing.

I promised my wife that I would take our five-year-old son to a doctor's appointment early one morning. For various reasons, we were delayed, so much so that by the time we were ready to leave, it was close to noon.

A minute before we left the house, the phone rang. It was my brother reminding me that it was the yahrtzeit of my grandfather's grandfather, one of the forbears of our family who traced his ancestry directly to the holy Ba'al Shem Tov, and that I should light a candle in his memory.

Although I was in a hurry to leave, I rushed to light a candle. I figured that what I hadn't accomplished until then would eventually get done.

Unexpectedly, my five-year-old son said to me, "Tattie, I also want to light a candle."

I wondered a little at this, for he had never made such a request — although he had seen many candles being lit in our home. I was in a hurry, but he insisted. Seeing how strongly he felt about it, however, I finally agreed. He climbed up on a chair, lit the candle, and with my assistance solemnly pronounced the name of his great-great-great grandfather.

It was lunchtime when we returned from the doctor. We were standing on the sidewalk in front of our home when my son caught sight of his brothers returning from *cheder* on the other side of the street. Before I knew what was happening, he shook his hand free of mine and ran straight into the street — and into the path of a massive eight-wheeler truck bearing down on him.

There was a sudden screech of brakes... and my son made it unscathed to the other side of the street.

Our whole family — those who saw it with their own two eyes and those who heard about it — were struck by the connection. We couldn't put it into words, but deep in our hearts was the conviction that it was he whose yahrtzeit it was, in whose memory my son had lit a candle, who had surely advocated for him in Heaven.

The inexplicable delays that kept us from leaving, making sure I was home to get my brother's last-minute reminder about the yahrtzeit, the lighting of the candle, and especially the innocent desire of my young son to light a candle too — all this told me that the merit of our ancestors stood by us at a critical moment of danger.

May all of us children be helped in the merit of our parents.

Making Choices

A man is led in whichever
way he wants to go.
(Makkos 10b)

Choosing One's Burden

I BELIEVE THAT THE message of the story I am about to relate will benefit many Jewish families. I have altered some details for obvious reasons, but the essence is true. I will tell the story in all its myriad detail as the requisite background for revealing the *hashgachah*, which will unfurl only at the end.

There is a well-known saying that "one father can raise ten children, but ten children cannot raise one father." Whoever has not experienced the "pain of raising parents" — who in their old age often do not have the physical or mental facilitates to "raise" themselves — cannot fully comprehend the implications of this saying. Aside from the emotional stress a child feels seeing his parents in need of care, there are endless additional difficulties that need a tremendous amount of perception and wisdom to deal with, not to mention an abundance of *yiras Shamayim* to find the fortitude to cope with them.

When my father, z"l, was widowed after my mother, a"h, passed away, he felt as if his world had fallen apart. Now in addition to being ill and frail, he was faced with a sudden loneliness that was tremendously difficult for him. My father was a respected person, fastidious and refined, who had made sure throughout his life to always appear dignified. Thus, although his appearance revealed nothing, I, as the youngest child, born when my parents were older, sensed how disconsolate he felt. The teaching of our Sages that "A woman dies only to her husband" (*Sanhedrin* 22b) was embodied fully by him in a most tangible way.

When we realized my father's health was beginning to deteriorate, the first step we took was to have my son spend nights with him. Since I lived closer to him than any of my siblings, I also provided the meals. As the months passed, it was obvious that my aged father's condition required constant care, and that we could not let him live on his own any longer.

I hesitated — until my father slipped and fell. For two hours he lay there on the floor unable to rise. Who knows what the end of this story would have been had not a neighbor heard his weak calls for help? For me this was the final straw. Delicately, I suggested to him that he should consider moving into one of his children's homes.

Father became irritable whenever the subject was raised. He claimed he did not want to burden his children, and said it was better for him to remain in his own home, where he had lived for over fifty years.

I told him that he would be given a private room, and that no one would be disturbed on his account but that, on the contrary, the children would feel honored and privileged to have him live with them. Besides, I added, as long as he lived alone, we had no peace of mind and lived with a constant burden of anxiety for his well-being. Finally, Father promised he would at least think it over.

The next day he told me he was willing to live outside his own home on a two-month trial basis, to see how things worked out. Although my father was blessed with nine other children, *b'li ayin ha-ra*, it was only natural that I should offer my home, since I was the one who had suggested the move in the first place. Also, as I mentioned, my home was nearest his. It is also large and spacious, so it would be easy for us to give him his own room. And, naturally, I felt a certain closeness to my father since I was the youngest. I felt that what I could give him he would not receive anywhere else.

That was in the month of Adar. We agreed that he would arrive at our home for Pesach.

As I left his home after this agreement had been made, I intuitively knew that I had put myself into a not-so-easy aspect of the mitzvah of *kibbud av*. In the depths of my heart there was not the slightest doubt that this trial period would not end after two months, but would stretch out for many years to come — until the end of his days after a hundred and twenty. This truth glared at me from the very first, but I convinced myself that we were talking about a trial period with which we could, God willing, cope.

I prayed that my wife would stand by me. I knew everything depended on her consent. No doubt the difficulties she would encounter would be greater than mine — both because the main burden would ultimately rest on her and, mostly, because this was not her father but her father-in-law, and the difference is immense.

Hashem sent me the opportunity to broach the subject, and I was prepared to embark on a difficult journey of persuasion. But I was pleasantly surprised that my wife agreed with me with all her heart that this was the right step for us to take. "All of us will reach this stage, please God, and none of us want to be deserted in our old age," she said. "Hashem sent this great mitzvah to our doorstep, and it is up to us to take it upon ourselves heart and soul." I will never forget the *chessed* she did for me with that response; I felt as if a huge stone had been rolled off my chest. More than that, I felt renewed confidence and support.

At the Shabbos table, we told the children, with apprehension in our voices, that we were about to undertake a great mitzvah, in whose merit all of us would have a share. I told them about the great respect Rabbi Tarfon accorded his aged mother, and I expanded on the subject of the great dividends of the mitzvah of *kibbud av*. I explained how difficult it is for an elderly person who is used to a quiet life to live with young children, and that they should respect him and show him at every opportunity that we were happy to have him among us.

My children were not overly enthusiastic about the decision, especially the oldest among them, who were none too happy to relinquish their room. Their relationship with their grandfather was not that close, since Father was by nature an introvert. I sensed their reluctance, and this pained me greatly. Only my little daughter had the sense to act excited. Innocently, she announced, "Abba, when you will be old and sick, I will invite you to come and live in my house!" This sweetened my disappointment a little at my less-than-enthusiastic children.

The two-month trial period commenced with the onset of Pesach. During *chol ha-mo'ed*, all the members of the family came to visit. I spoke to each of my siblings and told them that Father had come to stay for a while.

Some of my siblings agreed with what I had done. One of my brothers-in-law nobly offered to give any necessary financial assistance. Yet how bitter it was to hear another brother-in-law argue that, in his opinion, the matter wasn't settled. "An adult feels better in his own surroundings," he insisted.

I had decided on my initiative to bring Father over without sharing my anxieties with my siblings. Now my brother-in-law's words pierced me like a knife. I bit my tongue so as to keep from crying out, "Aren't you ashamed to talk to me like this? Here I am doing all the work and you are not doing anything! Where's your gratitude?"

To make a long story short, each family member reacted differently, but the underlying conclusion was that no one wanted to host Father for another two months. Basically they were saying, "All the more power to you for taking this great burden upon yourself, and best wishes for success." But what I longed to hear was, "We're with you every step of the way. Don't think you're alone in this." To my chagrin, I heard nothing along those lines.

The day after Pesach was Father's first "regular" day in our home. That morning I arose and tried to shake off the cloud of disappointment and doubt caused by the cold reactions of my siblings, not to mention my children, who seemed to silently and resentfully accuse me of thrusting this unwanted burden on them.

I felt on shaky ground. I was no longer so sure of the step I had so boldly taken. I berated myself for making such a rash move. After all, I could have informed my siblings of Father's failing health and included them in the decision. Why had I voluntarily appointed myself his primary caretaker? Now I would be encumbered with numerous difficulties for an indefinite period of time.

The *yetzer ha-ra*'s insinuations festered in my mind, and I felt pangs of regret the whole day. I sat in my office, but my mind was not on the work. It distressed me to no end that this was how the first day with Father in my house was turning out.

When I returned home from work, I found that Father had gone to the *beis midrash* nearby. The children, too, were not at home.

This was an opportunity to share with my wife everything that had been raging in my heart that day. I unburdened all my pent-up pain and frustration, so unlike my usual self.

Again, it was my wife who lent me the Heaven-sent support I so sorely needed.

"This is your *yetzer ha-ra* at work," she concluded. "If we took something upon ourselves, let's do it joyfully. We never dreamed it would be easy. Remember, we didn't do this in order to get other people's approval, and we didn't make our decision on the basis of getting your siblings' support. We did it for your father's good, and this is what we have to keep in mind."

I marveled at my wife's strength of character. I recalled that in her childhood her father had devoted himself beyond the call of duty to his own father, who had lived in their home for several years. It must have been this vivid example that led to her staunch stand on the issue.

"I am happy that it is we who are privileged to show an example to our children. Nothing else could benefit them as much in their education," she said.

I felt I was slowly getting back to myself, and clarity of thought emerged from the clouds of self-doubt in which they had been enveloped. At that moment, we heard the sound of Father opening the door. I went to greet him with a cheerful expression and a lighter step; I welcomed him in warmly and respectfully. He told me that he had been invited to attend a daily *daf yomi* class at the shul, and happily related that many of his acquaintances davened there. That evening, Father thoroughly enjoyed the children's lively behavior at suppertime, and the atmosphere was very pleasant. Yes, I thought to myself, a woman's wisdom does truly build her home.

I elaborate on the description of this first day with Father, for it is an example of what was to come. The highs and lows continued. From time to time I'd need a burst of encouragement, especially after I encountered what appeared to be a lack of familial support. Many times my siblings warned me that my wife could not continue in this fashion. Hashem helped me, in His infinite mercy, to draw support from His overflowing wellsprings and to stretch the two-month trial period to seven years!

Father loved the warm atmosphere in our home and the pleasant treatment he received from us. After the two months were up, it was not difficult to persuade him to postpone his departure indefinitely. The change seemed to invigorate him. It cast a ray of light on his suffering. It was easy to sense how his plight was considerably alleviated. I must point out that it was my wife's intuitiveness that promoted this. Father was made part of the household activities to an amazing degree, until he was an integral part of our life. Also, he still occupied himself with all sorts of activities. He had a daily routine, and despite the occasional difficulties, he adapted well to the house and to the children. Thus matters continued for a year, until the following Pesach, when my father's health began deteriorating.

It began with an ache here, a complaint of pain there; at times I was dismayed to see him very confused. All this brought us to discover that his blood sugar level was unacceptably high, apart from the other ailments from which he was suffering. The visits to the doctor became more and more frequent, causing me to miss precious hours from work.

At the beginning, I received assistance from one of my siblings, who offered to take Father to the doctor. But I sensed that Father prefered that I accompany him; he insisted that I understood medicine better than the others did and that I was more capable of investigating the benefits of one medicine over the other. I tried to respect his wishes, realizing how fearful he was of the future, and I discovered that I was his arm to lean on. Like a baby leans on its mother, father leaned on me. He did not verbalize this, but I recognized the signals. Whenever possible, I would drop everything — even for hours at a time — to make the trip to the doctor with him.

With time, Father became steadily weaker. It became increasingly difficult for him to perform even the most basic tasks. Sometimes he would lose balance due to a sudden attack of weakness. I found myself in the delicate position of having to perform certain unpleasant tasks with him in the presence of the children, all the while trying to preserve his dignity and uphold the regard in which

I held him as patriarch of the family.

My anguish was heightened by the fact that Father realized the impact his presence in our home was making. It was heartbreaking to see him so helpless. When an accident occurred, he would redden with embarrassment. I would tell him, "Father, don't worry, nothing happened." I tried to encourage him and bring a smile to his downcast face. "This is what you did for me when I was a baby," I would say. Father would not respond. He would remain silent or pretend he had suddenly dozed off.

"One thing I ask of you," he implored me a number of times, "don't send me to an old-age home, please." And each time I would faithfully promise him that I would never take this drastic step.

Difficult times now reigned in my home, times that were difficult for all of us and that sometimes drove us to the brink of endurance. "Abba," my son once burst out, after he had been forced to summon a doctor in the middle of a Shabbos meal, "I don't want Saba to be here." He was only expressing what his brothers and sisters were thinking. I explained to the children that it wasn't easy for any of us but that it was the right thing to do. What compounded the difficulties was that Father, as an introvert, could not open up and express his gratitude. At times, we got the impression that he was dissatisfied with the service accorded him. We never knew whether he was content or not.

Admittedly, there were good times, too. I will never forget one *erev Shabbos*, after I had washed Father and dressed him *lichvod Shabbos*. I seated him at the head of the table with all of his medical apparatus, and opened up a *Chumash* before him. I served him a glass of tea and a piece of cake, and my heart was filled with joy at the mitzvah I was doing. I told him I felt so fortunate that, *baruch Hashem*, he was with us, and told him what a privilege it was for us to have him here.

To our surprise, my father lifted a trembling finger to my older son, and in a quivering voice said to him, "You see, *bachur'l*, that's how one should behave."

My amazement knew no bounds. That moment was a glorious compensation for the countless difficult hours in the past: when Fa-

ther had lost all sense of time and insisted on a Wednesday that it
was Shabbos, rebuking my daughter for playing a cassette tape;
when I had finished washing him and his soup spilled once again,
splattering him and the tablecloth, and we had to change everything while all Father did was complain.

There were times when Father became enraged at one of the
children and harshly reproached him in a loud and angry voice,
wagging his finger and expressing his disapproval for the childish
misbehavior. At those instances I didn't know who of the three generations was having the hardest time — my father, myself, or the
child being chastised. Most times, after such an incident, I would go
out with the scolded child to the balcony and console him, explaining about Father's short temper, and telling him that it stemmed
from the hardships he was going through.

Sometimes one of my siblings would come with his family to
visit Father after a meal. Everything was pleasant and relaxed then;
not one of them could imagine what it had been like during the
meal: that the tablecloth had had to be changed three times, and
that not one of the children could get a word in edgewise about
what had happened in school — for Father in his confusion had
kept up a running monologue. At times I longed for such incidents
to repeat themselves, so that my siblings would see what was going
on and offer to invite Father for a couple of days to give us a respite
from the heavy burden.

I imagine you are condemning my disgraceful thoughts, but I
want to tell you honestly of the bitterness toward my siblings that
sometimes surged up within me. I longed for a good word, and I
longed for my wife to hear from someone other than me the praise
due her, that Father was treated like a king in our home.

I am reminded of another pleasant incident. From the time Father began staying at our home, my wife used to bring each of our
children to him on Friday nights — from the oldest to the youngest
— so that he should rest his hands on them and bless them that
they should grow up to be worthy people. One Shabbos, when Father was very weak and could not join me when I went to shul, he
felt very despondent. When the children came to him to get their

blessing, however, he felt so uplifted by this honor accorded him that in his weakness tears formed in his eyes, and he said aloud to me, "I bless you that they should behave like you — the way you behave to me."

Words like these hardly ever left his lips. I was so overjoyed to hear them, and I was so happy that my children had heard them, too. At moments like this I felt I was the luckiest of men, that I was privileged to do a wonderful mitzvah which I would not exchange for anything in the world! When I observed Father sitting in his designated place looking so content, clean, and relaxed, listening with pleasure to a *daf yomi* cassette, sipping his tea and enjoying the sugarless cake that had been especially prepared for him, I would silently watch him and muse, How did I merit all this, that he wasn't placed in an old-age home and treated like a number among all the other elderly residents there?

I know that sometimes it's impossible for an elderly person to be taken care of at home. I know, too, that there are homes where it may be out of the question for various other reasons — and no condemnation can be made. I also know that there are many wonderful residential homes for the aged. Each family has to find the solution that works best for them. I gave thanks to Hashem that He tested me with this burden, and that I was given the opportunity to take care of my father.

At one of these wonderful moments, there arose in my heart a firm resolution that I would eradicate all traces of complaints against my siblings from my heart. I would be happy that this mitzvah had fallen into my hands, and from then on I would never surrender it to anyone else.

I discussed this with my wife, asserting that I would never again express disappointment at my family's indifference, and that we were lucky to have been privileged to do this mitzvah despite all the hardships involved. I took pen to paper and recorded for myself, with renewed spiritual strength, that I wholeheartedly forgave them for the past and that I regretted all that I had complained about to them verbally and in my heart. I resolved that from then on I would be happy to fulfill the mitzvah of *kibbud av*, about which we were commanded by Hashem. I stored the paper away, and still treasure it to this very day.

Heaven tested me soon afterward, when my daughter became engaged. We had the vort at my home. Innumerable times I considered the possibility of celebrating the *simchah* outside our home. But I knew that Father would understand all too well why I didn't have the party at our home, and for this reason alone everything was done at the house.

In the midst of the *simchah*, at one of the most delicate moments, Father entered the room and stubbornly insisted on testing both the groom and his father. I flushed with embarrassment and escaped to the kitchen, stuck my head in the refrigerator, and beseeched Hashem that He should have mercy on our family and calm down my overexcited father. Then I opened a drawer and removed the folded piece of paper which had been hidden there — the paper where I had written two weeks ago, "...and from now on I will be happy to fulfill the mitzvah of *kibbud av*, about which we have been commanded by Hashem." The words seemed to taunt me, as if to say, "Now let's see you be happy about it!"

With renewed strength, I returned to the dining room and lightly tapped Father on the shoulder. I told my new *mechutan* and his son, the groom, who seemed slightly overwhelmed by it all, "Do you know what a merit it is to have a father staying with you? I am *zocheh* to this each and every day, and I have no greater pleasure than this." I poured a *L'chaim*, and asked Father to tell us something about the family.

While he spoke, the goblet of wine slipped from his trembling fingers, forming an unsightly puddle on the festive tablecloth. But I continued to extol Father's praises as if nothing had happened, drawing resources from a willpower I never knew I had, while calmly mopping up the result of the unfortunate accident. Nothing of the stormy tempest raging in my heart was apparent in my demeanor.

Later, my daughter's husband told her that the deep respect I had accorded my father at that time had made a tremendous impression on his father, and he spoke of the incident on many occasions for a long time afterward.

My brother entered the room at this awkward moment to extend his good wishes. He took in at a glance all that had happened and noticed I was close to tears. The next day he called me up and offered for the first time to take Father into his home for two weeks.

I turned down the offer. I knew it was better for Father to remain in our home, as that was what he was used to. If we had managed until now, Hashem would help us in the future.

I think I have sufficiently elaborated with my narrative, but this is merely a drop in the ocean of the saga of taking care of the elderly. I have barely touched the tip of the iceberg. I have drawn upon my memory to relive several incidents so you could get some idea of what commonly transpired. On the other hand, I tried to transmit the occasional moments of joy I experienced in fulfilling a mitzvah that served to strengthen me during trying moments.

Father spent most of the last two years of his life in and out of hospitals and rehabilitation centers. During these years I spent entire days nervously pacing outside operating rooms, and many nights at his bedside. From time to time, he would return to our home, a shadow of his former self, totally confused.

These years were extremely difficult for us, both because of the taxing physical toll they demanded and the emotional hardships involved. Almost every night Father would summon me two or three times for assistance. During the day, assisting him proved to be grueling both physically and emotionally. I had a house full of children then, we were usually standing between one wedding and the next, a busy office was under management, and at the same time I was under the constant obligation to help Father.

An elderly person who is ailing is sometimes like a child: he feels cold even when you do not; he becomes increasingly paranoid and afraid, even when there is absolutely nothing to be afraid of; and it is difficult for him to control certain functions — just like an infant. And if he or she is like my father, it is also difficult for him to express his needs.

But an elderly person differs from a child in two aspects, which makes the situation even harder: first, he understands everything, even when it seems that he is totally oblivious to his surroundings. This is heartrending for his family. Second, while a baby has the constant support of his parents, who are ready to do anything for him because of their love for him, the elderly person doesn't have this.

Of course, all the physical labor that had to be done for Father had emotion behind it. I wanted to show respect for him, to show him in every possible way that my regard for him hadn't waned one iota. I tried to ask small favors of him so that he would consider himself needed.

There were moments when I thought that perhaps the time had come for him to be placed in an old-age home, or that I should hire a private nurse. But I always told myself, If we managed to get to this point, let's continue with the mitzvah. After all was said and done, Father was very much aware of his surroundings, and I knew how much he wanted to stay with us.

What can I tell you? It was a constant, unrelenting burden. At moments of pressure and moments of pleasure, my mind was always preoccupied with thoughts such as, Has everything been done for him? Has he taken his medications? Does he feel good? I rarely attended *semachos* during that period. Before every meeting or *simchah* that took place in our home, there were endless considerations to be taken into account. The burden was so firmly entrenched in my mind that until Father left us, I didn't realize how heavily it had pressed on me.

One morning on *chol ha-mo'ed Pesach*, at the conclusion of the seventh year that Father was in our home, I was spoon-feeding him breakfast when he suddenly showed no signs of life. My heart immediately told me that Father was no longer with us. Until the ambulance arrived, I braced myself to have the necessary presence of mind, and davened that Hashem should grant me the resources to deal with this. I knocked at a neighbor's door and told him what had happened. I asked him to summon my children to his home to show them something interesting, and got another upstairs neighbor to ask my wife for help with some matter, fully aware of the nightmare that was to come.... When the house had been emptied,

I closed the door, hurriedly phoned my brother-in-law, and prayed to Hashem to be with me at this critical time.

Within twenty minutes, Father, z"l, was transported by ambulance to the funeral home, accompanied by my brother-in-law. Then I went to get my wife from upstairs, and quickly informed her that Father had left, never to return. I also had to somehow explain to my children that Saba died ("Daddy, what does that mean?"), when less then an hour ago he had still lain in his bed. I had to inform my siblings, so that somebody else would take care of the necessary procedures.

During that bitter day, there were many instances of *siyata diShmaya* that enabled me to control everything calmly and with self-restraint, and not to explode at anyone.

During *shivah*, which took place in our home, my siblings heaped no end of praise upon me of having taken care of Father with such devotion. I accepted it all serenely. I refrained from any sarcastic retorts. Inside, I was totally at peace with myself. Looking back, I can only thank Hashem for the great privilege I had been granted.

The days of *shivah* passed, and I organized Father's belongings while remembering all the time that an extremely important saga had just been closed behind me forever.

About three months after Father passed away, I found myself at a PTA meeting facing my son's teacher, a devoted, expert rebbe with many years of experience. He told me about my son's progress, and then surprised me by telling me that he had a tendency to hyperactivity that was creating problems. He told me of a certain expert who would be able to advise me on how to deal with it.

Since I had no prior experience of or knowledge about it, I consulted the expert and was told how to go about handling the situation. I somehow found the available time to make these various appointments. As I sat in one of the waiting rooms, while the expert spoke to my son, the thought struck me, "Had Father still been alive, how would I have found the available time to sit here?"

I found myself thinking along the same lines when I took my daughter to the dentist. While I waited outside, I was requested to fill out a form. One of the questions asked was when the last time a member of the family had been treated at the clinic. Try as I might, I couldn't remember exactly when a member of the family had last been there. I vaguely recalled visiting the clinic at various times with one or another of my children — some of whom were already married — but the memory of the exact dates eluded me.

As I handed in the form, the receptionist filled in the indicated slot, making the date of the last visit. It was seven years previously.

"Interesting," she pointed out. "Until seven years ago, you paid frequent visits to our clinic. One son received a retainer to straighten his teeth, a daughter had several root canals done here, your wife had a tooth extracted, and another child had some X-rays taken. During the past seven years, though, we haven't seen you folks here even once."

Her words rang in my ears. It was true; my children and wife had encountered no dental problems in the past seven years. Being occupied with taking care of my father all that time, how would I have had the time or money for crowns or braces?

The third incident happened last year. Less than two years had gone by since Father's passing. My wife and I were on a plane traveling abroad for a number of days to arrange a shidduch for one of our children. Recently the workload in the office had grown considerable, apart from the many household obligations that had sprung up after Father's passing. We had barely found the time to steal away from home to undertake this trip. At the last minute we had made the final decision to leave home from Thursday until *motza'ei Shabbos*.

Seated on the plane, soaring between heaven and earth, the thought crossed my mind: Had Father been alive, how would I ever have found the time to make this journey? I thought of another son of ours who had gotten engaged to a girl from abroad while Father was still alive. The entire process from beginning to end was arranged in Israel, where we live, without anyone so much as suggesting that we should travel abroad. My son's father-in-law made the trip to Israel to conclude the shidduch, instead of requesting that we undertake the journey. How remarkable that this time just the opposite was true.

Thinking thus, I also realized that when Father was alive I did not have the time to spare for all the business obligations that occupy me today from morning to night. Today I sit in my office from 8:30 A.M. When Father was alive, I could not leave the house earlier than 10:00 A.M., having to wait until he awoke in order to clean him and feed him, to put on his tefillin and help him daven, to bring him to the senior citizens center, and to make sure that everything was in order.

Today I am overcome with commitments. The burden of raising children and providing financial support for the family is a demanding one that leaves me with almost no time to relax. My mind is filled with ideas on how to handle the complex projects I head, so much so that I barely have time to think of myself.

Where were all these pressures during the seven years that my father lived with us? I realized that the office had not undertaken projects that demanded so much input on my part since subconsciously I knew my limits, that taking care of my father was top priority. It must have been this knowledge at the back of mind that had saved me from too heavy a workload at the office and left me with more time for the mitzvah of *kibbud av*.

From that time onward, I became increasingly aware of how many things which presently occupy me during the day — household duties, the children's education, the myriad obligations at work, all the responsibilities entailed in marrying off children — simply didn't exist in the past. I could continue filling up page after page with lists of the endless obligations, part of my daily schedule today, that never had to be seen to before.

It's not as if I wasn't a successful breadwinner during those years, or that I didn't marry off any children at that time, or that I didn't manage an office. It was that all those responsibilities took a back seat to my top priority, caring for my father, and that is why I was relieved from bearing the brunt of the other burdens. It was as if I had someone at my side in the office who assisted me in its management so that I was free to serve my father.

My eyes didn't open until my father passed away: it was a pat-

tern! The burden that Hashem had allowed me to place upon myself had relieved me of many other burdens. The trouble I was put
through by having my father with me saved me from facing so
many other troubles in different areas, which with my father's passing came rushing back at me.

Sure enough, I began to notice this pattern in other areas as
well. I learned that many problems had solved themselves without
my involvement. Only recently was I informed that one of my older
children had also been slightly hyperactive when he was younger,
yet even though I had regularly attended PTA meetings, not a word
of this had ever been mentioned. *Baruch Hashem*, in time the problem solved itself, without my having to worry about it or take the
time to run around looking for help. That child's rebbe had decided
to take matters into his own hands and treat the problem as he saw
fit. I did not know anything about this. I was spared this particular
burden, which the Ribbono shel Olam took care of for me, so that I
could devote myself to my chosen burden.

I discussed this subject, of how one burden relieves us of another burden, with someone I am close to. I told him how it seemed
to me that Hashem had spared me many burdens while I was taking care of my father. He responded that this phenomenon does indeed exist and can be seen many times in life. He then told me an
amazing story about his brother, the director of a very busy institution.

One day, this brother's car was in the garage for repairs, which
forced him to use public transportation. Unaccustomed to traveling
by bus, he left his briefcase, which held many important papers and
personal items, on the bus. Before he realized what had happened,
the bus drove off.

It's not hard to imagine how he felt. He had planned on tack-
ling a full day of business meetings in the town to which he had
traveled, but was now forced instead to waste the day tracking
down his briefcase.The prospect of its recovery was remote. To his
chagrin, not only were there important documents, a full wallet,
and checkbooks that didn't belong to him in the briefcase, but his
cellular phone was inside, too. That meant that all his detective

work had to be done from other people's phones. He called home to say he would be unavailable for the next few hours, and told his office to cancel the day's meetings. Toward evening, after many exhaustive hours of searching that had cost him a pretty penny, he recovered his briefcase. It had been a frustrating day that had seen many pressing matters postponed. Not only that, he had barely eaten a thing. If only I hadn't lost that briefcase, everything would have turned out so differently, he sighed. Well, as we say, man has many thoughts, but it is Hashem's wishes that will prevail.

On the way home, as he sat on the bus, briefcase on his knees, he took out his cellphone to listen to his messages. Fear gripped his heart as he hastily played message after message: "Shalom," said the crackling voice talking above the babble of background noises, "this is Simchah Cohen, your son Dani's rebbe. We are now on a class trip. I must get in touch with you urgently. Please call me now at...."

Message Number Two: "Shalom, this is Simchah Cohen again. The matter is very serious. Please contact me at...." The voice sounded tremulous and anxious.

Message Number Three: "Shalom, this is Simchah Cohen again. I have no choice but to tell you the news this way. Our class went on a trip to the mountains. Suddenly, we discovered that Dani had disappeared. We've been combing the area for him for the past two and a half hours, but we see no trace of the boy. We have no idea what happened. We do not want to call your house and alarm your wife. The police have arrived and we pray for good news. Please call me immediately...."

Message Number Four: "My dear sir," a loud voice boomed over the line, "this is Uzi from the police. Your son was found after three hours of search lying in a bush. He was lightly injured after a fall. He appears to have fainted and is suffering from dehydration and shock. He was taken to a nearby hospital accompanied by his teacher, Simchah Cohen. Please get in touch with him at the following number...."

Message Number Five: "Shalom, this is Simchah Cohen. We are at the hospital. Your son is alive and well, *baruch Hashem*. He fell and injured his foot. He is being treated wonderfully and is on intravenous for dehydration. Please get in touch with us. Your wife has still not been informed. The doctors say Dani will probably be released in a few hours."

Message Number Six: "Hello, Abba, this is Dani. Everything is okay. You won't believe the miracle that happened to me today! I'm on my way home in a taxi with my rebbe. I just called Ima to tell her what happened, so she wouldn't be worried. She told me about your lost briefcase. Shalom."

Message Number Seven: "Mordechai! Where are you? Dani had a slight accident today, but *baruch Hashem*, now everything is fine. Please call home right away."

"That's the story," my friend concluded. "If he hadn't lost the briefcase, if the cellphone hadn't been in it, would my brother have been seeing to his meetings and business affairs? No! He would have been busy worried about and searching for his lost son. See what Hashem prevented! He exchanged a frightening search for his son for a hunt after a leather briefcase and paper documents."

Now, you may ask, dear reader, why couldn't I have told you the briefcase story at the beginning of my tale?

I could have. But the story about the lost briefcase is the kind that a person reads, is impressed with, and then comments, "Yes, there is a God Who runs the world."

On the other hand, the lengthy narrative related at the beginning about my father depicts the circumstances of many Jewish families who are carrying a burden that taxes them both physically and spiritually, with many difficulties similar to the burden I carried.

For their sakes, I have told it all and for them I offer words of encouragement. They should realize that every burden spares a person. They have no idea what would have gone on with their time and money if not for this responsibility sent them from Above.

Plus, they are assured of the reward for a mitzvah in this world of which the principal remains intact in the World to Come.

When One Saves a Thousand

A PERSON NEEDS TO REALIZE that he is destined from above to experience certain setbacks and disappointments, but these relieve him of other — sometimes greater — aggravations.

There is a certain scribe — we'll call him Sa'adiah — who has taken it upon himself to set aside a portion of his work hours every month to voluntarily teach two young men the art of his trade. He teaches them all the intricate details of this holy work without taking a penny in return.

His colleagues say he's foolish to spend long hours teaching others and give up his valuable time that could be spent writing and making money. On top of this, he finds it difficult to make ends meet each month.

But Sa'adiah has a different way of thinking: "I have no doubt that what I take upon myself to do during these hours that I set aside out of my own free will release me of other burdens that I otherwise would have been forced to do."

"What would you say," he asks friends, who never fail to express their astonishment at what he's doing, "if instead of sitting and writing I would be forced to wait with my son at the dentist for long hours? Isn't that a waste of valuable time? Isn't that a waste of money?

"My reasoning is that it's part of life that sometimes a person is forced to be busy with things that take him away from his work. And if so, if I am destined to lose a number of writing hours every month, then why should it be at the expense of my poor son's aching teeth? Why should I have to spend these hours in places I would much rather not be in? That's why I willingly undertake to lose a certain amount of time and money, letting fellow Jews benefit from this...I am confident that these hours are anyhow lost time...."

This might sound odd, but look at what another scribe who works alongside Sa'adiah said about the matter:

"One month, after I saw him devote six hours of voluntary

work and once again heard his explanation that this burden relieves him of others, I decided to find out if it were really true.

"I asked him to take note of all the times he is interrupted in his work during the coming month, and to record all the hours he loses from his writing time. I, too, would record precisely how many hours of time I lose from occasional interruptions that pop up for various reasons. At the end of the month, we would tally our hours and compare results.

("Incidentally, this is advisable for every scribe; keeping track of these details once in a while will help improve the pace and intensity of your work.)

"Anyway, both of us work about eight hours a day. Taking into account the absolutely essential interruptions, the total hours of remaining work time is about one hundred and thirty hours a month. During that month, I recorded the time I missed from work every day. My month looked something like this:

"One day I came to work a little late because of a wedding that had ended very late the previous night. Another day I was delayed because of a family *bris*. On most days, the loss of working time was attributed to having to fix or sharpen my quill. And then there were times when a little shopping here and there, or other errands, caused me to leave work early.

"Like every scribe, I had many 'dark days' where everything that could go wrong did: one day some ink spilled, and on another I had no patience to continue. Another time, some letters were printed incorrectly, and yet another more than the usual amount of halachic questions regarding my writing arose.

"In short, my writing hours that month totaled only ninety-five. This wasn't a month where I had been interrupted more than usual; it was a regular month, and it was more or less illustrative of the way things tend to go every month.

"With my number of hours in hand, I approached my colleague, the volunteer tutor who wrote at the same table. I presented him with my monthly tally and asked him to show me his. Sa'adiah withdrew a notebook from his pocket and calculated the total amount of hours he had missed from his work, which he too had conscientiously recorded.

"Like me, he too had missed time here and there for various reasons. That month his father had been hospitalized with a heart attack, and this had taken a large chunk of time from his working hours. He had also devoted one full day's work of eight hours to his volunteer tutoring, which naturally had reduced his total number of working hours.

"But I jumped when I heard him say that the total amount of his work hours that month was one hundred and fifteen.

"I was astonished to discover that he, even with this volunteer tutoring, had worked more hours than I, though our writing ability is about the same. I wanted to understand this phenomenon, so the next month we again recorded our hours. It seemed very odd that although I missed time for the usual reasons, Sa'adiah didn't miss even more time, especially since his father had been sick.

"The next month, I was again faced with the startling reality that what Sa'adiah lost in volunteer work, I lost because of various other reasons. Even his father's illness didn't cause Sa'adiah to miss extra time. The implication was clear: what is destined to be lost, one anyhow loses, but there are people who wisely utilize this loss of time for mitzvos. Moreover, with his acts of kindness for others, Sa'adiah saved additional hours he might have lost in other ways.

"This is what ha-Rav Eliyahu Roth, *zt"l*, used to say in the name of his rebbe, Reb Shlomke of Zvill, *zy"a*: every step a person takes to help another saves him from having to take a thousand on his own behalf.

"It's a fact: one saves a thousand. And who isn't interested in such a lucrative deal?"

Treat Us with Tzedakah and Chessed

(from the Avinu Malkeinu prayer)

Profiting from Tzedakah

E FEEL BLESSED. We have a large family, *baruch Hashem,* and we have succeeded in implanting strong Jewish values in all our children. Until recently we even considered ourselves financially comfortable. We are not extravagant people, and although we always tended to buy only what was really necessary, we were well able to afford whatever we wanted.

The wheel of fortune turns slowly but inexorably, and it seems that Heaven decreed it was time for a change. We firmly believe that everything Hashem does is for the best, and we have no complaints, God forbid.

Slowly, over a period of time, we noticed that our income was gradually dwindling. We had been involved in a car accident, and, although no one was seriously hurt, we were suddenly beset by large expenses we were not used to dealing with.

At first we hoped our insurance would cover the expenses of the accident, but the insurance company balked at making a payment. We had to hire an attorney to negotiate for us. The attorney's fees were not low, and unfortunately he was unsuccessful in pleading our case. The insurance company would not assume responsibility because there was no personal injury involved. Naturally, we accepted Hashem's will, grateful that He had granted us the greatest gift of all, our lives, our limbs, and our health.

We realized we had no choice but to cut down on our expenditures. This signified instituting drastic changes in our lifestyle and giving up many comforts we were used to. We now had to watch every penny. We no longer thought, What do we need? but rather, What can we do without?

It actually came down to a choice between new clothes or new shoes before holidays, and often we decided to make do with what we had. We were determined not to borrow any more money if we could help it, and in time, we became relatively accustomed to our new restrictions.

We had, of course, explained the changes to our children, each according to his ability to understand. We said money was not the most important thing in life, and it certainly was not the arbiter of happiness. The really important things in life, we told them, are things like family togetherness, peace, faith, and joy. Money, we explained, is like a guest. When you have it, you can enjoy its presence. When Heaven decrees that it is time for the guest to depart, you just have to get used to living without it.

Of course, it wasn't easy. At the beginning of the school year, for instance, we were under great pressure with the need to purchase school supplies for all the children. We tried to solve this problem by saving money during the summer. We took no trips and managed to entertain ourselves and our children at home. We tried very hard to keep our children's spirits up by involving them in inexpensive games and projects. As a result, not only did we save some money, but we spent a lot of time with our children and had a lot of fun doing it.

One evening, shortly before Rosh Chodesh Elul, we sat down to estimate our expenses for the ensuing holidays and plan how to deal with them. After discussing what we could do without and what was absolutely necessary, we drew up a detailed list of probable expenses. We decided that in honor of *Yom Tov* we would allow ourselves to splurge somewhat and buy one or two extras. We would somehow spread the cost over a period of three months.

We set ourselves a clear limit, naming a specific sum we felt we could handle within the framework of our three-month plan. It felt good to be prepared, and we faced the holidays in a calm and happy frame of mind.

Only one thing cast a shadow over our pre-*Yom Tov* spirits. Before the accident, we had always given sizable donations to *tzedakah* before the holidays. It had given us great joy to know we were helping others enjoy the holidays. Now our situation was such as to make our former generosity impossible, and that disturbed us greatly.

Giving *tzedakah* is a great *segulah* for wealth. "Honor Hashem with your wealth," said King Solomon, "then your storehouses will be filled with plenty" (*Mishlei* 3:9-10). And in the next verse, the wisest of men issues specific instructions for those who have merited to give *tzedakah*: "My child, do not despise Hashem's discipline...for Hashem admonishes the one He loves...."

Rabbeinu Yonah explains the verses as follows: "If one who gives charity sees that his own financial position deteriorates or that he is suffering, he should strengthen his faith in Hashem. He should realize that the troubles that beset him benefit him more than success and wealth, for Hashem gave him the troubles to cleanse and purify him of guilt and sin and increase his reward in the World to Come."

We had always appreciated our ability to give *tzedakah*, and we certainly never gave in order to receive a reward in the World to Come. However, since we had always considered *tzedakah* to be part of our *Yom Tov* expenses, we found it difficult not to be able to do so this year.

Requests for *tzedakah* came in the mail in a flood as usual before the holidays. We were inundated with letters describing the plight of poor families who could not afford to prepare for *Yom Tov* at a time when we were just barely making ends meet ourselves. However, we knew that there were many families far worse off than we, and we burned with the desire to help them.

Our discomfort at the thought of not being able to give *tzedakah* this year gave us no rest. Finally, we decided to incorporate an additional sum of money for *tzedakah* into the framework of our three-month plan. We scraped together 350 shekels, a sum that amounted to more than the obligatory 10 percent tithe, and gave it to our local rabbi to distribute to the needy.

The 350 shekels we contributed were really more than we could afford, but, *baruch Hashem,* we merited to give.

A few days later, we were astonished to receive a telephone call from the lawyer we had engaged to deal with the insurance company. We had not heard from him in a long time, and we assumed the case was closed.

The lawyer had good news for us. "The insurance company has acceded to the request of your insurance agent, and although they are not legally obligated to pay you for damages, they have decided to award you a token sum. Your insurance agent persuaded them in view of the fact that you and your family have been good clients for many years. Just call up and make an appointment to go in and pick up your check."

We picked up the check the same day.

The token payment was 3,500 shekels — exactly ten times the amount of the *tzedakah* we had given.

We thanked Hashem from the bottom of our hearts, for we felt we had personally witnessed the truth of King Solomon's words. He who takes pity upon his fellowman, Heaven takes pity on him.

Giving When Times Are Hard

7HE BEST *SEGULAH* for wealth is generosity. We are well-aware that Hashem is the true Banker Who dispenses His treasures as He sees fit, yet Rabbeinu Yonah tells us, "One who gives much *tzedakah* adds wealth upon his wealth."

Eliezer is a young man who studies in *kollel*. He is the father of a growing family, and finds it difficult to make ends meet. Whenever he finds himself in a particularly tight situation — when expenses suddenly pile up and he has no clue how to pay — he goes to a particular *tzedakah* distributor in his area and increases his regular monthly donation by a few shekels. Yes, you read that right: he doesn't decrease the amount he gives to *tzedakah*; he increases it.

"I know that when one gives *tzedakah*, Heaven grants him special blessings for livelihood," Eliezer told me. "If my financial situation is bleak, if I urgently need Hashem to send me more money, the first thing I do is give *tzedakah*.

"Sometimes I see immediate results. Sometimes I notice that somehow or other, after a while, I have managed to work something out. Sometimes things do not work out. But still, I believe in the power of giving *tzedakah*. A man never knows what he may have accomplished by giving generously, what decree he may have averted.

"I thank Hashem," added Eliezer, "that I have the merit of giving a considerable sum of money to charity each year. *Baruch Hashem*, I live comfortably. My family and I lack for nothing."

I told him that, as a matter of fact, I was going through some financial difficulties myself at that moment. As a result, I was planning to phone the bank and instruct them to stop paying the monthly fees I had pledged to a number of *tzedakah* organizations. I was afraid I would not be able to keep up with these payments.

"Why," he asked, "is *tzedakah* the first thing you want to cut out of your budget? Why don't you first try to minimize your phone bill or avoid purchasing any extras? Why don't you consider canceling your savings plan payments or your insurance?"

"I consider those things vitally important," I said.

He told me that my *tzedakah* payments were even more important — in fact, necessary.

"Why don't you try to help yourself by increasing your monthly *tzedakah* contribution by twenty shekels?" he suggested. "See what happens. See if Hashem doesn't reward you by opening wide His treasure house."

I did as he said. Soon after that, I was asked to do some private tutoring that paid extremely well. I now not only had a new source of income, but a big load was removed from my shoulders.

When I bumped into Eliezer a few days later, I told him about the improvement in my income.

"The next time I feel pressed for money," I said, "I'll increase my monthly *tzedakah* contribution by twenty shekels."

Tzedakah Is Returned Tenfold

7HERE WAS ONCE A Jew of old Jerusalem who was the epitome of the *middah* of caring for one's fellowman. Whatever meager funds came his way were quickly distributed to his even needier neighbors. Somehow, with the help of God, he managed to feed and clothe his own family as well, though they survived on the barest minimum. He was never able to accumulate anything for "a rainy day," as they say. It was evident from the way this worthy Jew freely distributed his money that he firmly believed his purpose in life was to act as Heaven's messenger in ascertaining that the money reached the right address.

In spite of the fact that the pressure to sustain his own family should have weighed down heavily upon him, this fine Jew continued to give. He had upon Whom to rely for his own sustenance, so why not give to others?

His righteous wife had attempted, as the years passed, to save a few pennies, bearing in mind the far-off day when they would have to marry off their children. She pinched and scrimped from their already meager earnings and discreetly harbored her growing treasure in one of the hollow iron poles that served as a footpost to the iron bed in her bedroom. After a lengthy period of time, during which her young children were growing into adulthood, the hidden coins grew to a sizable amount. She hoped to please her husband by presenting him with a respectable sum of money when the time was ripe.

The inevitable day was drawing closer. Their oldest son was of age, and they started receiving many suggestions for matches. It was almost time to make use of their hard-earned treasure, and the worthy Jew's wife finally shared her secret with him. He, however, had recently heard about a poverty-stricken widow who was forced to clothe and feed her children all on her own.

Taking his wife quietly aside, he earnestly explained the situation. A poor widow was struggling to put food in the mouths of her hungry children, while in their very own home lay a large pile of coins gathering dust. Was it fair to deny the widow the money?

Silence reigned in the house. The clock ticked its steady beat, allowing no time for second thoughts or doubts. They removed the bedpost and poured the dusty coins into a sack.

The bare walls of the house were used to witnessing greatness. This latest occurrence, however, was unprecedented even here. Who knew better than they how many repairs were required but ignored because of lack of money? They had seen the children of the house go without new shoes; they had seen the wife's toil as she worked to earn each precious coin to place in her hiding place. They had rejoiced along with her as the collection had increased. Now they watched the radiant faces of this saintly Jew and his wife, and they couldn't help but whisper to each other.

> Giving tzedakah to the poor is likened to lending money to the Shechinah Itself. Their money will probably be returned twofold. Hashem will definitely reward them well for this loan, though that is not what they seek. The needs of their fellowman are paramount to their own. These two know what it is to give for the sake of giving rather than to give for the sake of receiving.

Not more than two weeks passed when, amid much excitement, the couple's oldest son became engaged. Neighbors, friends, and relatives came to extend heartfelt Mazal tovs. It was only when the excitement died down a bit and the house emptied of all its well-meaning visitors that the blatant truth of the family's situation came home to the worthy Jew and his wife. They knew that they had nothing but the mercy of their Father in Heaven to rely on.

Were they worried? Far from it. They staunchly believed that ha-Kadosh Baruch Hu would provide for all their needs. In the meantime, they were grateful to Hashem for blessing their son with such a wonderful shidduch.

As we all know, not all stories end well. There are many righteous people who don't merit to see the fruits of their labor in this world. These individuals will certainly gather strength from the selflessness we have described. They will hear about others who, like them, give without expecting anything in return.

This story turned out well and the couple were repaid tenfold for their kindness to the widow. How did they manage to pay off all the debts from the engagement and the wedding? The true conclusion of this story may sound like the happy ending of a fairy tale. The couple we have described in this story were people of valor, who gave without expecting a thing in return. So why should we continue the tale and destroy the picture we have painted of an altruistic couple?

Do people think they can sign a contract with Hashem when they give *tzedakah*? Do we need to be assured of receiving a reward when we help our fellowman? No. The only thing required of us is to be faithful servants of Hashem and constantly fulfill His wishes. The groom's parents personified this trait, and that is what we are meant to derive from this story — that one must give of oneself without questions or doubts.

With the hope that others will benefit and learn from this story, we will now describe what transpired shortly after the couple parted with their hard-earned money.

During the early weeks of the engagement, a businessman approached the worthy Jew with a business proposal. He was about to embark on a lengthy trip abroad, and he needed a trustworthy person upon whom he could rely to oversee his business at home. He was a real estate agent and wanted someone to see that his commissions and rents would be collected while he was away. He also had property that might be sold or rented in his absence. An office worker would see to the details, but he wanted an honest, responsible person to supervise.

The worthy Jew accepted the job and promised, "with the help of Hashem," to do his best. The businessman gave him a large enough advance to pay for his share of the shadchan's fee, the wedding, and the first payment on an apartment for the bride and groom.

The businessman promised to send him a regular monthly salary as long as he was gone, which he did. The advance served as immediate relief, and the money that poured in in abundance afterward enabled the couple to marry off all their children.

All It Takes Is a Little Rachmanus

ZEDAKAH COLLECTORS make the rounds, collecting for all sorts of tragic causes. Once, one of them sat in my house telling me his story, and my heart broke. I took out a small sum from my wallet and offered it to him hesitantly, explaining that if only I could, I would give more, since I understood the depth of his tragedy. On hearing my apology, he told me a wonderful *d'var Torah* in the name of the *tzaddikim* on the saying, *Kol ha-meracheim al ha-brios, merachamim alav min ha-Shamayim*, "One who treats other people with compassion will be shown compassion from on High" (*Shabbos* 151b). The simple meaning is that if Reuven treats Shimon mercifully, then Heaven will treat Reuven mercifully. But the novelty of this particular *d'var Torah* was that the word *alav* here refers to the one to whom the mercy was originally shown. In other words, if Reuven shows mercy to Shimon, then Shimon is also treated mercifully by Heaven. If ha-Kadosh Baruch Hu sees that a Jew has mercy on a certain unfortunate individual, then mercy is also aroused on High toward that same needy person. All it takes is a little *rachmanus*, compassion.

"Therefore," the *tzedakah* collector continued, "when a Jew hears of another Jew's anguish and his heart is moved, and he gives as much as he is able and even adds a blessing from the depths of his heart, this causes Heaven to shower mercy upon the very person who needs help."

The impact of his words has stayed with me. In the past, whenever I gave a small sum to charity I would think, "What good can my five or ten dollars do for a man who is bowed under the weight of enormous debts?" But now I know that these few dollars, coming from a caring heart, are a form of human mercy and compassion. And who knows? Maybe as a result, Heavenly mercy will be invoked.

In Heaven, there exist limitless possibilities for helping people, far more than what we can ever imagine. When we do our share, then there is a fulfilment of *Hashkifah mi-me'on kodshecha*, "Look down from the seat of Your holiness" (*Devarim* 26:15), and mercy is shown from Heaven. I think the following episode is a perfect example.

There is a broken man who often sits in the doorway of my shul, collecting charity. His expression is one of total misery and suffering. He hardly speaks. His face twists with pain from his back when he stands up, and sometimes he even needs to use a cane to walk. He holds a paper plate in his hand and his eyes turn pleadingly to passersby as he silently gives thanks for every coin thrown his way.

In Hashem's mercy which He shows to all His creatures, He put it into my head to pay attention to this pauper who caught my eye, and on several occasions, I struck up a conversation with him about his predicament. He told me that his home was bare in the most literal sense; he and his wife, he said, did not have a penny to their name. Any money that came in from unemployment insurance or social security was used up on the numerous medications he had to buy because of his various health problems, which cost a fortune to treat.

Every loaf of bread that he bought, he told me, was eaten to the last crumb. Likewise with every bag of milk or container of cheese. They tried, he said, to minimize expenses in every way. They hardly bought anything, in order not to get into a debt they would be unable to repay. Their only income, he said quite frankly, came from charity.

I wondered whether I should believe the man, whether he was really telling the truth. If he was, I decided, something should certainly be done to help. The man gave me his address and invited me to come and visit him at home whenever I wished.

I took him up on his invitation and made a surprise visit to his home. I was shocked to find out how bad things really were.

In crossing the threshold I felt as if I had stepped into another world, one I thought no longer existed in this day and age. The poverty in the house was awful. Everything was faded and dusty. The refrigerator was empty save for some milk, cheese, and a bottle of water. The breadbox had a few slices left in it from the week before but that was it. The kitchen cabinets were almost bare: all I saw was a little sugar in a bag, a few raisins, and some rice.

The man pulled out a bundle of medical records from under his bed testifying to his muscle disease and various other ailments, and their treatment. In one corner of the room sat an elderly woman, his wife, wringing her hands.

I left the house aghast. In a bountiful generation such as ours could there be such poverty? Most of us think nothing of spending a few dollars here and there, money which, when added up, could put that home on its feet. Why, I thought to myself with mounting excitement, even one full grocery bag would brighten up that impoverished house and its inhabitants.

All of this took place shortly before Pesach. After seeing what I saw, I spoke to a friend and told him about the troubling situation, which to a certain degree had become my own trouble. We decided that we would go to a supermarket together and do a major shopping for the elderly couple, even if it cost a couple hundred dollars. Let me just add that both my friend and I are ordinary working people, certainly not men of means.

We met the next day at a local supermarket and pushed a shopping cart through the aisles, filling it with every imaginable item, from canned goods of all sorts, to staples such as oil, sugar and flour in large quantities, to cleaning supplies and toiletries, along with cooking basics and various pots, dishes, and utensils.

The pile in the shopping cart grew to the point where we had to take a second shopping cart. A quick calculation toward the end of our "shopping spree" showed that we would indeed be spending several hundred dollars.

As we were standing in line at the checkout counter, trying to remember if there was something we had forgotten, a wealthy looking religious man with a trim beard came over to us and said in a French accent, "Your purchase seems to be for *tzedakah* purposes, no?"

We nodded. My guess was that he figured two poor-looking fellows shopping with such abandon could not have been shopping for themselves.

The man said that he had heard of a *chessed* organization run by a local rabbi that gave out food in hospitals and also helped the needy. We told him we were not part of that organization, but chatted with him about what we knew of its good work in the community.

At this point we still assumed he was waiting in line, as we were, to make his own purchases. It didn't even cross our minds that he was standing there just to talk to us. That's why we were floored when he said, "I would like to take part in your purchase."

My friend and I looked at each other. We were speechless.

The gentleman proceeded to remove three one-hundred-dollar bills from his wallet. He then handed them to me, thanking us for the opportunity to share in the mitzvah.

By the time we recovered, the man had left the supermarket, disappearing before our eyes without our having asked his name or even having had a chance to thank him.

The groceries and household items reached the poor man's home via a messenger, who identified himself as a volunteer from a certain charity organization that distributes food to the elderly before Pesach. We accompanied the messenger until just outside the door to make sure all went smoothly. We couldn't help but walk around to a side window to see the couple's reaction to their gift.

The sight that met our eyes was a poignant one. The elderly couple burst into tears and raised their hands heavenward in gratitude to Hashem for remembering them in their misery and not forgetting them in their plight.

I wiped away a tear and thought about how there really was no one to thank except ha-Kadosh Baruch Hu, Who had given us the idea of helping these people, and had then sent an anonymous emissary to pay for the help in full.

Yes, it really is true — all you need is a little *rachmanus*.

THE POWER OF CHESSED

A Life for a Life

Who knows where an act of chessed can lead? Whether a small favor done for a stranger, or a gigantic act of selflessness such as saving a life, Heaven records each and every deed of man. We are repaid, measure for measure, for the acts of chessed that we do — perhaps not right away, or perhaps not even in our lifetime. Sometimes it is only after several generations that the recipient of the chessed is finally able to repay his or her benefactor, favor for favor. And sometimes, the beneficiary is even zocheh to be an agent of rescue.

A NUMBER OF YEARS AGO, I was in London doing some fundraising for a worthy institution right after the disastrous Pan-American Airlines plane crash. On board the ill-fated London–New York flight were a number of Jews who lost their lives. Many more, though, were saved. The One Above, in His mercy, found unique ways to keep each one of them from getting on that particular plane.

The stories of these amazing rescues were the talk of town during my trip to London. One family reported that their son had gotten locked in a bathroom at the terminal and was only released from his "prison" after the flight had already taken off. Others missed the flight because for "some reason" traffic on the highway to the airport was unusually heavy that day, and dozens of taxis and cars couldn't get through. In fact, a whole group that was traveling together was saved in this way.

One person related that when he heard that another airline had built a new terminal, he on impulse canceled his flight with Pan Am and booked with the other airline, just to see what the new building looked like.

These stories and others inspired the Jewish community, for it was obvious that the traffic jams and accidents were not just chance occurrences, but that each and every delay had come straight from Hashem.

When word of the Pan Am tragedy reached America, hundreds of relatives and friends of the supposed passengers thronged to the airport, anxious for news of their loved ones. At first, no one knew that by a miracle, some of the passengers missed the flight. People were in a complete panic.

Meanwhile, another plane left London for New York, carrying many of those whom *hashgachah* had saved from the doomed flight. They arrived in New York while the airport was still in an uproar. Many of those who had come to the terminal hoping for news of their lost relatives were stunned to see them coming off the second plane, alive and well, in a veritable *techiyas ha-meisim*. The drama repeated itself again and again, as passengers who were supposed to have been on the first flight met relatives who were sure that they would never see them again.

The Stage Is Set

On one of my rounds about London in the wake of the crash, I stopped in to see an old friend. Practically before shaking hands, he pulled me into the house and took a plane ticket out of his pocket. Waving the Pan Am ticket folder in the air, he exclaimed: "I am keeping these tickets in my pocket right over my heart. They are witness to the miracle of my rescue!"

And with that, he began to tell me the following incredible story:

"On Thursday night of the week of that flight, I had a family wedding in New York. I planned to fly to New York Thursday morning, which would get me to the wedding on time. The Thursday morning flight is always overbooked, so I reserved tickets well in advance.

"On Monday of that week, I was suddenly hit with terrible pains in my back. My doctor diagnosed a mild slipped disk, and advised me to take a two-day course of treatment in the hospital to ease the pain. Although I was very busy, I was forced to take his advice. The pains were so bad I couldn't function.

"The treatment worked well and I started to feel better immediately. *Baruch Hashem*, the slipped disk was caught early and could be treated properly. I stayed on at the hospital the second day, Tuesday, just for observation. For all intents and purposes, I was well, and I spent the day ambling around the hospital and arranging my discharge papers.

"Thus it was with great surprise that on one of my tours of the corridors I bumped into an esteemed acquaintance, a respected *talmid chacham*, who had taken the trouble to come all the way out to the hospital just to visit me. True, I daven at the shul he heads, but that didn't justify his taking so much trouble to come see me. Besides, I wasn't even in the category of an ill person who deserved or needed *bikur cholim*. I was just in the hospital to get some back treatment.

"Embarrassed, I thanked him for coming to visit me, and we looked for a quiet corner to have a few words. My visitor, whom we can call Reb Haskel, showed an interest in my condition, listened as I told him about it, and sympathized with my pains.

"At some point, it occurred to him to ask, 'Don't you have a wedding in the family this week? Are you going to be able to attend?'

"I answered that I hoped to be discharged from the hospital that evening, and that I had booked a flight for Thursday morning. If all went well, I would indeed be able to attend the wedding on Thursday night.

"Surprisingly, my distinguished visitor expressed dissatisfaction with my plan. 'You plan to leave London Thursday morning? You'll arrive at the wedding Thursday night exhausted from the trip! You won't be able to dance and to gladden the bride and groom at your family's *simchah* if you do that!'

"'Besides,' he continued in a fatherly tone, 'you've had a hard week — the pain, the hospitalization, the treatment. That alone is enough to exhaust a person.'

"'So what should I do?' I asked him. 'Miss the wedding?' I already had the tickets in hand and couldn't imagine in my wildest dreams what he would suggest.

"'In my opinion,' the rabbi declared with a decisiveness that surprised me, 'you should leave London on Wednesday morning. You'll arrive in New York the day before the wedding and be able to rest up. Then you'll be able to attend the wedding refreshed and in a happy frame of mind.'

"I made a quick calculation. It was really no problem to do as the rabbi suggested — switching flights is easy enough — and so, given his stature and personal interest in my well-being, I decided to take his advice. I thanked Reb Haskel for his concern and help, and escorted him back to his car, where we took friendly leave of each other."

Why Change Flights?

"On further thought, though, I was a bit surprised by the rabbi's whole suggestion. Why was he so concerned that I attend the wedding 'refreshed and in a happy frame of mind'? Was this enough of a reason to push up a flight by a whole day?

"But even if I thought otherwise, I couldn't dismiss Reb Haskel's obvious care and concern for me. So I picked up the nearest phone and called to cancel my Thursday morning flight and reserve instead a seat on the Wednesday morning flight.

"I wasn't the only one who was surprised by Reb Haskel's concern. I later heard from his driver that the rabbi himself had also been surprised. On the way home from the hospital, he told his driver that he had no idea why he had come to visit me. He was also puzzled by why he had suddenly had the urge to visit an acquaintance who, after all, had just been admitted to the hospital the day before, and then just for minor back treatment, and who furthermore was going to be released that very day.

"However, the fact remains that I was released from the hospital that evening and I flew to America Wednesday morning, just as Reb Haskel had suggested."

Joyously Alive

"On Thursday, in the United States, I heard about the terrible disaster from which I had been saved. I was astonished at the *hashgachah* bestowed upon me in the form of Reb Haskel, who had directed my steps and saved me from death. Understandably, I called him immediately and in a voice choked with tears thanked him for having acted as Hashem's emissary in sparing me from the grave.

"Reb Haskel was astonished and overcome. Jokingly, he began to protest that he had no *ruach ha-kodesh* or anything like that. It was just that Hashem had directed his steps and put the words into his mouth in order to save another Jew.

"And sure enough, I found myself 'refreshed and in a happy frame of mind,' and dancing at that wedding as I had never danced before in my life.

"But if I thought that this was the end of the miracle, when I returned to London, alive and well, I discovered that what I already knew of the story was just the beginning. Or to be exact, it was just the second half.

"I was stunned to learn that, apparently, the story of my rescue had a first half, which had occurred decades before I was even born, and that my gift of life was the closing of a circle, a repayment of a debt, arranged by the One Above, Who never forgets anything.

"Soon after I returned to London, Reb Haskel asked me to visit him, which I did with alacrity. 'Do you know,' he began, with a far-away look in his eye, 'for some reason, I was recently reminded of a "minor" incident that happened during the Holocaust, which can explain a lot.'

"The tension and excitement of the week before had taken their toll on me, and I held my breath and waited for him to continue. He began again, almost in a whisper, and this is what he said:

What I Never Knew...

During the first days of the war, I hid out in a certain apartment. The Nazis, *ym"sh*, were still at the stage of rounding up men and boys to send to forced labor camps, or worse. I hid in a double hideout in the apartment, and spent my days learning Torah.

In the apartment across the hall lived a *tzaddekes* whose husband had already been taken. She supplied me with all my needs, for she saw it as a privilege to protect me since I was involved in learning Torah. She took it upon herself to be on guard for the soldiers. When she saw them arriving on their searches, she always ran to warn me not to come out of my hiding place.

Once I was standing out on the landing when suddenly I heard the sounds of stomping boots running up the stairs accompanied by terrifying, vicious shouts. My blood froze and I couldn't think. I didn't know what to do with myself.

Just then the *tzaddekes* from across the hall opened her door and motioned me to enter her apartment without making a sound. Then she pointed at a ridiculous hiding place: against the wall behind the opened front door.

With time of the essence and having little choice, I stood flat against the wall. When the first fist began pounding on the door, the *tzaddekes* opened it wide, covering me behind it. She stood calmly, leaning on the door, and asked the SS men what they wanted.

"Where is your husband?!" the evil one roared at her. "Where are your grown sons?!" He pounded on the doorframe so hard I was afraid he would take it off.

The *tzaddekes* stood her ground at the door and answered quietly, "My husband and sons have already been taken away from me. No one is here but the little children."

Through the door, I heard the soldiers burst into the house and storm though the rooms, overturning closets, breaking, plundering, and screaming all the while. "Listen," I heard one of them shout at my hostess, "we are going to search the house again. If we find anyone, both he and you will pay with your lives. I'm giving you one more chance," I heard the voice roar just on the other side of the door.

I almost died on the spot from terror.

"Tell me right now: is anyone hiding in this house?"

I heard a thud and the sound of something smashing to pieces. I was shaking. Was my benefactress finally going to turn me in? She certainly didn't have to sacrifice her life for me. I was scared to death. All the murderers had to do was move the door and they would find me.

But the door stayed where it was, opened up against the wall with me behind it and the *tzaddekes* standing there in front. She answered firmly, "There is no one here, sir. My husband and older children haven't been here for a month. Only I and the little ones are left."

The soldier thumped his rifle on the floor threateningly but the brave lady only repeated her words. "Search as much as you please. You won't find anything in any case."

I was overwhelmed by the realization that she was willing to sacrifice her life for me. I held my breath tensely for what seemed like an eternity, and then I heard the footsteps of the wild beasts charging down the stairs and out of the building.

White as chalk, the righteous heroine finally closed the door and with a sigh of relief, released me from my hiding place. I was too paralyzed to thank her for the greatness of her *chessed* to me, and I could only silently beseech the Ribbono shel Olam that He repay her for her goodness and save her from the war. And then I ran back to my own shelter.

I endured the horrors of that monstrous war and in Heaven's mercy came out alive. This "minor" incident receded to the recesses of my memory along with the thousands of other miracles that I had seen day after day. I was happy to hear, years later, that that *tzaddekes* had also survived.

The End Was the Beginning

"Reb Haskel stopped speaking for a moment and took a deep breath. I had been following his story with bated breath and only now stopped to wonder what all this had to do with me. Why had he called me to hear this fascinating tale?

"'Ah, life!' I thought. 'We all want to live. That's how it has always been.'

"'And so,' Reb Haskel continued, his voice trembling, 'I must tell you, my friend, that the *tzaddekes* was…your grandmother.'"

The Exact Amount

MENDEL IS ONE OF a pair of young men who voluntarily visit families who want to strengthen their *Yiddishkeit*. On one of these visits, he discovered that the mezuzos in the house were invalid and needed to be replaced immediately. There were six mezuzos, and neither the family nor the volunteers had the means to replace them.

Nevertheless, Mendel wanted to take care of the matter right away, if his fellow volunteer would accompany him. They decided to go to a religious neighborhood and try to collect money to purchase the mezuzos. They began knocking on doors and explaining to their fellow Jews why they needed the money and that they were only seeking a relatively modest sum. The coins started to pile up, and soon they felt they had enough money to take to a store that sold religious objects. They stopped collecting and went to make the purchase, figuring that if they were short they would simply go back and collect some more.

When the salesman calculated the cost of one mezuzah times six, they were astounded to discover that the total exactly matched the amount they had collected, down to the last shekel. They saw this as a powerful sign from Heaven that for the sake of the mitzvah they had undertaken they did not have to go out of their way even one step more than necessary.

It Never Hurts to Do a Favor

THE ROSENBUSH HOME was in a flurry. Rabbi Rosenbush, a well-known rosh yeshiva and esteemed personality in the Torah world, was due to fly abroad in just a few hours.

If the truth were told, the Rosenbush home was always a beehive of activity. Students came and went all the time;

one group was just leaving from a *mussar* lesson while another was entering to discuss a complicated piece of Gemara. On a typical day, Rabbi Rosenbush might receive someone inquiring about a particular boy as a prospective son-in-law, a delegation of community leaders seeking the Rav's advice, a scholar needing help with a personal matter, and a young married man asking a halachic query.

The door to the Rosenbush home was always open. Rabbi Rosenbush greeted everyone with a warm smile and a pleasant manner. He was known for his endless patience, which people sometimes took advantage of. It was therefore not in the least unusual that Rabbi Rosenbush was still welcoming visitors with his characteristic smile in the hectic hours before his journey.

Not one of the numerous callers was aware of the real reason Rabbi Rosenbush was leaving. His demeanor remained calm and untroubled the entire time, giving nothing away. Only his nearest and dearest knew that recent X-rays had revealed the presence of a malignant tumor that posed a serious danger to the Rav's life. Only those closest to him were aware that he was going to a large hospital in Canada for surgery.

The Rav's family was anxious to close and lock the front door. They were concerned about the Rav, who was frail, and wanted him to rest before his flight. They felt that he really ought to be conserving his strength for the ordeal that lay ahead.

In one room, Rabbi Rosenbush's wife quietly packed his suitcases, while in another his son made telephone calls to check up on the medical arrangements. In the Rav's study, visitors sat and unhurriedly discussed whatever matter it was that had brought them there. From the Rav's demeanor, it seemed that he had all the time in the world to devote to them.

At long last, the family was able to retire. They were all tense and anxious, worried about the Rav's health, but he remained calm and in control. Just when his family thought they were finally settled for the night, the shrill ring of the telephone proved them wrong. Rabbi Rosenbush's son hurried out of his room to pick up the receiver — perhaps the caller had a message regarding the flight, or perhaps it was a call from abroad.

"Hello?" A tired voice sounded through the receiver. "Can I please speak with Rabbi Rosenbush?"

The Rav's son was annoyed. Wasn't the caller aware that it was after midnight? Controlling his irritation, he asked who was speaking.

"Menachem Raful. It's rather urgent. I've been trying to get through for hours but the line was constantly busy, so I assumed the Rav was still awake."

The son was about to explain that Rabbi Rosenbush couldn't possibly be disturbed when the Rav himself picked up the extension in his room.

"Hello," began the caller, "this is Menachem Raful speaking. I apologize for calling so late."

Rabbi Rosenbush quickly assured the caller that it was perfectly all right. "We're all still awake," he replied, "happily awaiting your call."

Mr. Raful's relief was obvious. In an anguished voice, he related that he had a four-year-old son who was learning-disabled. Things had become so difficult that they were strongly advised to place him in an institution for special children. The family had looked into the matter and decided that the Shorashim institution was the perfect place for the little boy, but a technical problem had come up. Because Mr. Raful was not an Israeli citizen, they could not accept his son.

"I was about to give up," continued Mr. Raful, "when a friend of mine who works at the institution mentioned that if a certain member of Knesset, who serves on the board of the school, would personally recommend the boy, he would be accepted despite the fact that I'm not a citizen. My friend also told me that the Rav is a good friend of that Knesset member.

"Please," pleaded Mr. Raful, "would the Rav try to help? We would be so grateful. As matters stand now, we are all under great strain and are really desperate to get help for our son."

Rabbi Rosenbush was greatly distressed by the man's plight. "Mr. Raful, would you be able to come to my house tonight? Right now?"

"I'm on my way," said the delighted caller. "I'll be there in fifteen minutes, God willing."

The family protested. Sunrise was but a few hours away. The Rav would need to daven *vasikin* and immediately thereafter set out on a long and tiring journey. He was a frail, ill man. How could he, now of all times, take up another burden?

But Rabbi Rosenbush would not be swayed. "I can nap on the plane tomorrow," he insisted, "but this poor Jew cannot sleep at night. How can I refuse to help him?" Despite his frailty, he rose from his bed, switched on the light in the living room, and sat down to write a moving letter to the Knesset member Mr. Raful had mentioned.

He explained the Raful family's problem, and pleaded with the Knesset member to see to the matter as soon as possible. The fact that Mr. Raful was not a citizen, argued Rabbi Rosenbush, was not a justifiable reason to prevent a Jewish family from gaining some measure of relief. For several reasons, he explained, it would be best for the child if he were to receive his care outside the home. In conclusion, Rabbi Rosenbush showered the Knesset member with blessings, once again urging him to "move heaven and earth" to see that Menachem Raful's son was accepted into the superb Shorashim institution.

Rabbi Rosenbush felt drained and exhausted from the effort of writing that letter. At 12:15 A.M., when the peal of the doorbell sliced through the stillness of the quiet house, the letter was all ready. Menachem Raful could not find the words to thank Rabbi Rosenbush sufficiently. His tears of gratitude, however, expressed more than words ever could.

After a few hours' sleep, Rabbi Rosenbush got up to daven with the early-morning minyan. Immediately upon returning from shul, he and his son prepared to leave. It was a moment of keenly felt emotion. The family bade them goodbye and wished them a safe trip and, more important, a healthy return.

Rabbi Rosenbush arrived at the hospital and spent the next few days undergoing a battery of X-rays and tests. Several top specialists examined him to determine whether the operation was feasible or even necessary. They first tried various noninvasive treatments, but it soon became clear that there was no alternative. They had to operate.

Rabbi Rosenbush asked the cost of the operation. He found out that as a private patient, the surgery would be extremely costly. The surgeon said there was little he could do to help, as the price was determined by the head of the hospital and it was often a question of what the market would bear.

Rabbi Rosenbush listened thoughtfully, weighing the information. How could he possibly come up with so much money? Would he be forced to accept charity? Where might a man of modest means find even half the sum? He prayed fervently to Hashem, Who grants life as well as sustenance, to help him in his hour of need. The surgeon read the concern on the rabbi's face.

"You know," said the surgeon thoughtfully, "rumor has it that you are something of a VIP in Israel. I believe the hospital has a policy of reducing its fees for important people. You see," he explained, "it has to do with P.R. If a celebrity chooses our hospital, it's good for our reputation and our public image. Why don't you go down and speak with the hospital director and explain that you are an esteemed rabbi in your own country?"

"My father is far more than just an esteemed rabbi," interrupted Rabbi Rosenbush's son, who had not left his father's side. "He is the dean of a large educational institution with a student body in the hundreds, and he is extremely well-known both in the Orthodox community and in government circles. His door is always wide open to accommodate the steady stream of visitors who come to seek his advice. It is indeed a great honor for this hospital to have the privilege of caring for him. Just pick up the phone and call any public figure in Israel."

The surgeon listened attentively. He explained that if the matter were up to him, he would immediately approve a reduced fee. However, he explained that only the hospital director had the authority to do so.

Rabbi Rosenbush's son set up an appointment to see the director the following morning.

"What good will it do?" the rabbi dismissed the idea with a wave of his hand. "The director himself will not have heard of me. What will he do to determine if I am all you say I am? Test me on *Shulchan Aruch*? Initiate a discussion on a *sugya* in *Yevamos*? How can he possibly judge whether I am a 'distinguished personality,' deserving of a reduction? After all, anyone from abroad could make the same claim." Rabbi Rosenbush's tone made it plain that he did not place great hopes in achieving anything in this manner.

"But Abba," protested his son, "it's certainly worth a try. Even the hearts of Canadian hospital directors are in the Hands of Hashem. Who knows? Perhaps it will be easier than we think."

The next morning Rabbi Rosenbush and his son sat down in the hospital director's office and introduced themselves.

"Rosenbush, you say? Rosenbush? The name rings a bell. I'm certain I've only just recently come across the name somewhere," the hospital director said.

Rabbi Rosenbush recalled his son's words: "Even the hearts of Canadian hospital directors are in the Hands of Hashem." But how could the director of a large Canadian hospital complex, even if he is Jewish, be familiar with the name Rosenbush from distant Jerusalem?

"Are you by any chance involved with the Shorashim institute?" inquired the hospital director, still trying to figure out where he might have come across the name Rosenbush. "I saw the name Rosenbush just a few days ago, and I think it was in connection with a letter I received about Shorashim."

The director drew out of his desk drawer an impressive looking folder with the word *Shorashim* stamped on it in gold. Opening the folder on his desk, he explained that he was honorary chairman of the board of directors of Shorashim. Flipping through the letters and documents in the folder, he stopped at one particular letter and quickly scanned the written lines. "I knew I had seen your name somewhere recently, Rabbi Rosenbush."

He handed the letter to Rabbi Rosenbush, who was staring at him in great surprise. It was a fax of none other than the letter he himself had written in the middle of the night to his friend in the

Knesset on behalf of Menachem Raful.

Rabbi Rosenbush was confused. Why was the director showing him a letter he had written on behalf of someone else, when it was he who needed the recommendation?

"The member of Knesset you wrote to," explained the director, "forwarded this letter to me as chairman of the board, and asked me to instruct the Shorashim management to accept the Raful child despite the fact that his father is not an Israeli citizen. He added a note explaining that Rabbi Rosenbush is a highly respected member of the Orthodox community in Jerusalem, and a letter of recommendation from such an esteemed person was not to be taken lightly."

The hospital director seemed amused at the interesting turn of events. Rabbi Rosenbush had caught up with a letter he himself had written only a few days before on the opposite side of the world! He immediately began pleading Mr. Raful's case in person, as if he had come to Canada especially for that purpose. He explained that he was personally familiar with the family's difficult situation, and that it would be a great kindness on the hospital director's part if he were to set the wheels in motion so the child would be accepted into the institution.

"Consider the matter taken care of," said the director. "And the matter you originally came to see me about is taken care of as well," he added, quickly scribbling his signature on a form authorizing a sizable reduction in Rabbi Rosenbush's hospital fees.

"*Refuah sheleimah*, Rabbi Rosenbush."

Mercy for the Merciful

Every day in the Modim blessing we offer thanks to the One Above for His "miracles that are with us every day." What could be more of an ordinary everyday occurrence than to give someone a lift? Yet who can guess the benefits of doing such a chessed? As the car wheels turn, so too do the wheels of destiny.

T WAS A *MOTZA'EI SHABBOS* early in the winter of 1994, and I was on my way back to Jerusalem from Bnei Brak.

The weather was stormy. Between bursts of rain, the fog hung too thickly to see the road. Traffic moved at a snail's pace as the cars slowly chugged along the highway, bumper to bumper.

Just before the steep climb up to the Castel Junction, I noticed a van parked on the shoulder with two men standing alongside it waving for help. I pulled over, in total sympathy with their unfortunate plight of having to stand there in such weather.

"The motor died," they explained, "and we've been waiting out here for two hours. No one stopped," they added bitterly. It turned out that they were supposed to be in Jerusalem for an awards ceremony, and the prizes were in the van with them. I'm no mechanic, so all I could offer the two men was a lift to Jerusalem with all their parcels, but they were grateful just for that. I dropped them off at the hall where the ceremony was being held and they thanked me profusely as I drove off. In the dark, I hadn't been able to make out their faces, and I hadn't asked their names.

About a month later, I was in Bnei Brak again, at the end of an exhausting day of errands. Before setting off home to Jerusalem, I stopped in one last store to pick something up. As I stood waiting at the cash register, a stranger approached me and stuck out his hand with a hearty "Shalom Aleichem!" I shook hands, with a blank look on my face, and was introduced to one of the fellows to whom I had given a ride on that rainy night several weeks before.

"You have no idea what a *chessed* you did that night," he said with emotion. "You were a messenger from Heaven sent to help us." And then he began to heap blessings on my head: "May the mitzvah you did protect you and watch over you!" he called after me as I smiled and nodded goodbye, too tired to answer.

My son, who was with me, had *baruch Hashem* become engaged that week, and was at least as tired as I was. He figured he would sit in the back seat and try to take a nap on the trip back up to Jerusalem. At the last minute, though, he changed his mind, and decided to keep me company up front in the passenger's seat. We set out on the highway, taking the shortcut to Jerusalem's northern neighborhoods through Ben Shemen.

At some point, I must have dozed off, because the car swerved out of the right lane into the oncoming left one. We experienced our first miracle right there, as the other lane was empty at that critical moment. My son started screaming, "Abba! Abba!" and I woke up in time to swerve off the road, to where the guardrail ended next to a cliff face. The car was still moving so fast, though, that we hit the rock wall head on and were bounced backwards, down the side of the mountain.

It is hard to describe what happened in the moments that followed. I can only thank Hashem that I am the one writing these lines. This was one of those moments that you read about but never dream could happen in real life.

The "tin can" containing me and my son tumbled downhill like a leaf in the wind. It was tossed violently from rock to rock and fell with loud, terrifying crashes punctuated by the sound of smashing glass, crunching metal, and piercing cries of "*Shema Yisrael!*" and "Ribbono shel Olam!"

And then, after a minute that seemed to last an eternity, there was silence. Nothing moved. It was over.

I couldn't speak. My body was wracked with pain but I was happy for every pain I was able to feel. From my awkward position, I could see my son lying over me, looking back at me, every bit as alive as I was.

"Listen," my cracked voice came out, "I filled the tank just before we left Bnei Brak and it could catch fire any minute."

With unbroken hands, we unbuckled ourselves from our seat belts, and with whole legs, we crawled out of the shambles and onto the hillside. We stood up and looked at each other and were amazed to find that not only had our lives been spared, through Heaven's mercy, but our limbs had been spared as well. We were bruised and battered, but there was not even a cut or a scrape on either of us.

Up on the hilltop, some Arabs started to run down to us from their nearby village. We waved to them to show that we were okay.

We started climbing and stumbling back up the slope toward the road, tripping over thorn bushes and falling into pits, balancing from rock to rock, until we finally made it. The twisted heap of metal — our former car — lay two hundred feet below.

Up on the shoulder of the road, my son flagged down a car, and when the driver heard our story and peered down at the wreck below, he could not believe that we had come out of the crash alive. He took us to the hospital, where they released us that same evening for "lack of evidence" of any injuries.

The following morning, my older son arranged for a tow truck to fetch the remains of our vehicle, at which point we were appraised full-scale of the miracle we had experienced. The entire back section of the car was completely crushed, and the roof was flattened to the floor of the back seat. I shuddered to think what might have happened if my son had decided to doze off back there after all. The entire car was completely destroyed except for the two front seats, which were in perfect condition, as if a loving Hand had cradled them and protected them.

When the driver of the tow truck saw the damage, his first question was, "What about the passengers?"

My son answered, "Nothing," which the driver took to mean the worst, and shook his head with sympathy. But when my son corrected him and told him about the miracle, the man at first could not believe his ears. Finally, after much persuasion, he was convinced, and he was so moved that he took out a camera and memorialized the miracle on film. With his years of experience as a tow truck driver, he was ready to attest that coming out alive from such a wreck was an enormous and extraordinary miracle.

As I lay recuperating at home for a few days after the ordeal, the words of that anonymous Yid who had blessed me for giving him the ride echoed in my mind.

"May the mitzvah you did protect you and watch over you," he had said, just moments before I set out on the road. I felt that it must have been in the merit of my having done a *chessed* that I was given such a *chessed* in return. Because I had had the merit to show mercy to others, Heaven had shown mercy to me.

The Last Minute

YONAH WAS A young boy when he first stepped onto American shores. His parents had sent him on such a long journey in order that he could study in one of the many yeshivas that were sprouting up in the United States. But although he was thankful for this great privilege, right now Yonah felt helpless. He stood at the side of the noisy expressway, not knowing in which direction to turn.

His watch indicated that the hour was late. He had been informed that the yeshiva doors would be open day and night for *bachurim* who were scheduled to arrive from all over Europe. However, he had mistakenly alighted from a taxi at the wrong address, and now found himself utterly alone in a strange, bustling neighborhood. His suitcase was heavy, but what made him more despondent was the thought that there was every chance in the world that he could walk for hours — only to find out that he had been heading in the wrong direction.

He had been walking for a long time already, and still did not see any figure with whom he could possibly exchange a few words. His English was not too good, and his Yiddish he knew would not be understood by any non-Jew whom he stopped. His heart began to pound in fear for his fate.

In such situations, Hashem sends help through one of His many messengers. While Yonah was still walking, his heart full of prayer to the One Above, a religious man suddenly stopped near him and asked in Yiddish if he could be of any help.

Yonah explained his situation, and the friendly Jew told him that he was now very far from his yeshiva. Even if he took a taxi right then, he would find nothing to eat at such a late hour.

"May I suggest that you come to my house, which is not far from here. My family and I are spending our summer vacation in this neighborhood. You can bring all your things to my house, have something to eat, and get a good night's sleep. In the morning, I will get you on your way."

Yonah did not refuse. In his host's home, he was the recipient of warm Jewish hospitality, as he had never before experienced. The transition from the busy, unfamiliar roads to the quiet Jewish home relaxed him completely. After a hot, kosher, nutritious meal, Yonah settled down to sleep in a pleasant room, and slept better than he had ever imagined.

Yonah could not find the words with which to express his heartfelt thanks. The kindness of his host and the Divine Providence that had dictated his meeting such a worthy Jew, had rendered him speechless. It was all so spontaneous, his host was so gracious and friendly — definitely one of the friendliest people Yonah had ever met.

The next day, his host warmly saw him off on his way. Before he left, Yonah learned that the man's name was Gavriel Berman. This name would ring in his ears for many years to come, since he never forgot that night.

During his years in the yeshiva, Yonah often tried to locate Gavriel Berman, but he recalled that the house he stayed in did not belong to his host but was rented for the summer vacation. At every available opportunity, he tried to find out more, but he was told that the summer home was rented out to many people, making it difficult to locate any of the short-term tenants.

Although he persisted in his efforts, Yonah eventually concluded that he would never find the man. After all, he did not even know where he lived.

Years passed and Yonah married and moved to England. He was successful in business and soon became a wealthy man. Although he never met Gavriel Berman again, he adopted his style of hospitality as his life's goal. The warmth that he had felt in his heart that night radiated outward to others for the rest of his life. The community leaders in London, where he lived, knew that a guest could always be sent to Yonah's home. His was an open house and guests were part of the family.

Whenever Yonah told his children about the warm hospitality he had experienced in Gavriel Berman's home that night, he always added that he hoped he would have the opportunity to meet him one day and repay him for his kindness. There was no doubt in his mind that it was Gavriel Berman who had sowed the seeds of the mitzvah of *hachnasas orchim* in his heart.

However, as time went by, Yonah resigned himself to the fact that he would probably never see Gavriel Berman again. Yet, although thirty years had passed in the interim, every guest reminded him of his host, whose face he could no longer recall but whom he would never forget.

It was the same with the current guest, an older man who was accidentally delayed in London and found his way to Yonah's door.

The noise in the plane was loud, and the weary steward tried in vain to raise his voice above the commotion. The passengers on this Friday morning, New York-bound flight were distraught when their plane made a sudden, unscheduled landing in London. The flight staff announced that due to unexpected technical complications, the flight would be delayed by a few hours. In the meantime, each passenger would be provided with comfortable hotel accommodations.

When the traveler heard the words, "delay of a few hours," he knew he would have to abandon this flight and spend Shabbos in London. He could not take the risk of boarding the plane after those "few hours" were over, when the clock was speedily advancing toward the arrival of Shabbos. However, he did not know anyone in London; it was the first time he had ever stepped onto English soil. Still, he hoped he would manage.

The concerned passenger informed the flight staff of his plans. A cordial steward helped him locate his baggage immediately, and escorted him through Customs. An hour later, the passenger was flagging down a taxi to take him to an Orthodox Jewish neighborhood — actually any Orthodox Jewish neighborhood — in London.

The driver left him off near a shul, but the imposing building was still locked. Having no choice, the weary traveler decided to wait near the door until someone came and showed him where to go.

He put his suitcase on the sidewalk and sunk down onto a

nearby bench. Sitting made him feel his exhaustion even more. It had not been easy for him to get here, but he surely didn't want to risk desecrating Shabbos. He had called his family to let them know what had happened, and now he waited patiently for one of the local Jews to arrive.

About two hours before Shabbos, a man appeared dressed in his Shabbos finery. From the rattling of his keys, the man on the bench surmised that he must be the *gabbai*. After a short conversation, the *gabbai* explained that he could not host the stranger himself, for his house was already full of guests, but he promised to find him suitable accommodations for Shabbos. The *gabbai* went into an inner room of the shul and began calling various congregates. For some reason, every household he called was overflowing with guests.

The *gabbai* put his finger near the next name on the list, dialed, and waited for the enthusiastic response he always received when he called this particular family about taking in a guest.

Yet when someone finally answered, the *gabbai* was informed that they, too, were already full and that he should try the next person. After thinking some more, he unthinkingly dialed Reb Yonah's number. The telephone rang once, twice, and was then answered by one of Reb Yonah's sons. The *gabbai* identified himself, and was about to open with his regular greeting of, "Can I speak to Reb Yonah?" when he almost dropped the receiver.

Had he forgotten? Had he lost his senses? How could it have slipped his mind that Reb Yonah had been sent home only yesterday from the hospital in critical condition, in accordance with his wishes to spend Shabbos at home? Reb Yonah was certainly not in a position to host guests now! The *gabbai* did not know what to say. How could he have dialed this number? Such a thing had never happened to him before. He must be getting old.

"Uh..." he stammered. "I dialed your house by mistake. You see, some guest showed up here, and out of habit, I called your home. I'm really sorry. I hope we will soon hear good news." He tried to end the embarrassing conversation, when the son interrupted him.

"Wait one moment, please."

The *gabbai* heard the son tell his father what had happened. The telephone was probably located near the sick man's bed, and he wanted to know what was going on.

"Listen," the son said, "send the guest here. We will be happy to have him."

"But...but..." the *gabbai* protested, wishing the floor would open up and swallow him then and there. He couldn't believe the uncomfortable situation he found himself in. "I can find someone else; the list is still long."

The son's voice was resolute. "My father asked that you send the guest here. I will come immediately to take him home in my car."

"Your host is a wonderful person," the *gabbai* told the traveler as he stepped into the larger room of the sanctuary. "Reb Yonah is one of the most respected members of the community." He said nothing more, not wanting to disconcert the guest with the sad tidings of Reb Yonah's illness, which had recently disturbed the tranquility of the entire community.

Reb Yonah's son soon arrived. He smiled at his guest, lifted his luggage, and placed it in the car.

The guest enjoyed a wonderful Shabbos. There were moments when he felt it was worth enduring the flight delay that had stranded him in London just so that he could experience Reb Yonah's outstanding hospitality. An ordinary man was not often privileged to experience such excellent treatment, and did not always realize what a difference it made when the household was so warm and welcoming.

He didn't meet the man of the house almost the entire Shabbos. When he asked about him, his sons, who directed the Shabbos table, explained that their father was lying down in a nearby room since he wasn't feeling well.

Only during *seudah shelishis* did his host's condition improve somewhat, and he was taken into the dining room in a wheelchair, accompanied by a private doctor who had spent Shabbos with him.

When Reb Yonah saw his guest, his suffering face lit up. "Shalom aleichem!" he called out in a weak voice suffused with joy.

"Make yourself at home. I am not doing so well today, but God willing, everything will be okay."

The guest felt a pang in his heart at his host's friendly greeting even under such circumstances. He blessed his host that the great merit of *hachnasas orchim* would influence his health and that he would soon recover.

Reb Yonah did not ask the guest for his name, for that was the custom of the house. Many paupers, who were forced to go collecting from door to door, spent Shabboses here without having to embarrass themselves by revealing their identities. Reb Yonah had taught his sons to do the same and not ask any unnecessary questions.

While they recited the Grace after Meals, Reb Yonah's eyes began to roll. The doctor leaped up and propelled the wheelchair back to his room, and his sons ran after him. Additional doctors were quickly called, but they left after a few moments. A cloud of mourning soon spread through the house.

Reb Yonah had returned his soul to his Maker. One moment he had been sitting with his guest, and a minute later he was no longer there.

The guest entered the room. At their father's bedside, the sons were sobbing bitterly over their loss. The man approached them somewhat hesitantly.

"What was his name?" he asked.

"Reb Yonah," he was told. "Reb Yonah ben Reb Yitzchak."

The guest asked the sons for permission to speak. He went closer to the deceased and called out, "Fortunate are you, Reb Yonah, that your soul left your body in the midst of performing the mitzvah of *hachnasas orchim*. May it be Hashem's will that this mitzvah accompany you to the World of Truth, and that in its merit, you will be privileged to greet the *Shechinah*."

A fervent chorus of "Amens" echoed in the room.

One of the sons could control himself no longer. He approached the guest and asked him his name.

This son, who told us this story, realized that the unexpected visitor had been his father's last guest on earth. This man had completed the long chain of hospitality that his father had extended all his life. The guest would probably never forget this Shabbos, just as they would never forget it. This time, it would be interesting to know who he was.

"We don't usually ask our guests for their names," he excused himself in a soft voice. "But could you perhaps tell us, if you don't mind...."

"Tell you my name? Of course I don't mind. I didn't realize that I hadn't done so until now."

And closing a circle of thirty years, he said, "My name is Gavriel Berman."

THE POWER OF PRAYER

Two Points of View

YONASAN WAS DEPRESSED. One day seemed to melt into another with no purpose. His eyes seemed always to be looking downward, or at least on the same level. He found no joy in the beauty of Hashem's world that surrounded him, for that is the way he had been brought up. If he was not playing a game or engaged in a sport, doing something or watching others do something, he was bored. He had never paused to think about what he was doing or why he was doing it.

Fortunately, just at the point in his life when he was becoming so depressed about the pointlessness of it all, Yonasan met some wonderful people who introduced him to *Yiddishkeit*. They explained to him why his life had seemed so empty, and they taught him how to fill it with Torah and mitzvos and begin to live a bit for his fellowman. His life became sweeter, and he began to feel he no longer wore blinders that limited his vision. He appreciated the miracles he began to see all around him, he enjoyed the satisfaction of being able to help, in a small way, other people, and he learned to thank Hashem for his newfound happiness.

Yonasan also felt greatly indebted to those who had helped him climb out of the depression his secular lifestyle had engendered. They were dedicated and righteous people whose help had extended to many others for many years. In particular, he was grateful to the warm and understanding staff of the yeshiva he had studied in, and he still maintained close contact with them — though he had gone on to study in a more advanced yeshiva.

You can understand how distressed Yonasan was, then, to learn that "his" yeshiva was in dire financial straits. The situation was so bad that they might even be forced to close. Yonasan worried about the yeshiva's fate and the fate of all those who needed the yeshiva.

Yonasan had a secular friend, Gabi, who was more than well-off. Gabi had been in business for many years, and his head was always swimming with original ideas about how to make more money. The two men were still fond of each other even though Yonasan's life had changed so drastically. Yonasan therefore felt justified in asking his friend's help for the yeshiva.

Yonasan knew, however, that an ordinary request would elicit a meager response from Gabi, because the latter was not very big on giving charity. Yonasan felt that the great need of the yeshiva demanded some originality on his part, and an approach that would feed into Gabi's interest in making money.

Yonasan went to see Gabi. "How would you like to make a profit on something I dreamed up?" he asked.

Gabi's eyes gleamed. He was always investing money in various schemes in the hope of finding a gold mine someday. "Of course I'm interested," he chuckled. "But that is usually my line," he added. He was amused by Yonasan's question, and just as obviously did not have much faith in his business acumen.

Ignoring Gabi's friendly jibe, Yonasan told his friend that he was serious and that he had a tempting offer for him. Gabi was always ready to make a deal. "I wouldn't mind earning twenty thousand dollars right now," he said.

The figure he mentioned fit in very nicely with Yonasan's idea. He explained the deal he had in mind. Starting from that very day,

Yonasan would pray to Hashem every day that He grant Gabi the means of earning the sum of money he had just mentioned: twenty thousand dollars. Yonasan assured Gabi he didn't want anything in return, but when he earned this sum, he only wanted Gabi's promise to give one quarter of it — 25 percent, five thousand dollars — to the yeshiva.

You may think this was the height of presumption on Yonasan's part, but he was determined to help the yeshiva in any way he could, and he sincerely hoped that he would thereby merit earning Hashem's *chessed* on its behalf. He was entirely confident in the limitless power of Hashem, and he prayed with all his heart that Hashem send the money to Gabi through one of His numerous messengers. The "business deal" immediately appealed to Gabi.

"It's a deal," he said. "You pray for twenty thousand dollars, and your yeshiva will receive five thousand. Even if I make fifteen thousand, this deal is worth it." They shook hands, and the deal was closed.

We all know perfectly well that if the yeshiva was destined to receive money, Hashem had it in His power to send the money to the yeshiva through any one of an infinite number of messengers. He certainly didn't need Yonasan as an intermediary.

Yonasan had learned, however, that Hashem often performs miracles in the guise of natural occurrences. He was not a business-man, and for him to acquire five thousand dollars suddenly would have to be counted as a miracle. On the other hand, large sums of money passed through Gabi's hands daily. For him to earn a profit of twenty thousand dollars on one particularly successful deal would not seem out of the ordinary at all.

So, far away from probing eyes, especially Gabi's, Yonasan quietly launched his unique campaign for the yeshiva. He recited *Tehillim*; he beseeched Hashem in his own words to send the salvation the yeshiva so desperately needed. He begged Hashem to ensure that the institution would not be forced to shut down, and to allow him the privilege to have a humble part in it.

"Ribbono shel Olam," Yonasan prayed, "see how Your son Gabi is ready to change his usual behavior and donate 25 percent of his profits to *tzedakah*. May that qualify him to deserve Your bountiful blessings."

Naturally Yonasan had some misgivings about his prayers. He knew it wasn't right to demand that Hashem fulfill a particular request. But he felt the shared pain of the yeshiva so keenly, and his belief in the power of prayer was so strong, that he continued praying heart and soul to help the yeshiva. If he did his part, perhaps Hashem would find him worthy. This spiritual haven for so many must be allowed to continue its awesome work. Maybe Hashem was waiting for a sign from just one of those who had benefited so greatly from the yeshiva.

There was not the slightest doubt in Yonasan's mind that Gabi's primary interest in this venture was to fill his own pocket. Yet the power of *tzedakah* and *tefillah* is so great that he hoped it would assure the success of the deal. We know that Heaven deems any act of charity worthy even if the giver's benefits are commensurate with those of the taker. The taker is dependent on the giver, regardless of the giver's ulterior motives.

It appears that Yonasan's instincts were correct. Not long afterward, Gabi informed him that he was offered the position of agent representing two large firms in a bid for a particular contract. It was too early to tell if the deal would go through, and if it did, Gabi still would not know what his commission would be.

Yonasan continued to pray daily.

A few days later, Gabi called again to say his prospects looked good, and he was almost certain the deal would go through.

Yonasan knew that only Hashem knows what is truly best for us, and all deals "go through" only if He wills it, but he kept his thoughts to himself.

The good news arrived a few days later. The contract was signed, and Gabi's commission was twenty thousand dollars. To the penny.

When Yonasan went to see Gabi and congratulate him on his success, he was therefore utterly shocked to receive one thousand dollars in cash from Gabi.

Gabi noticed Yonasan's look of disappointment and said,

"Now, see here. A thousand dollars is a lot of money." Yonasan did not say a word, but inside he grieved. He had done his part faithfully, and he had expected Gabi to do his. What could the yeshiva do with one thousand dollars?

Nevertheless, if he tried hard, Yonasan could understand Gabi's point of view. As far as Gabi knew, the money he had earned from this particular business deal was the fruit of his own labor. It never occurred to him that the business deal he had just completed was only the means through which Hashem was shifting the money into the right channels. He could not truly conceive that the business deal had materialized solely because it was Hashem's will.

If a person understands that the assets in his possession are only placed there by Hashem, and the role he plays resembles that of a simple servant guarding the King's treasures, he will be more easily able to part from his money by giving *tzedakah*. Paradoxically, when one believes that his fortune is solely his, and was acquired through his own toil and sweat, he will be extremely hesitant to part with even a small fraction of it.

Yonasan was still standing in front of Gabi, just looking at him. Sometimes, maybe, silence is more eloquent than words. Gabi obviously was in a terrible quandary. With a sigh, he quickly withdrew the wad of bills from his pocket and painstakingly counted out another forty one-hundred-dollar bills. Yonasan now had fifty crisp green bills lying in the palm of his hand. With heartfelt thanks, Yonasan left Gabi's office and headed straight for the yeshiva.

Everyone in the director's office was downcast and despondent. Like a Heaven-sent messenger, Yonasan placed the stack of one-hundred-dollar bills on the desk. Everyone looked up in astonishment. Yonasan quickly told his story and looked around in satisfaction. The faces around him gradually lit up with hope.

Until that moment, the harsh reality of the yeshiva's financial situation had painted everything black before the staff's eyes. The future seemed so unpromising that they had lost every vestige of energy and enthusiasm they might still have possessed, and they no longer had the will to continue. The five thousand dollars — equal at that time to twenty thousand shekels — that Yonasan had suddenly thrust in front of them, injected them with a new surge of hope, and renewed their motivation to continue their holy work. The mere fact that someone had gone out of his way to help the institution boosted their spirits and filled them with new resolve as well.

From that day onward, things started to climb steadily upward for the yeshiva. The five thousand dollars served as a signal that there was indeed a light at the end of the long tunnel. It inspired the staff to continue trying and, naturally, they and Yonasan continued praying daily. With Hashem's help, the situation continued to improve.

Yonasan's prayers had succeeded. Today the yeshiva continues to reach out to our lost brethren and spread the word of Hashem's greatness to all corners of the world.

There Are Tefillos and There Are Tefillos

There are *tefillos* and there are *tefillos*. There are prayers that are answered after a day, a week, or a month, and there are prayers that are not answered until years later, when the one who davened them is no longer alive to see their results.

There are *tefillos* of *tzaddikim* and those of Jews of simple faith. There are ordinary daily prayers, and there are *tefillos* that burst forth from the heart of their own accord, whether that happens when we are in the middle of the street, at work, or whenever we feel a need.

Jews who believe in the power of prayer are always sending up *tefillos* from the depths of their hearts to the One Who hears prayer, they are forever pouring out their troubles, and they have faith that no prayer goes unanswered.

"If a *tefillah* doesn't help right away," *tzaddikim* say, "it will help many years later. If it doesn't help the one who davened, it will help another Jew across the world, now or at some other time. He Who hears all prayers, accepts them all and makes use of them, at a time of His choosing."

But there are also prayers that are answered immediately, as in this story.

For many years I have been a typical father with children to marry off, borrowing and lending, repaying and renewing loans, rolling over debts, covering one hole only to discover a new one. In this fashion, I, like many others, have managed with great *siyata diShmaya* to help build *batim ne'emanim be'Yisrael*.

My beard may be a little whiter, but *baruch Hashem*, my *emunah* has stood by me. The One Who gives life gives a living and so too the One Who gives children covers their expenses. Ha-Kadosh Baruch Hu has been with me every step of the way.

For one thing especially I thank Hashem, and that is that I have always been able to keep my word. Whenever I've promised to return a loan by a certain date, I might have had to move Heaven and earth, but with Hashem's help, I was always able to return the debt on time. This fact alone has been enough to open many doors for me. People are willing to lend me large sums of money without hesitation because they know from experience that they will get it back on the date promised.

One day, between one child's wedding and the next, I found myself in urgent need of $13,000 cash to pay back such a loan — and I had no idea where the money was going to come from. As always, I turned to my merciful Father in Heaven during the *Shemoneh Esreh* prayer, and asked Him to help me get the complete sum that very day.

I had no sooner finished davening and was busy folding my tallis when a friend of mine, the principal of a yeshiva, walked over to me and said, "A wealthy donor just gave me a check for $13,000. We don't need the money until next month. Could you use it as a loan until then?"

Was I surprised? Not really. Was I grateful? Very.

But ever since, when I approach that friend from time to time and, with a smile, ask whether a check has arrived from any donor and am answered in the negative, I am not surprised either. I have always known that there are *tefillos* and there are *tefillos* ...

You Satisfy the Desire of Every Living Thing*

*I*T IS ALMOST MIDNIGHT in the Bikur Cholim office. The telephone rings again. The callers on the other end of this line are always people in desperate need of help, hoping that whoever picks up the phone will be able to assist in some way. Sadly, the phone never stops ringing.

"Ha-Kadosh Baruch Hu's office is always open," the dynamic woman who directs the activities of the Bikur Cholim organization told me, "and we must follow in His ways."

"I have nine children, *b'li ayin ha-ra*," the voice on the phone said, "and my wife recently gave birth to two more — twins, *baruch Hashem*." The man on the line was struggling to keep his voice steady. "Two weeks after she brought the twins home, my wife had a nervous breakdown." The man's voice broke. "Now she is in the hospital again and I have ten little ones to take care of...."

"Surely you mean eleven children?" the director said. In her mind, she could picture the tragic scene. She imagined an empty refrigerator; the fast-food substitute for dinner the children probably had eaten — or didn't eat; the mess; the heaps of dishes piled in the sink. Although she did not hear the newborn twins wailing, she could easily imagine the father going from one to another of his nine other crying children trying to calm them down. She pictured the children going to *cheder* in mismatched clothing without their sandwiches.

In answer to her question, the man on the other end of the line

---

* *Tehillim* 145:16.

cried, "No, no. I have only ten children at home."

The director's heart filled with pity. "Reb Yid, please calm down. We're with you now all the way. Ha-Kadosh Baruch Hu is with you; He's holding your hand. Just tell me, where is your eleventh child?"

"Yirmi, one of the twins, is in Hadassah hospital in Jerusalem. He developed serious respiratory problems, so we had to take him there for tests. He's there all alone. My wife is in another hospital and I cannot leave the house...." The man fell silent, but the director knew instinctively that he had more to say. *He has not finished unburdening himself,* she thought. Her experience in helping so many unfortunate people had taught her to read volumes in each sigh and sob.

"I understand that you haven't yet finished giving me the whole picture," she said encouragingly. "Let us try to help you with all your troubles. We will soon send a wonderful, caring woman to sit at Yirmi's bedside and take care of him like a mother. She won't leave him for a minute. And whoever relieves her in turn will be just as dedicated. They will take good care of Yirmi, I assure you.

"As for your difficulties at home, we will dispatch teams of *heimishe* women to help you out. They will work in shifts, two at a time, taking turns to keep the house functioning normally until this difficult period passes. And it will pass quickly, *b'ezras Hashem.* You did the right thing in calling us to ask for help. Everything will be much easier from now on."

Nevertheless, she made a mental note to find out where the mother was hospitalized and who her doctor was. She wanted to consult the organization's experts in the medical field about the case. Perhaps they could help in that respect as well.

The other phone lines in the office were ringing, each call bearing news of yet another sorrow. The caller she was speaking to was just one of five cases that had cropped up that day. All five homes would be functioning smoothly by tomorrow, *b'ezras Hashem.*

"Thank you so much for everything...it's so hard," the caller continued. "What really troubles me is that my neighbor called the municipality's social services, and they told me a social worker will come tomorrow to take Mendy, the second twin, to a foster home, 'so that he doesn't suffer the neglect that caused Yirmi to develop breathing problems.' I don't know what to do.

"I told them that Yirmi's problem had nothing to do with Mendy, who is *baruch Hashem* healthy, but they said I have no choice in the matter. They are going to give Mendy to a 'proper babysitter' by tomorrow morning, and they said they would bring the police if I refused. I'm afraid they will place him in a non-Torah home. No one in my family can help me. They all have problems of their own. One of my cousins happened to hear about your organization from a friend and told me to call you. Can you help me with Mendy as well?"

"We will do our best to help you solve all your problems," the director said. "Give me your name, address, and telephone number, and we will start working on it immediately."

Time was short and there was much work to be done. The director's first call was to the head of a well-known *chessed* organization, who had experience working with the social services department. "You will have to find a suitable foster home for the baby before the social workers take him," she said. "Once they place him somewhere, it will be much harder for you to remove him from the home where they have placed him and put him in a home that you think is more suitable."

It was already after midnight, but the director knew she could call her volunteers at any hour. After all, they are all part of the Bikur Cholim family. Her eyes scanned her list of volunteers. The house needs a temporary mother, she thought. Someone who will take over willingly and help this poor man cope with the difficult situation and return the household to normal. Her finger stopped at two names on the list that seemed suitable. She arranged for them to go to the caller's house first thing in the morning.

Then the director summoned two volunteers to the Bikur Cholim headquarters and assigned them the job of recruiting more volunteers and setting up a work roster to take care of the home and the family. She knew that the next day the older children would go to school warmly dressed and have a warm meal waiting for them when they returned. The house would be neat, the clothes laundered, the floors clean. Someone would be there to greet the children after school, feed them, bathe them, and put them to bed.

The director and her volunteers would make many more phone calls that night to ensure that a dedicated, warmhearted volunteer would be at Yirmi's bedside as soon as possible. Then they would contact people in the medical profession to oversee the treatment and care of the incapacitated mother. They would do everything possible to provide the family in crisis with a warm, supportive atmosphere until the mother was well enough to go home.

Even though their list of volunteers is a long one, it is not always easy to find enough volunteers available at a moment's notice. One woman may be busy with a wedding or other family *simchah*, another may be feeling unwell herself, and the next one may already be working on another case. Nevertheless, the director knows that Bikur Cholim's work is always accompanied by great *siyata diShmaya,* and that they have been able to help thousands of needy Jews.

Siyata diShmaya: that is the key phrase in the Bikur Cholim family. That's what the director of the Bikur Cholim organization hoped for at this late hour, when she knew she had to find a warm, loving home for a Jewish baby before dawn.

"I'll help you from Above," her illustrious father, Reb Avraham Yitzchak Kahan, the Rebbe of Toldos Aharon, *zt"l,* had promised her. And that night she knew she needed his *tefillos* before the Heavenly Throne more than ever.

A difficult night lay ahead for the director of the organization, but she would soon see the veil of *hester panim* lifted somewhat, and Hashem would provide her with a glimpse of the marvelous way He runs His world.

Ribbono shel Olam, where shall I begin? she asked herself. It's past midnight. How can I find a foster family to receive an infant starting tomorrow morning? If the baby is not under proper care when the social workers arrive, they will place him wherever they can, and it will be impossible to switch homes later.

She looked over her list of volunteers. Every woman on my list either has a houseful of children of her own, *baruch Hashem*, or is too old to take on an infant, she concluded.

The director made a few calls, but was unable to find someone who was both willing and able to undertake the task. She decided to ask the advice of a friend of hers who had been very active in the organization at one time but was now retired. Mrs. Helfer would not mind being awakened well after midnight for a good cause.

"Hello?"

"Hello, Mrs. Helfer. I apologize for calling you at this hour, but it's urgent. Somebody needs Bikur Cholim's help, and I need yours."

"Well, I'll be happy to help you," was the response, "but I think you may have the wrong number. Mrs. Helfer no longer lives here. She moved two months ago."

"Oh, I am so sorry that I disturbed you. As long as you are already awake, perhaps you can give me Mrs. Helfer's new telephone number."

"I'm sorry, but I don't have it. The Helfers moved out before we moved in and I never met them."

"That is a great disappointment," the director said. "Do you have any idea how I can reach her?"

"No, but perhaps I can help you instead," the woman said.

In the stress of the moment, the director began to tell the woman, who said her name was Orah, about the problem. "And so," she ended, "we desperately need a foster family to care for little Mendy by tomorrow morning and no later."

"You are not going to believe this," Orah said, "but I think I can solve your problem. My older sister, Rivkah, has no children, though she has been married for twenty years. I know she is not working right now, and I also know that she would love to care for a baby."

The director's heart filled with both pity and hope. "I hope you will forgive me, but it is my duty to ask you a few questions. First of all, do you think your sister has the patience to care for a newborn infant? And secondly, is her home a Torah home? I need to be sure of the conditions before I turn over such a precious treasure, you see."

Orah reassured her on both counts. "You can't imagine what a warm and loving person my sister is and what a good Jewish home she has. Rivkah is a wonderful woman, with firm belief and trust in ha-Kadosh Baruch Hu. She knows that Hashem knows what is best, and she never complains."

Heaven has obviously led me to this woman, the director thought. It could not be otherwise. "Would you mind calling her right away and then letting me know if she is willing?"

The director thought of her holy father, and his promise to her. When he had asked her to take over the management of the Bikur Cholim organization which her mother had founded, she questioned how she would manage. Her father, the Rebbe, had said, "I promise I will pray for you and help you at all times. I will always be at your side."

Orah called back a few moments later. "Rivkah is not home. She went to a wedding in another city and has not yet returned. But I told my brother-in-law why I was calling, and he was enthusiastic about caring for the baby. He said he was almost certain Rivkah would like the idea, but, of course, he cannot answer for her. He promised to leave her a note to call you as soon as she gets home, no matter how late."

While all of this was going on at Bikur Cholim, Rivkah was dancing joyously at the wedding of a couple who had recently returned to Judaism. All the participants felt uplifted by the great *simchah* experienced at such an affair. The parents of the bride and groom were not present at the wedding in protest against the path their children had chosen, and perhaps that was an added reason for all the guests to join in making the couple happy. Everyone there was certain that their prayers for the successful building of a new Jewish home would rise directly to Heaven.

Every passenger in the van Rivkah rode home in wanted to maintain this marvelous state of spiritual elevation, including the driver. "Does anyone mind if we stop at Kever Rachel?" he asked. "We have all just joined in a mitzvah, so now is an opportune time to pray for salvation."

No one objected. It was an opportunity too good to pass up, even though it was one-thirty in the morning.

Rivkah was especially grateful for the opportunity to pour out her heart at our matriarch Rachel's tomb. Perhaps tonight her prayers would be answered.

"Why did Yaakov bury Rachel on the road to Bethlehem?" asks the Midrash. "He saw, through *ruach ha-kodesh,* that the Children of Israel would pass this road on their way into exile, and he buried her there so she could pray on their behalf."

They entered the ancient holy site in silence. Rivkah began reciting *Tehillim.*

"Mamma Rochel," she whispered. "Dear, dear Mamma Rochel, you know my anguish. You too prayed and pleaded with ha-Kadosh Baruch Hu until He blessed you with a child. Please, daven for me before the Throne of Glory. *Hava li banim,* "Send me a baby from the treasure house of souls on High."

Unbidden, more words popped into her mind. In the midst of her impassioned prayer, she suddenly found herself thinking, "Even if it is not meant for me to have a baby of my own right now, please send me a baby to love so that I can share in the mitzvah of raising a Jewish child."

It was now two o'clock in the morning.

When Rivka arrived home, a light still glowed softly in the kitchen. There was a note on the table in her husband's handwriting:

> Hello and welcome home! Orah phoned at one-thirty with a very urgent message. Someone wants to know if we can take care of an infant for a few weeks or months starting tomorrow. I promised that you would call this person back as soon as you get home — no matter what time it is! Please call her immediately.

Rivkah dropped into a chair. She read the message again. The prayer she had just prayed at Rachel's Tomb was still ringing in her ears; her tears were not yet dry on her cheeks. Was this the answer to her prayers — so quickly?

She dialed the number with trembling hands and was soon speaking to the director of Bikur Cholim. Yes, it was true. Neither Rivkah nor the director slept at all that night. Rivkah's *sefer Tehillim* absorbed a gallon of tears. Only a brokenhearted father was finally able to rest a bit, relieved by the promise that the Bikur Cholim family would be sharing his burden and helping him and his family.

At seven o'clock the next morning, Rivkah and her husband came home with a precious bundle named Mendy. Within a single day, their home was filled with happiness and joy and the sound of a baby's cries.

When the social workers came to check on Mendy's welfare, they were well satisfied with the devoted care Mendy was receiving. Rivkah cared for Mendy with all her heart and soul, thanking Hashem for sending her this treasure on that wondrous night.

The Bikur Cholim family remained at the father's side the entire time, helping with the house, the children, the mother, and the infant twins. Yirmi still needed to be hospitalized from time to time, and he stayed at an aunt's house during the periods he was out of the hospital. Mendy turned Rivkah's home into paradise on earth. She had never had a more joyous period of time in her difficult life.

Three months passed. Rivkah called the director, telling her she needed to speak to her immediately and asking if the director would come to her house. The director was afraid something terrible had happened and went there immediately. Rivkah was very agitated.

"I'm sorry," she stammered. "I c-cannot care for Mendy much longer. You will have to find another foster home for him in a few months."

Six months later, Rivka and her husband were the proud parents of a baby boy, after having waited twenty years for that happy day. They named him Mendy, to remind them of the great *chessed* Hashem had granted them.

And where was the other Mendy? Mendy was at home in the arms of his happy mother, who had recovered from her illness. Yirmi was home, too, and the Bikur Cholim volunteers had said goodbye to the dear family they had grown so close to. There was not a hint of the disastrous upheaval that had shaken the happy household. It was as if it had all happened just so that Rivkah and her husband might merit their Mendy.

One Single Prayer

I ONCE VISITED THE United States many years ago, planning to be there only eight days. I made the trip a couple of years after the beginning of the Lebanon War, when the Israeli army had been sent to defend the northern border from constant terrorist attacks.

I had a return flight on KLM airlines that was scheduled to land in Amsterdam. Having successfully concluded my business two days before my scheduled departure from New York, I suddenly longed to return to the holy city of Jerusalem in which I live. Moving up my flight, however, even by one day, would be costly.

"Just stay in Brooklyn one more day," the travel agent advised. "There are plenty of places to go, lots of Torah institutions you can visit. Why should you pay so much more to leave one day earlier if you have no special reason to do so?"

His words made a lot of sense. I really didn't have a pressing reason to leave. I just felt a strong urge to return to Eretz Yisrael as soon as possible.

"Besides," the agent added, "if you arrive in Amsterdam on Tuesday, as you originally planned, you will have an immediate connecting flight to Israel. If you arrive on Monday, you will have to wait six hours for your flight. You will touch down in Holland at dawn, and the flight to Israel will not take off until the afternoon. You will be stuck in the airport all that time."

I could not explain it, but at that moment I felt an overwhelming desire to go home. I agreed to pay the extra charge, and accepted the penalty of sitting in the Amsterdam airport for several hours. The travel agent acceded to my request and changed my flight.

As a seat companion on that trip I drew an observant Jew who lived in Amsterdam. He informed me that we would arrive in time to daven *Shacharis* with the minyan in the large synagogue in Amsterdam. He offered to take me there. I was happy to join him, and even happier to know that I would be able to spend the next six hours in a *beis midrash* rather than at the airport.

My companion was a local resident, so he went straight through passport control. I had to wait in a separate line. We had agreed to meet as soon as possible in front of the airport building. When I emerged from the terminal, however, having received a permit to leave the premises for a few hours and return in time for my connecting flight, I could not find the man. I walked around and checked all the entrances, but he was not there.

It was still dark outside, and there were not too many people around. I was reluctant to try and find my way to the synagogue alone because I do not speak English well and Dutch not at all, so I reentered the terminal. I looked for a quiet corner where I could daven *Shacharis* undisturbed.

All the shops in the rotunda were closed and not one person passed by. I was able to pray with full concentration, even while standing in the lobby of the Amsterdam airport.

After an especially uplifting davening, I began to put on my Rabbeinu Tam tefillin. A young man emerged from a nearby elevator and stopped to stare at me. I assumed he was not Jewish, and could not imagine he had anything to do with me, so I ignored him and continued praying. He hovered nearby, apparently waiting for me to finish.

As soon as I removed my tefillin, he approached and asked me if I spoke English. Although I understood enough to know what he was asking, I shook my head to indicate that I did not speak the language. The young man switched to Hebrew, asking me if I spoke that language. When I answered in the affirmative, he said, "That's good. I am so glad to find a Jew who may be able to help me. I'm Jewish, too."

Before I could ask him what his problem was, he asked me what I had been doing and what were "those black boxes." Apparently, he had never seen tefillin before. I explained to him that the "boxes" were called tefillin and that Jews were commanded to put them on every day while they recited the morning prayers. While wearing the tefillin, I explained, a Jew connects with his Creator and prays to Him with devotion.

"I was born and grew up in Israel," the youth disclosed, "on a Ha-Shomer ha-Tza'ir kibbutz. The only thing I learned about Judaism was love of our homeland. Two years ago, when the war broke out, I was stationed just outside Beirut. My tank received a direct hit and caught fire. My buddies and I were trapped inside the tank.

"Out of the depths of my soul an unbidden cry escaped me: 'There is one God, and our souls are in His Hands.' I could hardly believe that the words had issued from my lips, so far removed were they from my belief. If God saves us from this furnace, I promise I will start to pray to Him, I thought.

"To this day I do not know exactly what happened, but suddenly an opening appeared in the side of the burning tank, and we were able to crawl out. We were all saved.

"We were taken to the hospital and treated for shock and mild burns, but basically we emerged unscathed — physically, that is.

"In the aftermath of that war, many of us who fought in it went through a great spiritual upheaval. We felt alienated from our people and our country, and felt that the war had not achieved a thing. Along with many of my friends, I joined the Peace Now movement, which called for the termination of the war and the cessation of bloodshed. I went even further than that. I decided my Jewishness meant nothing to me, so I would go and live in another country among gentiles. Now I live in Amsterdam.

"But do you know something? I can still hear my own words, the words I shouted out in the burning tank. I know there is a God and He is waiting to hear the prayers I promised to pray. I want to say a genuine prayer to Him, but I don't know what to say or how to say it.

"When I saw you standing here in the middle of this huge, empty rotunda, I knew you were praying to God. I just had to ask your help. Maybe you can help me to say that long-postponed prayer that I promised to pray in the burning tank."

Greatly touched by his account, I sat down with him to talk.

Maybe this is the reason I had to leave New York a day early, I thought to myself. Perhaps this is why my companion from the plane and I could not find each other outside the airport. And perhaps this is why I was so reluctant to try to find the synagogue on my own, and prayed here in the terminal just when this young man happened to pass by.

"Here are my tefillin," I said gently, offering him my tefillin bag. "They are very holy. I will show you how to put them on, and you can recite the *Shema* from the prayerbook. The recital of *Shema* while you are wearing tefillin is a genuine prayer that will fulfill your promise. It will also count as an expression of your heartfelt thanks to your Creator for sparing your life. While you pray, you can thank God and ask Him for anything you want in your own words or in the words of the prayers in the prayerbook."

As I watched this young secular Jew with the straps of my tefillin wrapped around his arm reading the words from the prayerbook for the first time in his life, I thought that this was testimony to the fact that every Jew possesses a soul more precious than diamonds, a soul that originates from ha-Kadosh Baruch Hu's Throne and radiates purity. Crowned by the tefillin, his eyes streaming with tears, he recited the words in a voice choked with emotion.

Perhaps the holy souls of his ancestors were crying along with him. Perhaps it was the exiled *Shechinah* Itself Who wept. I know that I was crying, too.

We do not realize how priceless our prayers are, how much value is attached to even one. We cannot begin to grasp the enormous privilege we are given three times every single day.

How dear is each and every prayer before ha-Kadosh Baruch Hu! How He craves to hear His sons call out to Him, even if it is only one single prayer.

One Who Comes to Purify Himself...

(Shabbos 104a)

That's Just the Way It Happened

I T HAPPENED IN MERON, near the grave of Rabbi Shimon bar Yochai, early in the year 1950. What a splendid *simchah* it was! Asher was celebrating the first haircut of his eldest son, Yisrael. Most of the family — parents, grandparents, aunts, uncles, nieces and nephews — were in attendance. Everyone glowed with joy and was in high spirits.

Yisrulik stood on a bench, and his face slowly took on the beautiful look of a *Yiddishe yingel*, a little Jewish boy, no longer a toddler. His *peyos* began to show themselves from between his newly shorn locks. The table was filled with good things, the cups were filled and refilled, and everyone blessed Asher that he should raise his family in good health.

Asher's glowing eyes spotted a familiar face. It was Kalman Rubler, a friend of his from yeshiva. Kalman was older than Asher, and, despite his good name, he was still unmarried — which was unusual for someone in his circles.

Asher smiled from ear to ear. "Kalman!" he called to his former schoolmate, "Shalom aleichem! Come on over and snip off some hair from my three-year old."

Kalman came over, blushing fiercely, uncomfortable at being the only bachelor. He nursed the hope that some of the people there might think he was actually married. It is difficult to attend such affairs. They remind you that you're old enough to be celebrating such a *simchah* yourself.

As Kalman held the scissors to Yisrulik's locks, Asher carelessly made a remark that devastated his friend. "Who would have thought, Kalman, when we were still in yeshiva, that we would be standing here one day together in Meron — you still a bachelor and I the father of a boy having his first haircut?"

Kalman's fingers clipped the ends of the child's hair, but he felt that his heart was being cut instead. Why did Asher have to say that? Kalman understood that Asher hadn't meant to hurt him, but his heart cried out silently just the same. He felt a heavy weight pressing down on him. It was as if all the years of his lonely bachelorhood had welled up in his yearning heart at once, at that moment, and sat themselves down with all their weight.

Kalman shook Asher's hand, mumbled some words of blessing, and ran out. His tears seeped into the clods of earth next to the building that housed Rabbi Shimon's holy grave. Asher's words reverberated in his head and skewered his suffering soul.

Kalman Rubler had a heart of gold, and he truly did not blame Asher for having wounded him. He also had tremendous *bitachon*, and he had no complaints against the Ribbono shel Olam either, *chas ve-shalom*, none at all. But the plain facts hurt so much; and when it hurts, it is hard not to cry out.

Kalman wept for a long time. All the hours that he had waited and hoped for a shidduch and been disappointed again and again rose up and poured themselves out straight into the listening ear that hovered over that holy place. His bitter heart leaned its full weight on Rabbi Shimon and was supported.

When Kalman stood up, a gentle Galilee breeze brushed his cheek, like a touch of comfort from Above. He felt as if a stone had been lifted from his heart. He felt he had needed to cry like that.

A closed heart collects bitterness aplenty, and as long as it remains sealed, it shrinks in upon itself and hurts. When ha-Kadosh Baruch Hu sends relief, He provides the right key, and then the gates of the heart are opened wide and everything comes rushing out, accompanied by sobs and tears. Deep in his heart, Kalman thanked Asher for his unheeding words, which had opened the lock of his heart.

His cries had been heard on High. That same year, Kalman Rubler became engaged to a young woman from a distinguished Jerusalem family, and by the following Chanukah they were married.

One *erev Rosh Chodesh*, during his first months as a married man, Kalman joyously returned to the grave of Rabbi Shimon bar Yochai. He felt he had to offer his thanks to the Ribbono shel Olam.

He had no doubt that the tears shed near the grave had been heard in Heaven.

He carried this feeling with him for many years, especially when he would go up to Meron. In 1956 he celebrated there the first haircut of his eldest son, Mottele, and the memory of that day in 1950 was still clear in his mind. In the late summer of 1960, when he was there to grace Yochanan, his third child, with *peyos*, the memory of his sobs returned even more strongly. It assailed him again three years later, on Lag ba-Omer 1963, when it was Meir'ke standing on the bench.

The years pass like a stream rushing by. One day follows another, and soon the next week's Torah portion is already being read on Shabbos in shul. One week follows another, and soon Rosh Chodesh comes around again. Another Purim and another Tishah b'Av, and the new year is already in sight. Another year and another, the children grow up, the family increases, the beard turns white, a decade passes, and then another one.

Fortunate is the Jew who knows how to plant substance into those years and so give a totally different meaning to their swift flight. The year was now 1974, and Kalman Rubler, who only yesterday had been a bachelor of twenty-five, was now forty-nine years old and bringing his firstborn, Mottele, to the *chuppah*.

Kalman was blessed with great *nachas*. His home flourished like a beautiful and fruitful vineyard. The many sons and daughters Hashem had blessed him with furnished him with tremendous pleasure and satisfaction. Five years after Mottele's marriage, in 1979, the entire Rubler family traveled to Meron to celebrate the first haircut of Avreimele, Mottele's firstborn, Reb Kalman's first grandchild.

Reb Kalman's heart overflowed with gratitude. What could he do to repay Hashem for all the blessings he had received? He was fifty-four years old, and he could see the second generation of his descendants following in the ways of their fathers.

He entered the building containing Rabbi Shimon bar Yochai's grave surrounded by his family. Avreimele was placed on the bench, and Mottele, the boy's father, honored his own father with cutting the first lock of hair.

Everyone was snipping, enjoying the cake and wine, and offering blessings and congratulations to the child, to his parents, and to Kalman, who was standing to one side watching the proceedings, his face glowing with happiness. Somewhere hovered in the back of his mind the unforgettable picture of the time young Asher had placed his son on the bench and offered the unmarried Kalman Rubler the honor of snipping some hair — and then, oh, how he had cried. Most thoughts come and go, but some come and stay and are never forgotten.

Kalman, his eyes shining with *nachas*, suddenly noticed a familiar figure entering the building. His heart stopped. It was Asher, his old classmate. Kalman smiled broadly. "Asher!" he called pleasantly to his old friend. "Shalom aleichem! It is a great honor to have you cut a few snips from my grandson's hair."

Asher walked over slowly, his face turning white and red by turns. He clipped Avreimele's hair as he was asked, and then shook Kalman's hand. Kalman inquired how his friend had been over the years since they had spoken.

Asher let loose a deep sigh and related his troubles. His eldest son, Yisrulik, was thirty-two and still waiting for a shidduch. "It has been thirteen years of anguish," Asher admitted in a choked voice. "*Tzaros* day and night. And for some reason none of my other children are married either."

Kalman was overcome with distress over the news. He could well understand that the situation was devastating to Asher. Who knew better than he how it felt to be an "*alter bachur*?" He mentioned, with half a smile, that he remembered being at Yisrulik's first haircut so many years before.

At the mention of the haircut, the color drained from Asher's face. He jumped as if bitten by a snake. "Yes! The haircut!" exclaimed Asher. Kalman was astonished at Asher's strong reaction.

"Until this very day I remember the hurtful comment that slipped out of my mouth here in this holy place. I saw how embarrassed you were, and I didn't know how to fix the harm I had done. I still think of it from time to time, but I assumed you had forgotten.

Maybe the time has come, after almost thirty years, to right the wrong and ask your forgiveness for the error."

The ancient memory came to life and Kalman's feet wanted to take him back outside to that spot behind the building to cry again — this time for his friend Asher's son Yisrulik — to shed tears that would melt the weight sitting like a stone on Reb Asher's heart.

Kalman pretended he had forgotten the incident. He didn't want to pain his friend further. "I forgive you completely," Kalman said in a choked voice. "Please consider that comment as if it had never been made. I never held anything against you, and if, *chas ve-shalom*, I unknowingly bore a trace of resentment, I remove it retroactively. From now on, may there be 'peace in your camp and harmony in your home.'"

Their hearts at peace, the conversation moved on to other subjects relevant to parents marrying off their children. Soon little Avreimele's face was framed with beautiful new *peyos*, and Mottele began gathering the family to head home. Kalman warmly took his leave of Asher, wished him many happy occasions in the near future, and joined his son.

That same year, 1979, Yisrulik became engaged to a fine girl from a fine home. The year after, Kalman Rubler was delighted to hear that Asher had found a bride for his second son. On Lag ba-Omer 1986, Kalman again met Reb Asher in Meron. This time they were both celebrating the same thing: they were sixty-year-old grandfathers of boys having their first haircuts — but for Asher it was the first time. The two danced together in a circle, expressing their thanks to Hashem.

Cycles begin and cycles end. Sometimes you can only see the beginning of the cycle, but not the end. At other times, you witness the end of a cycle without having seen its beginning. One passes through many cycles in a lifetime, but the main thing is to be satisfied with them all.

Whenever Kalman would tell this story to his children, he would always stress the following: He did not dare point to this or that event and say that this happened because of that thing, that this event was due to that one. We human beings are too limited and our minds too small to understand the ways of the Merciful One.

"I am just telling you the way it happened," he would say. "That's just the way it happened."

Signs of Heavenly Favor

DURING MY YOUTH, I often behaved in inappropriate ways. I thought a lot of myself, looked down at the people around me, and did nothing to improve my character. Today, having matured and gained life experience, I am ashamed of the disgraceful things I did, and I constantly pray to Hashem that He allow me to atone for them all. This is not so simple, however. Since my sins were largely committed against my fellow man, even Yom Kippur cannot atone for them until I personally appease those whom I wronged.

The Sages explain the verse (*II Shemuel* 24:14), *Niplah na be-yad Hashem ki rabim rachamav*, as, "May I fall spiritually only in sins against Hashem, since His mercy is great." The continuation, *u've-yad adam al epolah*, then becomes, "May I not fall spiritually in sins against man," since such sins are much more severe.

When I see yeshiva boys guilty of offending others, mocking them, hurting their feelings, and engaging in silly fights that so often develop into larger battles that cause untold damage, I want to cry out, "Stop! You're making a big mistake. You will end up toiling your entire life to atone for these sins — and still not succeed. Control your wild youthful urges, stop your tongues from shooting barbs, restrain yourselves for just one minute, and the danger will pass." But I don't dare tell them anything, since when I was their age I was just as biting and spirited.

I now know what young people sometimes forget but must be reminded: that the world is not ownerless. Ridiculing others is like playing with fire; everyone is harmed. Even at Purim or Chanukah parties, when jokes are made and mockery may be expressed in rhyme or in an offhanded fashion, the resulting hurt causes damage — just as an accidental shot, God forbid, can still cause injury.

Sometimes, when I try to remember how I harmed others, I am overcome by a feeling of helplessness. I have so much to atone for! I could compile a long list of telephone numbers of former acquaintances whom I have to appease and from whom I have to beg forgiveness. The problem is so complex — how I wish I could start anew.

In this story of mine, I would like to reveal to others what Heaven taught me — that one who corrects his ways is aided from Above. Even in my miserable situation, which I brought upon myself with my own hands, ha-Kadosh Baruch Hu assisted me and healed me.

One of the worst blots on my soul was caused by the following incident. Word once got around my yeshiva that a student named Reuven ben Yaakov was to be switched into our *shiur*. I didn't like this Reuven for many reasons, justified and not. I was offended at the thought that I would have to sit with him in the same class, and so I raised a hue and cry among the other yeshiva boys about this Reuven's terrible character and low-class family. I maintained that we could not allow him to feel comfortable in our *shiur*, and that the *mishnah*, "Greet everyone pleasantly," did not apply to him.

Reuven joined our class, but the boys treated him coldly and ignored him. I was aware of his discomfort and was delighted. I saw how Reuven tried to make friends with some of the boys and gain some attention, all to no effect. The class rebbe spoke to us about it, as a group and individually, but my one mocking speech had more effect than a hundred of his reproaches.

I was so involved in my own egoistic affairs that I gave no thought to the misery that I had caused Reuven. He never got along with the other boys, and eventually gave up and moved to another yeshiva.

More than twenty years passed. I was now a father and a busy working man, but I couldn't forget what I had done to Reuven in my youth. When I first resolved to correct my ways, I obtained

Reuven's telephone number, but I was afraid to call him. I doubted that he would be willing to forgive me. Could I blame him?

In my indecision, I pushed the matter off day after day. I wanted to rid myself of this burden, but I couldn't overcome my reluctance. One morning, when my pangs of conscience got the better of me, I decided that this was it. Later that evening, God willing, I would call Reuven. I wrote his phone number in large print, and pinned it up in a place I couldn't miss.

During the day at work, I kept thinking about my evening's venture. I found the task a heavy weight to bear, and I earnestly hoped that all would go well. In the tailor's shop where I worked, the clothes in need of repairs are labeled with their owner's name, address, and telephone number. My job was to do the mending. I sat at my table, and although my hands were sewing faithfully, my mind was elsewhere. I was continually rehearsing what I would say to Reuven, when in fact, quite possibly, there would be nothing I could say to assuage his old pain.

While mulling over my plans, I finished working on one article of clothing and picked up the next one. By chance, I happened to glance at the label bearing the name of the owner. My heart stopped beating. It was Reuven ben Yaakov, at the address and phone number that I knew all too well.

I thought I was hallucinating. Had Reuven actually decided to pursue me that day and reach me by whatever means he could? The black letters stood out clearly before me. That phone number had been hovering before my eyes all day, and now it appeared in full on a piece of paper, every digit, accompanied by the name Reuven ben Yaakov.

I recognized that Hashem's Hand was at work and that I could be sure of His help; He had unlocked the gates of repentance for me. With a pounding heart I went to the shop phone and dialed the number. I was resolved not to postpone the matter for even another minute.

Stuttering and shamefaced, I introduced myself and explained the reason for my call. In a voice choked with emotion I begged Reuven to forgive me. His voice removed the heavy weight from my heart. "Of course I forgive you. It was nothing but a youthful prank. I even forgave you back then, and I hold no grudge." I was happy to hear from our conversation that Reuven had gotten on well in his new yeshiva and had succeeded in his studies there. "Don't worry," he encouraged me, as we concluded the conversation. "Everything is perfectly okay."

I went back to work with a singing heart. I had pricked myself deeply, but the painful process had healed me. It hadn't been easy to loosen the inner tangle in my heart, but with a little effort everything was mended and shone like new.

I repaired the tear in Reuven's clothing, and with the help of Heaven, had repaired even more than that.

I pray that those who read my story will remove from their hearts all the grudges and hate that have been festering for years. You will be bestowing upon those who wronged you great favor both in this world and the next.

May such all-encompassing forgiveness eventually bring Heavenly forgiveness in its wake and an atmosphere of purity to unite all our hearts as one.

Judge Each Person Favorably

OWADAYS, CHICKENS ARE relatively cheap to buy and easy to prepare. They come nicely cut and packaged with the metal *kashrus* tag attached, and hardly anyone thinks twice before rinsing them and putting them straight into a pot.

But in the Jerusalem of my youth this was not the case at all. Chickens, purchased almost exclusively in honor of Shabbos or *Yom Tov*, had to be kashered at home, and every housewife knew how to determine if the chicken was questionable and needed halachic verification from the Rav.

Once, when I was seven years old, a question arose concerning the chicken my parents had purchased from Shaya's butcher shop.

My parents could ill afford to throw away such an expensive commodity, and the most natural thing to do when the status of a chicken was in doubt was to take it to the Rav. If the Rav decided that the chicken was kosher, well and good, and if not, the butcher would be obligated to exchange it for another one.

My mother was the one who brought up the chicken's questionable status. After examining it, my father claimed that he could detect no problem at all, and that from his standpoint the chicken was perfectly kosher. Nevertheless, my mother was not placated, and my parents called me over and told me to take the chicken to the elderly Rav Berneman, to whom we brought all our halachic queries.

I was mortified. Being extremely bashful by nature, I almost never opened my mouth to speak in front of strangers. I was too embarrassed to pay the bus driver or even return a borrowed item to a neighbor. My father tried at every opportunity to help me overcome my shyness, and would push me to speak and act in public even though it went against my grain. To be honest, I owe him great thanks for doing so; without his prodding I don't know how I would have managed in life.

The moment my parents saddled me with the job of going to the Rav, I felt as if my feet were rooted to the ground.

"Go, go," my father urged. "Don't worry. Rav Berneman will receive you very nicely and everything will be all right."

I just couldn't do it. How could I walk through the streets with a chicken in my hand? Everyone would be looking at me and laughing. How could I enter the Rav's house in such a condition? I shuddered at the very idea. My mother, seeing my hesitation, hurried me off, saying she needed the chicken urgently for Shabbos, not to mention that we might have to exchange it and so more time would be wasted. I had no choice. I had to walk out the door into the street — with the chicken — and go to the Rav's house.

My face alternately flushed and blanched. With the blood pounding in my ears, I walked, eyes lowered, through the city streets, in the direction of the Rav's house. I felt the stares of all the other pedestrians piercing me like red-hot spears, but I went about my errand as my parents had instructed. You may think I am exaggerating, but I can attest to the fact that these indeed were the feelings of a seven-year old with an overly developed sense of self-consciousness. Until today I cringe to think of it.

After what seemed like an eternity, I arrived and knocked on the Rav's door. As soon as the door opened I thrust the chicken in front of me and managed to blurt out, "A *she'eilah*."

The Rebbetzin explained kindly that the Rav was not home and that he was receiving people at the local shul. "You can go to him there and he will be happy to answer you," she said.

That was all I needed. To have to walk with the chicken down the entire aisle of the shul to where the Rav sat! I had always found it difficult to walk through the crowded shul under ordinary circumstances, and now with the chicken … it was just too much.

I returned home and told my mother that the Rav was not in and could not be reached. I begged her to free me from this burdensome errand, but my father was adamant that I see it through to the end and go find the Rav in shul. Neither of my parents were able to leave the house just then, and there was no one else who could take my place, so again I found myself in the street holding the chicken.

I reached a quiet, empty street corner and stood for a moment contemplating my predicament. It was clear to me that I would not go to the shul — no matter what. Just as no adult would dare walk through shul with a basket of cucumbers on his head, nothing on earth could make me walk through the shul with the chicken in my hand. So I resolved. But what should I do? My parents were awaiting my return.

I soon came up with a solution — a product of my paralyzing self-consciousness and embarrassment. Coming back home, acting as if I had just been to the Rav, I said, "The Rav says that the chicken is kosher, but he does not recommend eating it."

As soon as the words were out of my mouth I felt blessed relief wash over me, and my whole body seemed to relax from the tension that had gripped it for the past hour. I actually prided myself on the brilliance of my fabrication: the chicken was kosher, but it would not be eaten. It was all worth it as long as I didn't have to undergo any more embarrassment.

I quickly busied myself with a toy and watched from the corner of my eye as my father donned his coat and left for Shaya's butcher shop. I didn't know what had transpired there until that Shabbos, when I heard my father talking to my grandfather.

"I cannot understand how people can deride *kevod ha-Torah*," he began. "I went this week to a certain butcher shop with a chicken that Rav Berneman had ruled was not advisable to eat. I asked the butcher to exchange it, but after looking at it he insisted that the chicken was 100 percent kosher and that he would not exchange it. When I told him that Rav Berneman had ruled that the chicken was not perfectly glatt kosher, the butcher answered brazenly in front of everyone, 'If that's the case, then Rav Berneman is becoming senile! He is over ninety and obviously can no longer be depended on with *she'eilos*. I am completely certain that there is no problem with this chicken.'"

My father and grandfather went on to discuss *kevod ha-Torah* and the honor due to rabbis, but my seven-year-old conscience was left trembling at what I had done as a result of my fear of embarrassment. This story engraved itself in my heart and I never forgot it. All my life I wondered at the ramifications of my act and how I could remedy it. Perhaps my parents had stopped patronizing Shaya from that day on, and it was up to me to appease him as well as to clear his name in front of my parents. What's more, maybe Shaya did exchange the chicken in the end, and I needed to reimburse him for the monetary loss. And what about Rav Berneman's good name?

Years went by, and I learned to overcome my bashfulness, but the memory of that story continued to haunt me. When I was older I asked my parents what had happened after the incident with the chicken, but they had no recollection of it. I then went to Shaya the butcher, but he, too, could not recall the incident or its repercussions. Rav Berneman had passed away over twenty years before. No one was left who remembered a certain ill-fated chicken whose *kashrus* was in doubt.

Last year, thirty-five years after the incident with the chicken, the wife of Shaya the butcher passed away. (Shaya himself had passed away a few years previously.) I decided to go to the house of mourning and fulfill the mitzvah of comforting mourners. Maybe Hashem would have pity on me, and I would be able to find out what had transpired following that incident; perhaps I would be able to remedy my misdeed.

I addressed the eldest son, and we began discussing this and that until we arrived at the subject of the butcher shop, chickens, and eventually the issue of my parents' chicken. I had no sooner brought up the matter when Shaya's son told me that he distinctly remembered it, since he had been in the butcher shop when my father had come in with the chicken.

"Your father claimed the chicken was questionable and demanded a different one in accordance with Rav Berneman's ruling. My father was very surprised at the Rav's decision, and mentioned the Rav's advanced age and that he no longer could be trusted. In order to keep the peace, my father took back the chicken and gave your father a different one.

"Your father was satisfied, and left the butcher shop with the new chicken. Then my father sent me to a second authority, Rav Fisher, to clarify the issue. I was used to bringing *she'eilos* to rabbis — as the son of a butcher this was something I did almost daily. Rav Fisher took one look at the chicken and said, 'This chicken is glatt kosher. I don't see any *she'eilah* here.' He then smiled at me and said, 'Tell your father that the chicken is just fine, and I don't understand why he saw a *she'eilah* in a perfectly kosher chicken.'

"My father was happy that the ruling agreed with his opinion, so he rewrapped the chicken and sold it to another customer. So you see, he did not sustain any monetary loss. However, from that day on we stopped going to Rav Berneman with halachic queries. We thought that the Rav's advanced age had affected him to the point that he could no longer render correct decisions. Your father continued to patronize the butcher shop, and I assume he heard my father's opinion on Rav Berneman's cognitive abilities, but that's all I know."

I was grateful to Hashem for revealing the end of the story to me. I was relieved to know that I had not caused anyone any monetary loss. Shaya was able to resell the chicken, and my parents continued to give him their business. The only person to suffer injury was Rav Berneman, *zt"l*, whose honor was diminished in the eyes of my parents, Shaya, and who knows who else ever since.

Although Rav Berneman suffered no personal insult — no one ever told him that he was incompetent — it was enough that I, through my childish shyness, had degraded his honor and consequently that of the Torah. Additionally, Shaya had stopped going to him for questions, and perhaps others who were in the butcher shop that day stopped going to him as well. There is also the possibility that other people found out about the incident, and they too stopped coming to Rav Berneman with their queries.

I felt I must redress the wrong I had done so many years ago. I wanted to go to Rav Berneman's grave with a minyan in order to ask his forgiveness, but I had no idea where he was buried.

While searching for Rav Berneman's relatives, combing carefully through phone books for the address of his grandson, who had been a childhood friend of mine, Hashem, in His infinite kindness, brought me face to face with the object of my quest. While on the bus, I happened to start up a conversation with the young man sitting next to me, who turned out to be none other than one of Rav Berneman's grandsons.

I told him my story, and he promised that before the next yahrtzeit, when the whole family prayed together at his grandfather's grave, he would let me know so that I could accompany them. In the presence of their minyan, I would be able to ask the Rav's forgiveness and atone for what I had done as a child.

I am positive that had my father realized to what lengths I would go in order not to suffer embarrassment, he surely would have found another way to help me overcome my paralyzing shyness. Our wise King Solomon said, "Teach each child according to his way" (*Mishlei* 22:6). If a child is shy, we must take this into account, even if we think that his bashfulness is excessive.

I feel that there is a great deal more to learn from my story. First, of course, is that it is never too late to do *teshuvah*.

However, the most powerful lesson we can learn from this story is the danger of judging others unfavorably. Not one person involved ever thought that the whole story was the figment of a seven-year-old boy's imagination, and we'll never know the extent of damage I might have caused Rav Berneman, the subject of the *lashon ha-ra*.

Forgiveness

R EB YITZCHAK TUMILER, a forty-year-old man who is involved in disseminating Torah, entered his bank to withdraw some cash. He wrote a check to himself, filled in the date, and signed it. He then got into line to deposit the check and receive the money. It had been many months since he had stepped into the bank; since he learned and taught from morning until night and was very involved with his students, his wife usually took care of bank business. However, due to a family celebration in his home, he had no choice but to include this task in his daily schedule and take care of the withdrawal himself.

When Reb Yitzchak's turn came, he handed the check to the teller behind the counter. As he waited, he noticed that the clerk, a religious man, was peering closely at the check and seemed to be taking his time. His face changed to one of anger, and Reb Yitzchak was taken aback.

The clerk lifted his head after a moment of contemplation. "Tell me, who is the owner of this check?"

Reb Yitzchak replied that it was his check, and that he did not understand what the problem was. As far as he knew, there was still enough money in his account.

The clerk's voice grew grimmer, and his tone was sharp and frightening. "Are you Yitzchak Tumiler?"

Reb Yitzchak nodded. "I am Yitzchak Tumiler, make no mistake."

It seemed as if the clerk had forgotten where he was. "Are you the Yitzchak Tumiler who learned in Yeshivas Oholei Yeshurun twenty years ago?"

"Why, yes," Reb Yitzchak replied. He was indeed one of the alumni of Oholei Yeshurun, but he did not understand who it was facing him behind the counter and why he looked so angry.

"Well," said the clerk shortly, "I am Eli Simon. I am the one who does not forgive you and your whole group of friends from Oholei Yeshurun. Twenty Kol Nidreis have already passed and I still find myself unable to dislodge the grudge against you all in my heart. I had come from France, I was foreign and lonely, and you ridiculed and excluded me. I did all I could to get into your group. I desperately wanted to grow together with you, but I did not find favor in your eyes."

Reb Yitzchak stood there stunned, but Eli Simon was not finished. The words burst forth from somewhere deep in his heart, and the accompanying pain was as fresh and bitter as if it had all just happened. "You went on to spread Torah and raise generations of Torah students, while with your own hands you caused me to distance myself and fall away from a life of Torah. Love of money replaced the void of love for Torah in my heart. I'm a bank teller, while my friends from the yeshiva learn and draw tremendous pleasure from their studies. Because of this I have not yet forgiven you."

For a moment, Reb Yitzchak saw himself standing in the halls of Yeshivas Oholei Yeshurun twenty years ago. He was a young student, and facing him was Simon the French boy, hurling angry words at him. They had indeed formed an elite group there, they had sharpened each other's learning, and Simon had always been on the outside.

Behind Reb Yitzchak, people continued turning to other tellers, and only at this counter did the silence continue. Some more words of rebuke gushed forth from Eli's mouth, and Reb Yitzchak stood there stunned, not knowing what to do.

"I find no joy in my life, my children have no spirituality, and it's all because of you...."

When Reb Yitzchak recovered his faculty of speech, he began to plead for mercy as tears streamed from his eyes, but Eli Simon had already continued to process the cash withdrawal as if he had not heard. He took the amount of money that Reb Yitzchak had requested, meticulously counted out the bills , and slammed it down onto the counter. He then handed the pen to Reb Yitzchak Tumiler for a signature, seemingly oblivious to the man's trembling.

"Now you come? Now you tremble?" he hissed at him through years-long pain. "At the time, you knew how to keep a distance; you left me to tremble and cry alone during those long nights. What did I gain from that? How can you help me now? I have money but I have no Torah, and it is you who caused me to lose both worlds...."

In the end, Reb Yitzchak arranged to learn with Eli Simon every evening, in an attempt to atone for the pain he had inflicted on the bank teller so many years ago. Their learning session yielded fruit; Eli Simon experienced a newfound joy in his life. Reb Yitzchak had believed that it was possible to make amends, and he did so.

As time passed, Reb Yitzchak was astounded to discover that Eli Simon actually didn't work for his bank branch at all. However, exactly on that fateful day, there were not enough tellers at that branch, and the bank manager had to transfer employees from other branches. Thus, Eli Simon found himself in the branch into which Reb Yitzchak entered.

Aside from this, as we have mentioned earlier, Reb Yitzchak almost never entered the bank. It was only a particular situation in which he found himself that had brought him to the bank that day, just when Eli Simon was working there.

A bank that is short of clerks is forced to procure a clerk from another branch, a busy man is forced to enter a bank, and ha-Kadosh Baruch Hu sweetens a bitter incident. A pain-filled heart meets up with the one who caused the pain, in order to draw the hearts closer and bring about love and forgiveness through love of Torah.

There is a saying in the Gemara (*Kiddushin* 30b): "'...In the Book of Wars of Hashem: the gift of the [Sea of] Reeds' — through the book of Hashem, enemies become friends." The Gemara explains that the word *besufa*, reeds, should be read as *besofa*, "in the end" — and we can see it applied in this case. In the end, enemies became friends through studying the Torah.

Hashem Helps Those Who Return to Him

*H*E WAS AN ELDERLY immigrant from Russia who lived quietly and modestly in Rishon Letzion. His name was Leib, and that was just about all his neighbors knew about him. He was a widower, living alone, and no one had ever bothered to find out if he had family or relatives. His good health enabled him to be independent and see to his own needs. He cooked and cleaned for himself and never asked for favors.

Leib's golden years were truly a blessing. The shul-goers who had exchanged a few words with him were surprised to learn that he was over ninety years old. In spite of his years, his posture was still erect and he walked without a cane. He could read the small print of the *siddur* without eyeglasses, and his mind was as sharp as ever.

People were used to seeing him in shul, and no one thought much about him. He had become part of the scenery and aroused no more interest than did the frayed curtains or timeworn benches. But Leib didn't mind his anonymity. He seemed happy enough just to go to shul, daven, and then return home, even if no one inquired what he did before or after davening and even if none of the congregation thought to ask him if he would like an *aliyah* more than once a year.

Therefore, the Rav of the shul, ha-Rav Shmuel Trovitz, *zt"l*,*

---

* Ha-Rav Shmuel Trovitz, *zt"l*, was the author of *Ma'adanei Shmuel*, and passed away on 18 Nissan 1996. This story is based on one that appeared in his *sefer*.

was mildly surprised when Leib came up to him in shul one day after the Rav's *shiur* and said, "I have a confidential matter to discuss with the Rav. When can he set aside some time to see me?"

Leib went to the Rav's *shiur* regularly. He would sit in the back and listen with great respect, though he would hardly ever participate. Rav Trovitz held the elderly man in great esteem, and therefore replied, "I will be happy to come to your house, Reb Leib, whenever it is convenient for you."

"As you know, I've been living in Rishon Letzion for twenty-five years," Leib began later that afternoon after the Rav had seated himself on the couch. "All these years here I have done my best to obey the Torah and keep the mitzvos and learn as much as I could. I must confess, however, that this was not always so.

"I committed many transgressions when I was young. My home was not religious and for many years I knew nothing of *Yiddishkeit*. Since immigrating to Eretz Yisrael, though, I have been privileged to become Torah-observant, and can only hope with all my heart that the Ribbono shel Olam has accepted me. I hope that I will eventually be able to make up for my past wrongs. One thing in particular, however, weighs heavily on my conscience and gives me no peace, and that is why I wanted to speak to the Rav.

"It happened sixty years ago in Russia, in the aftermath of the revolution. The revolution was supposed to usher in equality, justice, and plenty, but it brought no relief to our suffering. People had no bread to eat.

"My elder brother and I were in the leather business. We traded in hides. We had to pay huge taxes to the government, and we barely managed to make a living. Circumstances drove us to deal in the black market, under the cover of a legal, nonprofit organization that we set up. Eight other men joined us, and my elder brother ran the organization. It seemed to us the only way we could continue to exist.

"Soon we found out that one of our group, Morris Tratch, was not carrying out the missions he was supposed to, and my brother was afraid to continue trusting him. We expelled him from the group and would not let him participate in our activities. Morris was deeply offended, and in retaliation informed on us to the Russian authorities. We were lucky to get off with a heavy fine.

"My brother, by now incensed at Morris' behavior, wrote a letter to the police giving details of a smuggling incident that only Morris had been involved in. My brother showed me the letter and asked me to mail it, which I did without a second thought. A few days later we heard that the NKVD had raided Morris' house and arrested him. They imposed such a great fine on him that he and his family were reduced to utter poverty.

"Many years have passed since then, but now my conscience troubles me greatly. I know that what I did left a stain on my soul. I could have refused to mail the letter and told my brother that it got lost in the mail. But I was a *moser*. I caused great financial harm to a fellow Jew, and I know this warrants serious punishment. I also know that if I do not make amends, I can never be forgiven for this sin.

"I am ninety years old and my end is near. Though I have led a blameless life for many years, I am burdened by the sins of my past."

Reb Leib broke down and begged the Rav to help him. "Tell me what I can do," he pleaded. Rav Trovitz thought for a moment and asked, "Is Morris Tratch still alive? Do you know where he came from and if he has any heirs?"

"Morris used to live in Tchernowitz," Leib said with a deep sigh, "but I heard that he passed away some years ago. No one I asked, and I have asked many people, could ever tell me anything about his family. Ten years ago an acquaintance told me he had met Morris' son in a certain town in Russia, and I immediately wrote to my two daughters, who still live in Russia, asking them to contact Morris' son. My daughters are in their seventies and did nothing to help me. I have the feeling that they think I am senile."

"I really do not know how I can help you, my dear Leib," Rav Trovitz said.

"Rabbi," Leib cried, "you are the head of our community. Whatever you *pasken* on earth is accepted in Heaven. Maybe you can promise me that, since I have done my utmost to find Morris and make amends for my sin, I will not be punished for it. If you can give me such a ruling, then maybe I will be able to stand before the Heavenly Court."

Rav Trovitz felt the full weight of his rabbinical responsibility. The words of Kol Nidrei echoed in his mind: "With the permission of Hashem and the congregation, in the Heavenly Court and the earthly court, we sanction...."

"Let me consult with other rabbis and *dayanim*," he said. "Come to me at the *beis din* in ten days."

Rav Trovitz left Leib's house with a heavy heart. How could he give a halachic decision for the Heavenly Court? How could he possibly cleanse a Jew of his guilt?

Rav Trovitz sought the advice of *dayanim* and other *talmidei chachamim*. He related the whole story to the chief rabbis of Rishon Letzion, ha-Rav Wolpe and ha-Rav Azran. They discussed Leib's request, and in the end asked for a ruling from the *beis din*.

When a person tries with all his might to do the right thing, ha-Kadosh Baruch Hu assists him in ways he never dreamed possible. *Chazal* say, "One who comes to purify himself is granted Heavenly assistance" (*Shabbos* 104a). Rashi adds, "And an opening is prepared for him."

On the eve of the tenth day, Rav Trovitz heard a loud knocking at his door. It was Leib. "I don't have to come to *beis din* tomorrow," he said with elation. "My problem is practically solved!"

Rav Trovitz invited Reb Leib inside and waited for him to explain. "A few days ago I was not feeling well, and, for the first time since I have lived in Eretz Yisrael, I decided that I had better see a doctor. I didn't know that I needed to make an appointment in advance, so I simply asked for directions to the local clinic and went there after davening *Shacharis*.

"I arrived at the clinic at six-thirty A.M. and found the door locked. Assuming that the doctor would arrive soon, I sat down at a nearby bus stop to wait. Another man was sitting on the bench waiting for the bus, and I had a feeling he spoke Russian. I was correct, and we were soon conversing in our mother tongue.

"His name was Leon, and he lives in Rishon Letzion. He said he came from Tchernowitz. As the Rav can well imagine, I immediately asked him if he had known a man called Morris Tratch in Tchernowitz.

"Leon burst out laughing. 'Morris Tratch was my father-in-law. I am married to his youngest daughter,' he said.

"I could hardly believe it. For a few moments I couldn't speak, but when I calmed down, I told him the story of what had happened in Russia so many years before.

"Leon stood up and said he would catch a later bus. He wanted me to go home with him and meet his wife, Morris' daughter.

"With a combination of joy and shame, I repeated my story to Leon's wife, who remembered clearly the NKVD's intrusion into their home. As young as she had been, she still recalled the amount of her father's fine — twenty thousand rubles, a fortune in those days. I immediately resolved to return that amount of money to the Tratch family.

"*Kevod ha-Rav*," Reb Leib said. "I am so happy. Praised be Hashem, Who saw my suffering. I have been searching for Morris' family for so many years, and all this time we have been living in the same city! After so many years of good health, Hashem caused me to get an infection that required medical attention. On top of that, if I had gone to the clinic at the proper time, Leon would have been long gone from the bus stop."

According to halachah, Morris' sons were the rightful heirs to the money. Leon informed Leib that Morris had two sons who were still living in Russia. The problem of transferring the money was minor compared to the difficulties Leib had confronted in locating them, but Leib was determined to see it through to the end.

An added twist to the long and complicated chain of events leading to Leib's happy discovery was that Leon recalled having left behind in Russia a savings account, which contained about the same amount as Leib owed the Tratch family. He had not been able to take the money out of the country when he immigrated to Eretz Yisrael, but he could legally transfer it to the account of another Russian citizen, and Leib could repay him.

Without further delay, Leon transferred the money in his Russian savings account to Morris Tratch's sons, and Leib's sixty-year-old debt was paid. Leib's only stipulation was that the brothers must send him a receipt for the money. That seemed a strange request after all that had transpired. When he received the receipt, Leib went straight to Rav Trovitz with it.

"Ha-Rav," he said, "I no longer need a halachic ruling, but I do have one request. When the time comes for me to leave this world, please bury this receipt with me. When it is my turn to be judged in the Heavenly Court, I want it to accompany me."

Rav Trovitz tried to explain to the elderly Jew that everything is already known to ha-Kadosh Baruch Hu and His Heavenly Court, and that He has no need of receipts. Leib's mind could not be put at ease, however, until Rav Trovitz promised to fulfill his request. "You can rest assured, Reb Leib, that you will come to Heaven as pure as a newborn baby."

Shortly after this Leib became ill, and a few days later returned his soul to his Maker. Rav Trovitz kept his promise, and placed the receipt in the grave beside the elderly Russian man.

Chessed shel Emes

*Acts of kindness that one does
for the dead are chessed shel emes,
"true kindness," because one does
not expect any reciprocal payment.
(Rashi on Bereishis 47:29)*

Pesach Cleaning in Shevat

SHIMON KAHN, the head of the household, returned home from work. All of the members of his family were waiting for him so they could sit down to eat their supper together. He was happy to see them, but extremely tired after a long day's work. It was *erev Rosh Chodesh Shevat*.

"Shimon," his wife said as they sat down to eat, "I want to start Pesach cleaning tonight." The tired man reacted as expected. He mumbled some blessings for a good beginning, reflecting that as long as the preparations did not involve him directly, he didn't mind if she started early. As far as he was concerned, his wife could have started the cleaning immediately after Pesach of the previous year. She usually did most of the preparatory work herself, certainly the early stages of cleaning, and though he was prepared to help as much as he was needed in the later stages, Shevat was a bit early to disrupt his regular routine.

For some reason, this year his wife was not content to receive only his blessings. She not only had a strong urge to begin early this year, she was also determined that he initiate the operation. Perhaps she thought it fitting that the one who completed the work, the one who performed the search and burning of the *chameitz*, should be the one to begin; or perhaps it was just "one of those feelings."

In truth, Shimon felt that he still had the taste of matzah and *maror* in his mouth from last Pesach, and he was caught unawares by his wife's plans for this Pesach. In any case, his wife seemed really determined, and Shimon could not refuse. The matter was settled: he was to start that evening by cleaning the upper, hard-to-reach bookshelves in the back room.

When he returned from his regular evening *shiur*, he was greeted by the sight of pails, brushes, brooms, and detergents. His wife and daughters had on their aprons and had begun to clean some closets. His sons had started to work on the bookshelves in another room. Once more he protested that it was only *erev Rosh Chodesh Shevat*, but it didn't help. Seeing no other alternative, he rolled up his sleeves and went to work.

Shimon intended to tackle the top shelf first, but for some reason, his attention was drawn to an old wooden cabinet wedged into the corner between the bookshelves and the adjacent wall. It was a filing cabinet, stuffed with old documents, used checkbooks, old bank statements, the family tree, and other such things that were rarely needed, perhaps only once every few years.

No one thought the file cabinet could actually contain *chameitz* because its drawers opened against the wall; in fact, they could hardly be opened. It was therefore not usually checked thoroughly, even before Pesach. Every year the drawers would be opened, and the file cabinet would be found in the same state as it had been left the year before. Whoever checked it would riffle through the papers to make sure there were no crumbs of food, and then leave it in the same disorder until the following year.

This time, Shimon suddenly decided that he would begin by cleaning out the file cabinet. As long as he had no choice in the matter, he would do a good job. He would dust off the old papers, examine them, and perhaps even find some interesting treasures to show his children.

His wife tried to dissuade him, but he persisted, arguing that it had been years since he had touched anything in these drawers and that he ought to go through them at least once every few years.

Shimon pulled the cabinet out of the corner, turned it to face him, and opened the first drawer. He began to cough from the dust that arose from the old papers.

The top paper caught his attention. It was dated Shevat 1979 and it read: "I, Binyamin ben Zevulun Morganstern, declare that I received from Shimon Kahn the sum of one thousand dollars, which I will return no later than two weeks after I am asked to do so." It was signed: "Binyamin Morganstern."

A thousand dollars? Shevat 1979? Binyamin Morganstern?

Shimon scratched his head, and a long-buried memory began to surface in his mind. Yes, he remembered a man who had once lived in the neighborhood. Mr. Morganstern had approached him in the courtyard of the shul and asked him for a loan of a thousand dollars. Shimon remembered that he had been able to help the man out, and he had forgotten all about the debt afterward. *Baruch Hashem*, he had been able to spare the money.

He looked at the name once again carefully. Many years had passed since he had last seen Reb Binyamin, for that was what he had always called him. But the name Binyamin Morganstern now rang a bell. Had he not just seen that name in an obituary notice in the newspaper the day before?

He went to the kitchen to find yesterday's newspaper. Yes, the *shivah* for Binyamin Morganstern, *z"l*, was to end that day, and the family was going up to his grave the next. Wonder of wonders! Heaven had caused him to look into that cabinet and find that I.O.U. so he could tear it up and cancel the debt.

Shimon decided to tear up the I.O.U. on the spot, and he would go to the grave the next day to declare his forgiveness to Reb Binyamin.

He was fairly shaken by what had just occurred, but he was in for a further surprise when his oldest son asked him a question: "Abba, did you hear what happened to the Tzion family this week? I heard about it in yeshiva today. Mr. Tzion passed away a short time ago; he recently appeared to his daughter in a dream and told her that he had borrowed some tools from their neighbor and had never returned them. He wanted her to look for them and return them for him and so be forgiven."

Shimon assembled his family around him and showed them the I.O.U. he had found in the cabinet and yesterday's newspaper announcing the death of and *shivah* for Mr. Binyamin Morganstern. Shimon said out loud in front of his family, "I hereby forgive Binyamin Morganstern this debt. He is forgiven, he is forgiven, he is forgiven! I bear no grudge against him for the thousand dollars that I lent him. I forgo them with a full heart!"

Shimon now realized why his wife was impelled to start Pesach cleaning on Rosh Chodesh Shevat, and why she felt that he must participate in the Pesach cleaning right from the beginning, and why he himself should suddenly be sidetracked into opening up the old file cabinet.

Shimon intended to remove some dust in honor of Pesach, but instead he merited to rescind a debt that was disturbing the peace of a soul in Heaven, enabling a Jewish soul to attain forgiveness and rest in the World to Come.

Last Moments

LTHOUGH REB YISSACHAR had neither child nor nephew nor pupil to see to his last needs on earth, *hashgachah pratis*, which oversees every step of every creature, saw to it that two distinguished Jews were at his side when his soul left his body. Thus, he had a smile on his face and he was not alone when he set out on his final journey. These two men were privileged to confer honor upon a fellow human being who had always avoided honor.

Few people were aware that Reb Yissachar was an outstanding Torah scholar and a unique individual, for he seemed to be quite an ordinary figure as he walked quietly past. Only a few people knew the secrets of his inner world, which he took with him to the grave.

Reb Yissachar was someone who might have honestly testified before Heaven that he had never tasted worldly delights. However, if you had asked about his life, he would have told you that all his days were full of pleasure and joy derived from learning Torah.

His home was a one-room apartment on the ground floor of a building in the Meah Shearim neighborhood of Jerusalem. He slept at night in the company of the many cats that gathered in his building. The cats may have troubled him, but we will never know for sure. It is clear, however, that he never bothered them, as this silent man had never disturbed any living creature.

He and his wife never had children, never enjoyed any *nachas* in this world. In the mornings, he would rise early to clean a nearby *mikveh* and heat the water. He derived his living from this, and it was enough for him. The Torah was his whole life, all his pleasure in this world. He had nothing else.

In truth, he did not require anything else. He ate little, and the small amount of money he carried in his wallet sufficed for his needs. He had hardly any expenses, just as he had hardly any income. He had no interest in money; it was not one of his priorities. He was one of those unique individuals whose life began and ended in the realm of halachah. Those few people who knew him well — as well as one could know such a self-contained person — could attest to the scope of his knowledge and describe the pleasure he found in it. Reb Yissachar was a genius in the field he had chosen. He was an expert in all areas of the holy Torah, in all its depth and breadth, and it was the joy of his life.

He did not smile much, for he usually kept to himself. The world kept on smiling all around him, but he remained on the sidelines. One of the volunteers attending him in his final illness told him that the entire community was awaiting his recovery. Reb Yissachar waved away the words with a motion of his lonely hand. "Who knows me anyway?" he asked. It was not a complaint — he was not a man who complained — but a statement of fact.

This great, humble man died quietly, but not alone, on one of the upper floors of Shaare Zedek hospital. Now, you will ask, how did that come about?

Reb Zerach, a noted Jerusalem educator, was one of those who knew and appreciated Reb Yissachar's true character. When Reb Yissachar's wife became sick at the end of her life, Reb Zerach made sure that a member of his family sat at her bedside at all times. And in truth, he was not the only one who cared about Reb Yissachar; a number of important and distinguished members of the community looked after Reb Yissachar after his wife's death.

Then when Reb Yissachar was hospitalized, Reb Zerach took it upon himself to notify the group and arrange for them to take turns visiting him. These men regarded it as a privilege to sit at Reb Yissachar's bedside. They cared faithfully for this living *sefer Torah* who was now suffering, and did everything they could to make him more comfortable.

Although Reb Zerach had made all the arrangements most devotedly and fully intended to visit Reb Yissachar himself, for some reason his visit kept being postponed from day to day, each time for a different reason. He knew Reb Yissachar was critically ill, and that he should not delay his visit, but every day some urgent matter detained him. The visiting arrangements ran smoothly, but Reb Zerach himself, the man behind it all, had not yet been at the hospital.

Reb Zerach finally decided one day that come what may, he would put it off no longer. He informed his learning partner that they would have to finish early that day, because he intended to visit Reb Yissachar. Reb Yoel, who was sitting nearby, overheard the conversation and asked Reb Zerach for more details about Reb Yissachar's condition. As Reb Zerach spoke, Reb Yoel sighed heavily, a painful sigh of pity for the man lying on his sickbed about to end a life that in an earthly sense had hardly been lived. Yet, how could a life of Torah, purity, and truth have been anything but a full life?

Reb Zerach set out for Shaarei Zedek in a taxi, before something else could happen to prevent him. When he arrived at Reb Yissachar's bedside, he was astonished to find that Reb Yoel had arrived before him. Reb Yoel had rushed to fulfill the mitzvah of visiting the sick.

Together they stood and watched the sleeping Reb Yissachar, who was breathing heavily. Their thoughts were on the sick man. How beautiful was the last stage of life when one approached it as innocent as a baby. How fortunate was the soul that was as pure at death as at birth, upon which the physical world had left no impression. King Solomon probably had just such a person in mind when he said, "The day of death is better than the day of birth" (*Koheles* 7:1).

Suddenly Reb Yoel said, "I don't like the sound of his breathing." Reb Zerach tried to dispel his fears. He told Reb Yoel that Reb Yissachar had been suffering from breathing problems for a long time; it was nothing new. However, Reb Yoel insisted that it sounded serious to him.

Reb Zerach went outside to question the nurses, who explained that they had just examined the patient and that there was no reason to come again. Reb Zerach insisted, however, and a nurse came in to look at the patient. She immediately rushed out to summon the doctors. And indeed, those were the last few moments of Reb Yissachar's life.

Reb Zerach and Reb Yoel stood together at Reb Yissachar's side and began to recite the *Shema*. A happy smile spread across Reb Yissachar's face, a rare smile, his last smile. Thus, he was taken from this world with a shining countenance, the words of the *Shema* echoing all around him.

Reb Zerach made all the arrangements. He called the *chevrah kaddisha*, he fixed a time for the funeral, he acquired an honorable burial plot, and he had the announcement broadcast in the streets so that the funeral would be well-attended on short notice, as is customary in Jerusalem. He arranged for distinguished speakers to eulogize Reb Yissachar, and did not forget to arrange for someone to say Kaddish throughout the year for the elevation of the dead man's soul. Everything was done in accordance with the halachah that had been so dear to Reb Yissachar. He was brought to his final resting place and accorded the honor and respect due him.

During the seven days of mourning, Reb Zerach even organized the learning of *mishnayos* in Reb Yissachar's memory. The *siyum* that Reb Zerach made was attended by many important and well-known rabbis. Honor had finally caught up with the one who had always fled from it.

Only afterward did Reb Zerach realize what great *hashgachah* he had experienced. Only later did he see why Heaven had delayed his visit to the hospital, and why he had mentioned the visit to his study partner out loud so that Reb Yoel would overhear him.

How great is Hashem, Who ordained that Reb Zerach, who did so much for Reb Yissachar and his wife, would have the merit to witness his departure for the World of Truth. And how fortunate was Reb Yoel, who decided to fulfill the mitzvah of visiting the sick immediately; for it was he who perceived that Reb Yissachar's life was ending. And because of this chain of events, he also merited to witness a Jew returning his soul to his Maker with such a radiant countenance.

In the Merit of the Departed

WE WERE ON OUR WAY home from my father's funeral. It was almost sundown and we were about to start *shivah*. It had been a busy, difficult day, and we were eager to get home in time to daven *Minchah*.

Our family group included only six men; we needed to find four more men immediately so we could say Kaddish. A friend volunteered to stand outside the building (we live in Bnei Brak, Israel) and ask passersby if they could join our minyan. The minutes ticked by while we waited upstairs.

We had just decided to give up and pray each man individually, without a minyan, when we heard a car pull up in front of the building. Looking out the window, I saw a man roll down the window of the front passenger seat and ask our friend something. Then four men got out of the car and came inside with our friend. We would have our minyan after all!

These four men, it seems, were not Bnei Brak residents. They had been driving around for some time looking for the Itzkowitz family. Not only were they lost, they were also anxious to get to their destination quickly because they had not davened *Minchah*.

Adding wonder to amazement, one of the four men immediately recognized one of the mourners and sat down to console him after davening. This visitor did not even live in Eretz Yisrael, and had he and his fellow passengers not stopped to ask directions in front of our house, he would have missed the opportunity to be *menachem avel*, to console his friend.

The Two-Hour Delay

HE SCENE IS THE Ukraine. The date is 19 Av 1997. The Vizhnitzer Rebbe, accompanied by hundreds of chassidim, has come to pray at the graveside of his ancestors. Today they are going to Anipoli, the native city of the holy Reb Zushya. Both the holy Maggid of Mezritch and the Ohr ha-Ganuz are buried there as well.

The bus arrives in Anipoli, and the chassidim disembark with trepidation. They tremble in awe at the thought that they are stepping on the same earth upon which the holy Rebbe, Reb Zushya, once walked. The area is unfamiliar to most of the chassidim, yet somehow everyone feels at home. After all, the grave of one of the exemplars of true service to Hashem is home to any chassid.

The visitors see a greenish sign posted before them that reads simply, "Cemetery." For hundreds of years, the cemetery was the burial ground for thousands of Jews. The Nazis, however, brought destruction to this quiet, peaceful area, and rendered it almost unrecognizable as a cemetery.

The chassidim wait patiently for the arrival of the Rebbe. For some reason, he does not come. One group of chassidim has finished reciting the entire *sefer Tehillim*; another has returned from a stroll in the city. One hour passes and then another, and still the Rebbe has not arrived.

While they are waiting, a group of chassidim notice a grave in the corner of the cemetery that is still intact. It appears that the Nazis somehow missed this grave on their rampage of destruction. A few men walk over to inspect it more closely.

The gravestone is covered with dirt. One young man tries to brush away some of the dirt with his bare hands. Obviously, no one has been here to visit this grave in many, many years. The young man manages to decipher the year inscribed on the stone: 5670, that is, 1910.

The men gather around to see what other information the tombstone may reveal. According to the dates, they realize that here lies a young man who passed away in the prime of his life. He probably left no offspring, had no continuity. His mission on earth was completed while he was but a youth.

Everyone in the group standing next to this grave feels that there must be a reason that this particular *tziyun*, tombstone, has remained intact. Most people, they are thinking, are blessedly able to leave children behind them when they pass away, and the generations that follow serve as a *tziyun*, monument, for their souls. Even when, God forbid, a tombstone is destroyed, the deceased has a living, breathing memorial of his existence in this world. This young man, who passed away with no descendants, has somehow merited having his grave spared when the entire cemetery was destroyed.

Almost ninety years have passed. The men stand in silence, deep in thought, while one of their number continues to scrape away the layers of dirt on the stone in an attempt to reveal the rest of the inscription. Suddenly he cries out, "Today is his yahrtzeit!"

Everyone in the group shivers with wonder. His voice trembling, the young man reads the words out loud: *Niftar le-veis olamo be-yud tes Av,* "Taken to the Next World on 19 Av." One of the men begins to recite *Tefillah le-Moshe* (Psalm 90), and the entire group recites chapter after chapter of *Tehillim*.

Divine Providence has arranged things so that this group of Jews would come to pray at the graveside of an unknown Jewish boy exactly on the day of his yahrtzeit. Who knows, they think to themselves, how long this soul has waited for Tehillim to be recited at his graveside? They then recite Kaddish.

Suddenly a cry is heard. The Rebbe has arrived! The men quickly stoop to pick up some stones and place them upon the gravestone. Had they not been waiting such a long time for the Rebbe, they might not have noticed the grave at all.

The Empty Plot

HEN MRS. ROSENSTERN passed away, her husband wished to have her buried next to her mother, Mrs. Lieberberg, who had passed away fifty years earlier. Why? He knew how close his wife had been to her mother, and he felt certain her soul would derive much pleasure from the fact that they were buried in close proximity.

The *chevrah kaddisha* representative he enlisted to help him told him it was highly unlikely that the spot would still be vacant.

"After all," he said, "the cemetery is very old, and a lot of time has passed since your mother-in-law died."

When they checked the burial society's records, they found that there were no empty plots next to Mrs. Lieberberg's grave. But something impelled Mr. Rosenstern to ask his sons-in-law to go out to the cemetery and see for themselves whether this was true.

At the cemetery, the two men could not find Mrs. Lieberberg's grave, though they had been told the exact location. They decided to split up and search further, each taking a different row. They checked the names on every tombstone in the surrounding area, and continued the search for a long time.

Finally one son-in-law shouted, "I found it! I found it!"

It immediately became apparent to both of them that there was indeed an empty plot on one side of Mrs. Lieberberg's grave, as if specifically intended for their mother-in-law. They immediately phoned the burial society, but the secretary insisted the plot was already taken.

"It was sold forty years ago," the secretary said, "to a woman named Rivkah King. She purchased it for herself."

"Rivkah King?" repeated one of Mrs. Rosenstern's sons-in-law. "I am positive I just saw that name inscribed on one of the tombstones I checked today while I was searching for Mrs. Lieberberg's grave."

He returned to the area and quickly found the stone. "Here lies Rivkah King," read the inscription. It appeared that someone called

Rivkah King had passed away several years ago, and for some reason had been buried in a different plot from the one recorded in the *chevrah kaddisha*'s books.

The two men hurried back to the burial society's offices to find out what was going on. After making a few telephone calls to veteran society members, the secretary found someone who recalled the incident. Rivkah King had purchased the plot next to the one where Mrs. Lieberberg was buried, and the transaction was duly recorded in the society's records. Some time later, Mrs. King changed her mind and asked to transfer her ownership to a different plot not too far from the original one, but closer to the graves of some relatives. Her request was approved, and Rivkah King received ownership papers for the plot she wanted, but her name was somehow never taken off the list as the owner of her former plot. It was an oversight.

The oversight, however, allowed the plot to remain unsold for all those years, yet caused the members of the burial society to mistakenly assume that the plot was taken throughout the forty years Rivkah King's name was listed in their records. They had simply forgotten to erase her name as owner of the first plot, even after she was buried in a different plot. It was this mistake that ensured the plot next to Mrs. Lieberberg remained empty until the time came for her daughter to be buried there.

"Had we found Mrs. Lieberberg's grave immediately upon arriving at the cemetery," his sons-in-law excitedly told Mr. Rosenstern, "we would have reported to the burial society that there was an unoccupied plot next to her grave. The *chevrah kaddisha* would have then informed us that the spot was already sold to Rivkah King, and that would have been the end of our efforts. Divine Providence saw to it that we did not have to return to you empty-handed, and that your good intentions would be carried out to the letter."

Final Judgment

HE ELDERLY MAN, let us call him Reb Ezra Doliner, was childless, a lonely figure who lived alone in a simple room in one of the corners of the Holy Land.

Everyone sensed that the walls of his house concealed a world unto itself, and acquaintances always felt that it radiated a special light. Beneath Reb Ezra's silent exterior lay a unique personality. He went about his business, spoke little, and almost never looked up, not even to those eyes that were constantly fixed upon him, following his actions.

However, the hearts of God-fearing young men were drawn to the aura of *avodas Hashem* that enveloped Reb Ezra and as time passed, they began to organize a weekly *seudah shelishis* in his home. On those occasions Reb Ezra would contribute a few measured words that were sure to penetrate his listeners' hearts.

By the time people began to recognize his greatness, Reb Ezra was an old man. Few knew that the childless Reb Ezra was a father to countless daughters and a grandfather to all their sons and daughters, having raised, together with his beloved wife, numerous orphan girls in his home. Whenever Reb Ezra heard about a girl bereft of father and mother, he would tell her that from then on she had no need to worry, for his home was hers and her needs would be fully provided for.

Because Reb Ezra and his wife had no children of their own, they resolved to fulfill the saying of Reb Yochanan in *Megillah* 13a: "One who raises orphans in his home is considered as if he bore them."

Over the years, orphans flocked to Reb Ezra's house, where he and his wife cared for them as would the most devoted parents. They extended themselves for the girls, and treated them as if they were their own children. Thus, they constantly performed acts of charity, as Reb Shmuel bar Nachmani says in *Kesuvos* 50a: "Who performs charity at all times? One who raises orphans in his home and marries them off."

Reb Ezra was involved in everything that went on in his

adopted daughters' schools. Like a true father, he spoke with their teachers and did all he could to help them grow up as the Torah would want. When they reached marriageable age, Reb Ezra's nights turned into days as he put forth tremendous efforts to find each orphan girl a suitable husband. He made no compromises, choosing only the best for his "daughters," and was not satisfied until he clarified the minutest details about each boy.

He succeeded in making excellent matches for all the girls, and only then did he relax, knowing that he had done all he could to help them make a new start in life. Reb Ezra did not do this for only one girl, or for three or four, but for many.

But since that period in his life, many years had passed. Now that the girls had established families of their own, in Reb Ezra's home there remained no trace of his previous activities, and save for a few close friends, no one knew anything about them. But in Heaven, where there is no forgetting, all was recorded and remembered.

The day came when Reb Ezra set out on his final journey, but not before he approached one of the rabbis of his acquaintance and signed an agreement with him that he would recite Kaddish in his memory and commemorate his yahrtzeit.

(Something amazing happened during this incident. Reb Ezra requested that an additional clause be inserted into this written agreement, stating that after this rabbi lived out his days and years, his young son was to continue saying Kaddish for Reb Ezra every year. At that time, no one understood the reason for this, for the rabbi was then in his fifties and in the prime of his life. Why did Reb Ezra ask for a provision concerning what would take place after the rabbi died? But when the rabbi suddenly passed away a few months later at a young age, everyone was stunned by the condition that Reb Ezra had insisted on adding.)

Reb Ezra grew increasingly weak, until he became sick with his final illness and was admitted to a hospital in Jerusalem. His days were numbered, and a few of his acquaintances stood around his bed, among them the "Kaddish sayer," the teller of this story.

The men began to notice signs that their friend's life was waning. They recited verses of *Viduy* and *Shema* over and over again, but they soon stopped when they realized that death might still be hours away. They organized vigils; another day and night passed and Reb Ezra was still alive. It seemed as if his soul refused to leave his body.

Thus he lay, neither alive nor dead, with no change in his condition. Even the doctors claimed they could do nothing to save him from a prolonged death. His friends did not know what to do. They saw for themselves that Reb Ezra's hour had come; all signs pointed to the fact that it was time for his soul to return to its Source, but the transition was unending.

There were other patients in that room, and their visitors came and went. A bed was removed and a new one brought in its place. Only they were still helplessly witnessing Reb Ezra's death throes. They prayed for his deliverance from death to life or from life to death, but his condition remained the same, with neither life nor death.

Among the various visitors who maintained a constant vigil at the bedside of the patient that lay near Reb Ezra was a certain man who came daily. It appeared that he had a close connection with the patient. When he saw what was happening, he stopped near Reb Ezra's bed and asked the young man on duty for the name of the unfortunate man whose death was so drawn out.

"Reb Ezra Doliner," came the reply.

"W-w-w-what?!" The visitor was shocked when he heard the name. His mouth went dry and he cried out in a hoarse voice, "Reb Ezra Doliner?" and promptly fainted.

The bewildered young man helped to revive him.

The man who had fainted opened his eyes and stood shakily on his feet. "Take me to the nearest synagogue! Hurry!"

Together they rushed to a synagogue, where the visitor ran up to the Holy Ark, opened it, and, standing reverently in front of the Torah scrolls, cried out, "I hereby forgive Ezra Doliner with all my heart! He is forgiven, he is forgiven, he is forgiven!"

"I, Nechemiah Deutsch, son of David, forgive Ezra Doliner with all my heart. May it be considered as if it never happened. All is forgiven — and just as I forgive him, so may he be forgiven in Heaven!"

No sooner had the two returned to the hospital room when they heard the news that Reb Ezra had just returned his soul to his Maker. Finally, he had been granted his eternal rest.

The incident left everyone shaken. Nechemiah Deutsch had many years before disappeared without a trace, but his name sparked a long-forgotten memory in one of the elderly acquaintances of Reb Ezra Doliner, of blessed memory. One detail followed another, and people listened in stunned silence to the story of what had taken place so many years ago.

It had all begun when Reb Ezra made a match between one of his orphan girls and a yeshiva boy by the name of Nechemiah Deutsch. This Nechemiah Deutsch was an outstanding scholar. Upon seeking information, Reb Ezra heard many good things about the boy, and he consequently signed an engagement contract.

A short time before the wedding was to take place, Reb Ezra suddenly heard an unfavorable rumor about the boy. Reb Ezra clarified the matter and found that it was indeed true; the boy's learning exceeded his fear of Heaven.

The news fell upon Reb Ezra like a thunderbolt. From that moment on, he felt obligated to cancel the match and send Nechemiah on his way. He had a heavy responsibility for the future of the orphan girl, and he knew that had her father been alive, he would not have allowed the shidduch to take place. Because of this, he immediately informed all those concerned that he had agreed to the match under a mistaken impression and that he was now going to break the shidduch.

The boy's rashei yeshiva rose up as one to protest this latest development. "To cancel a shidduch? To embarrass a Torah scholar because his evil inclination got the better of him? Who ever heard of such a thing? Was this fitting behavior for a fellow Jew? After all, the boy could be set straight and returned to the right path!"

Such were their objections, but Reb Ezra turned a deaf ear. If they were concerned about the welfare of Nechemiah Deutsch, they could take him for their own daughters. He, as an adoptive father, was not permitted to give one of "his" girls in marriage to one who had behaved in such a manner.

The controversy intensified and eventually became a public issue, involving the Torah leaders of the time. They considered the matter according to their understanding, and concluded that justice lay with the heads of the yeshiva. After all, calling off a shidduch was no small matter.

They summoned Reb Ezra and informed him of their decision, emphasizing that he was obligated to continue with the wedding. Such a thing was simply not done, they told him, and Hashem would surely have no complaints against him. If this Nechemiah Deutsch had sinned, he would repent fully, and would soon blossom as before. However, it was absolutely forbidden to shame him and give him a bad name. On the contrary, a groom was forgiven all his sins.

But for Reb Ezra, the issue was closed. He came to the homes of the Torah leaders only out of respect for them and their Torah, but he had no intention of changing his mind. He humbly told them that he had no choice, but his heart told him to cancel the shidduch. In addition, he had already begun to hear better suggestions for the girl.

Reb Ezra acted upon his decision. He sent the gifts back to the home of Nechemiah Deutsch, apologized for the error, and broke off the shidduch.

There is no doubt that Reb Ezra had only the best intentions. His sole purpose was the good of the orphan for whom he felt full responsibility. Yet matters between man and his fellowman are scrutinized under a microscope, and one must be careful about even the slightest thing. Thus, Reb Ezra the *tzaddik* was not allowed into his final resting place in Gan Eden until he atoned for his sin and received the explicit forgiveness of the one whose feelings and reputation had been hurt, Nechemiah Deutsch.

It was therefore arranged from on High that a certain patient, a close friend of Nechemiah Deutsch, would be hospitalized in the same city, the same hospital, the same ward, and even the same room. Thus, after so many years, Nechemiah would again meet the one who had caused him such humiliation.

As a member of our holy nation, Nechemiah understood that it was possible that the soul of Reb Ezra refused to leave this world only because it bore the stain caused by the incident. And so, he immediately hurried to declare that all resentment from his heart was gone. Consequently, Reb Ezra's soul was cleansed from this last small stain that had testified against him in Heaven, and attained its eternal rest.

There is a lot to learn from this story. When a person has only the right intentions, he is assisted from Above and is sure to obtain forgiveness while still in this world, so that he is not punished for his misdeed. What is also amazing is the chain of events that brought about a resolution.

At the same time, we cannot help but feel shaken by seeing the exacting judgment on matters between man and his fellowman, to the extent that even so pious a man as Reb Ezra needed final release from the one whom he had wronged.

Like a Fallen Leaf

THE RINGING OF THE telephone broke the silence late one *erev Shabbos* at one of the offices of the *chevrah kaddisha* in Jerusalem. The secretary was still there, and he answered the phone unenthusiastically. He had been hoping to go home. On the line he could hear the trembling voice of a man in tears.

Phone calls to that office do not usually bring good news. Hearing the choked voices of Jews in their most difficult hours was daily fare for the secretary. Too often, the voices were those of widows and orphans, sobbing of their need for *chessed shel emes*. In this case listening was somewhat easier, for the deceased had merited a long life before he had concluded his task on earth.

The caller asked if there was any way for the funeral to be held that very day, but a glance at the clock showed that it was so close to Shabbos as to be totally impossible. For lack of an alternative, they agreed to be in touch on *motza'ei Shabbos* and to hold the funeral then. The secretary understood from the conversation that the deceased had been an ordinary Jew, and he picked out a plot on the Mount of Olives accordingly. The rest of the arrangements, he decided, he would finish once Shabbos was over.

Motza'ei Shabbos arrived and with it the arrangements for a large funeral of an important and well-known *talmid chacham*. With one thing and another, the burial society began to deal with arrangements for the funeral of the simple Jew close to midnight. They completed the *taharah* and were on the way to the burial plot on the Mount of Olives, when they suddenly realized that they were missing a tenth man for the minyan at the graveside. They decided to stop at a certain *beis midrash* in the Meah Shearim neighborhood to find someone who would be willing to join them.

Rabbi Blau sat in the corner of the *beis midrash*, winding up his review of the books placed before him. He gave a daily Gemara class in a yeshiva, and he had just completed preparing his lesson for the following day. The request by the man from the burial society surprised him a little. Going out to the Mount of Olives at midnight to bury an unknown, ordinary Jew is not the most pleasant thing to do.

At first, he wanted to apologize for being unable to go: as a teacher, he had to be alert the next day. He was going to recommend that they ask some of the others in the *beis midrash*. But on second thought, he decided that here was a mitzvah to be pleased about. It didn't often fall to one's lot to do the mitzvah of *chessed shel emes* with a man one would never get anything from and did not even know. And so Rabbi Blau closed his books and hurried to do that which Hashem had assigned him.

It was dark on the mountain as the minyan of Jews walked with the bier of their dead Jewish brother toward his final resting place. One of those in front carried an electric torch to shed some light by which the funeral was held, as Jewish law requires. The grave was filled, someone recited Kaddish, and the burial society started to pack up and go home. It was very late and the place was chilling. The deceased would rest in peace, he would rise to his fate at the end of days; but they were anxious to get back home, alive and well.

Just as they were about to leave, one of the members of the burial society remembered that the widow has asked, had actually implored, that after the burial those present sing "Bar Yochai" around the grave. She said that her husband had requested it, and that he had desired it all his life. As the widow and children generally do not participate in the graveside service if the deceased is buried in Jerusalem, the widow had relayed her late husband's request to the *chevrah kaddisha*.

But they were tired and weary, the night winds whistled around them, the silence of death in the place urged them to leave as fast as they could, and no one felt much like singing "Bar Yochai" just then....

The torchlight flickered, and someone asked, legitimately, "We don't have a *siddur* here. Does anyone know the song by heart?"

No one could answer. It seemed that even if anyone had known it by heart, he wouldn't have been able to remember it under such circumstances as the middle of the night in a cemetery.

Rabbi Blau stood on the side, a bit uneasy after having participated in what was for him an unusual night's occupation. The burial society was still debating what to do and had almost given up, when he suddenly remembered that he had a copy of "Bar Yochai" in his pocket.

"Here," he called out to the group as he held the page. "I have it here!"

Someone took the paper, shined the torch on it, and began to sing weakly, "*Bar Yochai, nimshachta ashrecha...*".

If in the first few moments the song had been carried by a lone, lifeless voice, slowly all the rest began to join in. All in all, this was not something that happened every day. At their feet, clods covered some unknown Jew, and in their hearts, the hymn was plucking hidden chords. Who knew who and what the deceased had been? How could they have been so sure that he had been just an "ordinary" Jew? Is there any such thing as an "ordinary" Jew?

They continued from one verse to the next of the holy, kabbalistic song, and a sort of excitement grew in the air. The words echoed over the mountains and cut the silence. "*Ta'alumah ve'ayin kora lah namta ayin lo teshurecha.*"

They finished the song and climbed down the mountain with beating hearts. Rabbi Blau was overcome. "What a wonder," he whispered, "an absolute wonder." It was clear that he had been rocked by something. In the van on the way back, he told the members of the burial society of the powerful impression the amazing conclusion of his day had made on him. As the story unfolded before his astonished listeners, they too were aroused and forgot their exhaustion, for what had happened was truly wondrous.

"Listen, friends," he said. "It's absolutely amazing! '*Mah rabu ma'asecha, Hashem...*, How great are Your deeds, Hashem, You have done all with wisdom.' Listen and see how Hashem arranged it so that this Jew's request would be fulfilled and we would sing 'Bar Yochai' at his burial.

"I usually daven the earliest *Minchah* on Shabbos afternoon, right after lunch, at the nearest shul. This is something I always do, and I have made it an unvarying practice. For some reason, lunch today lasted longer than usual, and against my usual custom, I missed my regular minyan. So, after the meal, my son and I went to a different shul for *Minchah*. As we neared the shul, I saw a piece of paper that should have been in *genizah* lying on the ground. I bent down and picked it up, saw that it had the hymn 'Bar Yochai' printed on it, kissed it, and put it in my pocket...intending to put it in *genizah*.

"However, I immediately forgot all about it — which is how the page ended up still in my pocket — until just now, at the cemetery. Now I understand why this page ended up in my hands, and why I missed my regular minyan and had to go somewhere else. It was all so I could meet up with this lost sheet of paper, put it in my pocket, and have it with me to sing 'Bar Yochai' over the fresh grave of an unknown Jew!"

The members of the burial society were stunned by the story, for it was an amazing instance of *hashgachah pratis*. The Ba'al Shem

Tov, *zy"a*, taught his disciples that each leaf that falls has a destination and a purpose, like a certain tiny leaf that had fallen in order to cover the body of a worm and protect it from the heat of the sun. Now the members of the burial society saw with their own eyes that every page belonging in *genizah* also has a purpose and destination, and that ha-Kadosh Baruch Hu will send it to a particular man to pick up and carry for a particular purpose.

They were reminded of the lesson that nothing in the world happens by chance, that no one lifts a finger until it is decreed that he do so. No one delays a meal or comes late for a minyan unless it is decreed that he do so. No one picks up a *genizah* page until it is decreed that he do so.

But Rabbi Blau hadn't finished. "I experienced something else amazing today," he continued, "and I have a hard time digesting it. I always prepare my Sunday class at home in my living room. I do not ever recall doing otherwise. I never leave home *motza'ei Shabbos*, and for years, about an hour after Havdalah, I have gone into the living room to prepare my class.

"For some reason, the children's noise disturbed me this evening, and I was having a hard time concentrating. They were in the middle of a game that didn't look like it was ending soon, so I decided to go to the *beis midrash* to prepare the class. My family was surprised to see me leave, since they know that I'm used to the *motza'ei Shabbos* noise. I apologized, explaining that I had no choice, that tonight I just had to leave the house.

"Now I understand," Rabbi Blau concluded, "why I had to leave home with the song 'Bar Yochai' tucked in my pocket. I was wanted as a messenger to bring it to the grave for the deceased. In Heaven it was arranged that I would go to that particular *beis midrash*, so that the burial society could find me."

It had indeed been a wonder of wonders. Even those who were used to doing *chessed shel emes* felt that it had been a special evening for them.

In the Right Place at the Right Time

Despise no man, and find fault
with no thing; for there is no man
who does not have his hour,
and there is no thing
that does not have its place.
(Pirkei Avos 4:3)

If You Chance Upon Something

N 1984, I TOOK A trip abroad to carry out a certain mitzvah. It was the first time I had ever left Eretz Yisrael, and I hardly spoke a word of English. I packed my suitcases and placed my tallis and tefillin — both Rashi and Rabbeinu Tam — in a carry-on bag along with some travelers' checks and my return ticket.

We landed in New York earlier than scheduled and whoever was supposed to meet me had not yet arrived. I called my host and told him that I would just find a taxi on my own and save him the bother of picking me up.

Leaving the terminal with my carry-on bag and suitcases, I was approached by a man who appeared to be a taxi driver. He started talking to me and making various gestures, apparently pointing to a taxi that was parked some distance away. I didn't understand a word he said, but I took out a piece of paper with the address I wanted written down. Before I could show it to him, however, he walked away and disappeared into the sea of people streaming in and out of the terminal.

I shook my head. The world was full of strange characters. I kept looking around for a taxi, and finally one drew up in front of me. I bent down to pick up my bags... when I froze in a panic. My carry-on bag was missing! I looked desperately all around me and then retraced my steps all the way back to the baggage hall.

I was distraught. My tefillin were gone, my precious tefillin, with the unique *parashiyos* written by ha-Rav ha-Gaon Yisrael Rosenzweig, who was widely known for his *yiras Shamayim*. The Rashi tefillin had first been wrapped around my arm by the holy Rebbe of Biyale, *zya"a*. My tefillin! I had never let them out of my possession, I had never worn anyone else's tefillin, and I had never even left them overnight in shul.

To compound my distress, I was all alone in a strange country without knowing a word of the language. I barely gave a thought to the traveler's checks and plane ticket in the lost bag; I was concerned only about finding my tefillin.

A fellow traveler, a religious Jew, passed by and took pity on me. He saw how upset I was and asked me in Yiddish what had happened. He explained that I must have fallen prey to a pair of experienced crooks. They always worked in pairs, he told me; one would occupy the victim's attention with all sorts of nonsense and the other would come from behind and steal the victim's bag. The first one would continue talking just long enough for the thief to slip away, and then he too would vanish.

My rescuer insisted that I register a complaint with the police at the lost and found desk at the airport. It was a time-consuming, exhausting procedure, especially after such a long flight, but it was worth doing, he said. And it was all I could do.

He put my suitcases into the trunk of his car and drove me from one airport office to another. He registered my complaint for me in the proper places, helped me sign the necessary forms, and used up hours of his precious time to help me. Everywhere we went, we were told it was a waste of time; those crooks were too sharp to be caught. Nevertheless, my rescuer persisted, and I heard him speaking on the phone again and again, canceling appointments and telling people he was unavoidably delayed.

When we had done all we could think of, I expected my benefactor to go about his business and leave me to mine. Evidently, however, he had decided to complete the mitzvah that he had begun. The address I sought was in Flatbush, but he was going to Monsey, which I understood was in a totally different direction from the airport. He said it didn't matter, and drove me all the way to my host's house — which I found out later was at least an hour out of his way.

I thanked this angel from the bottom of my heart, shook his hand, and asked his name. "Shraga Newhouse," he told me. The name didn't mean anything to me at the time, and we parted.

Privately, I thanked the Ribbono shel Olam, Who had sent Reb Shraga Newhouse to me in my hour of need. I added a prayer that

He would help restore my tefillin to me, and I continued to pray for a miracle.

Treasure in a Trash Can

When I arrived at my host's house and he heard the story, he helped me cancel my plane ticket and set about finding me some tefillin to borrow. Though he soon found me a pair of Rashi tefillin, he could not find a pair of Rabbeinu Tam anywhere. For lack of an alternative, I decided that I would have to borrow a pair of Rabbeinu Tam tefillin every morning in shul.

I remained disheartened, and felt that my soul was missing something. I had never realized how much my own tefillin meant to me. Yet when I called my family in Eretz Yisrael, I never mentioned my loss; I didn't want to trouble or distress them. Every morning after davening with my borrowed tefillin, I would ask one of the men in shul if I could put on his Rabbeinu Tam tefillin. They were all good-hearted Jews and lent them generously without asking questions.

One morning, I traveled to the borough of Queens to see Rabbi Gelernter, *zt"l*, in connection with the mitzvah for which I had come to the United States. I davened *Shacharis* at a local shul in Queens and, as usual, I asked one of the men if I could borrow his Rabbeinu Tam tefillin for a few minutes. While wrapping up the straps after I had finished, the man asked me who I was and where I was from, and he took the story of my lost tefillin very much to heart.

As we were talking, the man, who told me to call him Chaim, asked whom I had come to see in Queens, and I told him. As we left the shul, I thanked him again for his kindness, and we went our separate ways. I had never met the man before and I never expected to meet him again. That night I returned to Flatbush and forgot all about our meeting.

About ten days later, I was astonished to receive a phone call from Rabbi Gelernter asking if I had recently lost a pair of tefillin. He gave me the number of a man in Queens who had found a pair of tefillin the day before.

I called the number in great excitement. Just because some stranger in Queens had found a pair of tefillin didn't mean they were mine, but it was certainly worth a phone call. The finder explained that he had found the tefillin without any identifying mark, but nearby he had seen a receipt from a carpentry shop on Tachkemoni Street in Jerusalem.

"Sure!" I said. "It's a receipt for four hundred shekels." The man confirmed that, and said the tefillin must be mine. Blessed is Hashem, Who heard my prayers and did not withhold His Mercy from me.

I immediately ordered a taxi and set out for Queens, with praise and thanks to Hashem on my lips. Everyone had said I would never get them back, but for Hashem all is possible. I recognized my tefillin on sight, even without their bag, and showed the man all the little signs by which I was able to identify them. He then astonished me with the story of how he had found them.

"It happened on Sunday," he said. "I don't work on Sunday, and since it was Lag ba-Omer, my children were on vacation too, so I decided to take them to the park.

"We had a wonderful time, and just before we headed home, I stopped to throw out the empty drink bottles and food packages in a small trash can. I had thrown everything out, replaced the trash can cover and turned to go, when I found my feet bringing me back to the can. I had caught sight of something in the can that just didn't seem right, but it didn't register until after I had closed the can. I went back to take another look inside. What had caught my eye was a red *tefillin* cover with the words *shel rosh* written on it!

"In shock, I reached in and pulled the treasure out of the trash. It was not only a tefillin cover, but a whole *tefillin shel rosh*, with its holy *bayis* and the letter *shin* of *Shadai* on it, complete with its black straps. I kissed the tefillin and the knot warmly, and immediately started digging in the trash to see what else might be down there.

"Sure enough, I caught a glimpse of a red *shel yad* cover, filled with a *bayis* and straps. Then I saw another *shel rosh* and another *shel yad*, this time of Rabbeinu Tam tefillin. With shaking hands I clutched the precious treasure. Who knew how they had gotten there and what kind of *siyata diShmaya* had sent me back to look in the trash can a second time to bring them up from its depths.

"I bent over the can once more, thinking I might find something else to identify the owner. All I found was the receipt from the carpentry shop in Eretz Yisrael.

"That evening in shul I sat down next to my friend Chaim and told him the amazing story. My friend told me that just a week or so before he had met a young man from Eretz Yisrael whose tefillin had been stolen at the airport. He told me to call Rabbi Gelernter, who made the connection. And that is how you found your tefillin."

If I had been able to borrow a pair of Rabbeinu Tam tefillin along with the Rashi tefillin, I wouldn't have been looking for a pair to borrow every day in shul. Thus, I would never have become acquainted with Chaim, and Chaim would never have heard my story. The man who found my tefillin happened to sit down next to Chaim in shul, and so the chain of *hashgachah pratis* was carried along until my precious tefillin were returned to me. The rest of the chain is just as amazing: the thief threw the tefillin away, and the finder threw his picnic trash away, in exactly the same trash can...and it all transpired on a Sunday when the collectors do not come around to remove the trash.

With praise and thanks to Hashem Yisbarach, I returned to my host's home in Flatbush and wrote my family a letter recounting the whole story, from my meeting with Reb Shraga Newhouse until the tefillin were returned to me. I began the letter with the words, "I thank Hashem with all my heart."

My story, however, does not end here.

Many years had passed since then, and the whole event was tucked away in the back of my mind. Then, on *motza'ei Shavuos* 1998 — fourteen years after the original incident — Hashem again showed me His *hashgachah pratis*, and displayed how there are no coincidences in this world.

Rabbi Shraga Newhouse

One evening, right before Shavuos, my youngest son had been looking all over the house for a place to keep the illustrated *Akdamus* he had received that day in *cheder*. All the storage places in our house were full to bursting with my children's treasures, which is why the little one had to look very hard to find a spot. His efforts bore fruit when he opened a drawer in an old chest and removed a bundle of papers in order to place his precious *Akdamus* within.

My oldest son passed through the room just then and picked up the papers his brother had placed on top of the chest. First he glanced through them, then he sat down and began to read from beginning to end. "Abba, I never knew that you lost your tefillin!" he cried.

I smiled. The memory of that story rose to mind, but I wondered how my son suddenly found out about it. He gave me the yellowed papers he was holding. I recognized the letter that I had once written to my parents beginning with the words, "I thank Hashem with all my heart."

That was the letter I had sent my family on the day I had found my tefillin, fourteen years before. It hadn't occurred to me that the letter might still be around. I was astounded to see it again so many years later. During those years, we had moved three times. The letter had moved along with us without my realizing it, and now here it was, just as touching as ever, bringing the whole incident to life again.

I sat down to reread the entire letter. Oh yes, Shraga Newhouse was the name of that man who had helped me, I now recalled. I would never have remembered it if I hadn't seen it again in my letter. *I really still owe Shraga Newhouse a great debt of gratitude that I have never repaid,* I mused. I couldn't get the name out of my mind during the entire Shavuos holiday.

The day after *isru chag* in Eretz Yisrael, I came home from shul in the morning and looked at the daily paper: "*Arono ba,*" began the funeral announcement, "Shraga Newhouse, *z"l,* of Monsey, passed away on Shavuos.... The funeral will be held today in Bnei Brak...."

The headline shocked me, but I soon understood what I had to do. It was clear that Heaven was giving me a final opportunity to honor Shraga Newhouse.

I cancelled every meeting and appointment I had scheduled for the day — just as he had done for me — and traveled to the airport, and from there accompanied the coffin to Bnei Brak. I stood alongside his bier and wordlessly thanked him for his goodness and kindness, which surely were standing in his merit now. Ha-Rav Povarsky, *shlita*, in his eulogy, told of Rabbi Newhouse's kindness and generosity. I followed the bier to its final resting place, and it seemed to me that the book had been closed on that story.

Another year passed, and it was the summer of 1999. Once again Heaven gave me another glimpse into an incredible cycle of *hashgachah pratis*. I had traveled to the United States once again, this time for a *simchah*. Since I was in the middle of writing a *sefer* at the time, I took my papers with me in order to work on them while I was away. In the evenings we celebrated *sheva berachos*, and during the day I sat in one of the shuls and worked assiduously on editing my work.

One day, a man sat down near me and began asking halachic questions. While we were talking, he started to leaf through the pages I was writing, and that led us to introducing ourselves. I discovered he was a relative of Shraga Newhouse.

I jumped at the name. "Do you mean Shraga Newhouse of Monsey?"

My new acquaintance nodded in surprise. How did I know the head of their family? I answered that not only did I know him, but I even remembered the date of his yahrtzeit — 6 Sivan 5758 — and I had even been at his funeral in Israel. I told Reb Shraga's relative that I had heard ha-Rav Povarsky's eulogy, and I had even been at Rabbi Newhouse's grave. Then I told him about my stolen tefillin.

We were both very moved. A hidden Hand from Above had shown itself so strongly!

"Listen," my new acquaintance said, "you are writing a book of halachah, isn't that so? I wish to memorialize the head of our family, Reb Shraga, in your *sefer*. Without a doubt, you have a connection to him."

On the spot, he took out his checkbook, and with trembling hands wrote out a check for the publication of my *sefer* "in the memory of Rabbi Eliyahu Shraga ben ha-Rav Avraham Newhouse of Monsey, z"l, Shavuos, 6 Sivan 5758."

I needn't mention how much this dedication and the accompanying funds helped me.

In 1984 I lost my tefillin and met Shraga Newhouse. The tefillin were returned to me by extraordinary means. Years later, miraculous financial assistance for the publication of my *sefer* came my way as a result.

Nothing happens by chance. Everything is decreed in Heaven.

Mutual Help

O NE SUMMER, MY FAMILY decided to spend a week vacationing in Tzefas. We were able to find an apartment to rent, and made our arrangements accordingly.

Our suitcases were packed with, we hoped, all we would need for the week. My sons and I carried the baggage downstairs. We then locked up the house and soon had everything packed in the trunk of our car. As we all settled down in our seats and buckled our seat belts, my wife asked me if I had packed the Havdalah candle and the *besamim.* I had not.

It was hot and I was tired. I could not face climbing the stairs again, unlocking the door, and searching for the candle and the spices. I told my wife that we would manage in Tzefas when the time came, and without further ado we drove off.

We enjoyed our stay in the beautiful and historical city in the north of Israel, and by the end of the week, we had forgotten about our lack of Havdalah candle and spices.

On my way home from shul on *motza'ei Shabbos* I remembered. We looked around our rented apartment, but saw no sign of either a candle or anything we could use for *besamim.* There were only four apartments in our building, and no one was home in the other three apartments, so I went outside to see if any passerby could help us out. Surprisingly, there was no one outside. I was uncomfortable about knocking on any other doors on our street.

Just then an elderly woman came out of the house across the street with a clear plastic bag in her hand. As she approached us I could see that the bag contained a bottle of wine, a Havdalah candle, and a small jar of spices!

"Excuse me," she said. "I wonder if you would be able to help me. I need someone to make Havdalah for me. You see," she explained, "I am really stuck this week. Usually my next-door neighbors call me in to hear Havdalah with them. This Shabbos they were not home. I haven't been able to eat anything yet this evening because I haven't yet heard Havdalah."

I then understood clearly why we forgot to pack our candle and spices, and then didn't think about them until the last minute. Indeed, ha-Kadosh Baruch Hu takes care of widows and strangers in the most unexpected ways.

Wrong Number

HAD BEEN WORKING IN education for decades in Lod. In 1981, however, I was sent to Beersheva with my family to found two elementary schools, one for boys and one for girls.

I rented an apartment in Beersheva and made arrangements to move. On the day of the move, at the height of the action — with the workers coming and going, taking furniture and boxes out to the waiting truck — the telephone rang.

Distractedly, I picked up the receiver. With my eyes on the movers, my ears caught the shrill voice of a woman complaining angrily.

"Is this Minsky? You should know that because of you I have no peace day or night!" she yelled. "My phone rings constantly. The callers all want Yaakov Minsky. As soon as I hang up from one wrong number, the phone rings a second and third time, all for the same Minsky. Don't you think it's time you did something about it?! How long do I have to suffer because of a Minsky I don't even know?"

She went on and on with her tirade, fuming about the disturbances that, she said, had been going on for quite some time. I couldn't get a word in edgewise, neither to explain nor even to apologize.

Finally, while she paused for breath, I explained to her that the problem was all because of a misprint in the telephone book. My number had been printed with 04 for the two final digits, instead of 94, making the listing her phone number instead of mine. I explained that the mistake wasn't my fault, and I assured her that the phone company had promised me that they would correct the misprint in the very next printing. In spite of all my efforts, however, she didn't sound too appeased.

I tried to cut the conversation short, for it was not a convenient time for me by any measure. Before hanging up, she asked, "By the way, what have you got over there? An institution? An office?"

"No," I answered, trying to mask my impatience, "it's a private home." At that moment, I thought to myself, the private home was about to fold up and ship out. I had no time for this!

But the woman on the line was not budging.

"A private home!" she exclaimed. "How can that be? Every wrong number wants to know about tefillin or mezuzos, *sifrei Torah* and shuls. Before Pesach, they ask about matzah and wine; before Sukkos, about *lulavim* and *esrogim*. Have you set up shop in that private home of yours?"

"Something like that," I answered her, shifting from one foot to the other and switching the receiver from ear to ear. "We're part of a well-known organization that tries to help people in need."

The moving men were trying to ask me something, but I could hardly hear them. With half-syllables and gestures, I asked them to repeat whatever they were saying. The noise was deafening. Hashem, I offered a silent prayer, please bring this strange conversation to a close!

Just when I was about to mumble an apology into the phone to the effect that I couldn't talk anymore, I was caught by a change in my caller's tone of voice as she said, her voice breaking, "You help people in need? Maybe you can help me. I am also in need!"

This was something else. I covered my free ear with a hand and tried to concentrate on what she was saying, encouraging her to tell me what was troubling her.

In between sobs, she told me of her ten-year marriage that as yet had not been blessed with children. As cautiously and tactfully as possible, I tried to find out a few pertinent details about the state of the tefillin and mezuzos in her home, but as she put it, "some rabbis" had told her they were kosher. I promised to look into the matter soon, and wished her with all my heart that we hear good tidings from her soon. I made a note of her name and number, and hurried to deal with the million things still left to do.

Moving On

After I put the phone down, I could hardly believe that the conversation was finally over. Even while I turned my attention to the logistics of the move, surprisingly, I found the strange coincidence very much on my mind. A few days later, I called my brother-in-law in Lod from Beersheva. I asked him to look into the matter of the woman who had called me, and check the tefillin and mezuzos in the house to see what could be done.

I had a year of intense, complicated work ahead of me in Beersheva: starting two schools, lining up teachers and rebbes, registering children. I was busy day and night, in addition to the basics of moving the whole family and adjusting to a new city. In the natural course of things, my moving-day conversation with that woman slipped my mind completely.

A few years passed, the schools became well-established, *baruch Hashem*, and our family returned to Lod. When we arrived back home, we were greeted by friends and family, including the brother-in-law I had asked to take care of the woman and her problem.

In the course of our conversation at this time, for "some strange reason," the incident with the phone call popped into my mind, clear as day. I asked my brother-in-law what had become of that family. He remembered the story well. He told me that when he came to their home, he found that their mezuzos and tefillin were not kosher at all, so he helped them replace everything immediately. He also spoke to them about whatever spiritual matters that needed strengthening, and that was the end of his connection with them.

We were both very interested in knowing how things stood, but it was too late at night to call, so we put it off. The following day was Friday and we were too busy, so we decided to wait for Sunday morning.

The Right Ring

Sunday morning, we made the call with beating hearts. An elderly sounding woman answered and asked whom we wanted. When she heard that we were looking for Mrs. Plonis she let out an exclamation of joy. She was Mrs. Plonis' mother, she told us, and said with obvious elation that her daughter had just given birth to a fine healthy son that very morning after many years of waiting.

We were suffused with an intense feeling of happiness and thanks to Hashem Yisbarach, for we felt that we had a part in this family's great *simchah*. But more than that, we were astounded at the amazing *hashgachah* that had merited us with hearing the good news on the very day it had occurred. We hadn't called on Friday or *motza'ei Shabbos*, even though so short a phone call could have been made, and now it was clear why we had decided "for some reason" to call on Sunday.

What was most amazing was to see yet again that nothing happens by chance. If Hashem wants to connect a woman in need with Jews who can help her, He can do so even by means of a "mistake" in a telephone listing.

Just in Time

MY PARENTS, may they rest in peace, merited to host at their Shabbos table a prominent rosh yeshiva of the previous generation, when he was visiting their hometown. This *gaon* suffered from diabetes, and due to his heavy schedule while traveling, his condition was not monitored as closely as it should have been.

That Shabbos, right in the middle of the meal, the rosh yeshiva suddenly lost consciousness and slumped over the table.

My parents were thrown into a panic. They were ordinary folk, unused to and uncomfortable with the unexpected. An incident such as this — especially involving as it did one of the *gedolei ha-dor* — was more than they could handle.

As my mother hurried to get a glass of water, a knock was heard at the front door. My father rushed to open it. Standing there was none other than one of our city's most prominent doctors.

"Run inside," he was greeted hysterically. "The Rav has fainted! He suddenly collapsed!"

Dr. Rosenberg quickly grasped the situation, and did what he could to restore the Rav to consciousness and stabilize his condition. Within an hour, the Rav had recovered and was once again sitting at the head of the table, weak but calm.

Now was the time to ask the doctor about his miraculously opportune visit.

"How did you know to come?" my parents asked.

The doctor, who was also amazed that he had arrived at this critical time, told us that he had planned to visit the Rav after the Shabbos meal, but in the middle of the meal he had suddenly felt a strong urge to be at the Rav's side.

Before even tasting the main dish, he prepared to begin reciting the Grace after Meals. His family was very surprised. Where was he rushing off to? Was he afraid the Rav would run away?

But once his mind was made up, the doctor would not allow himself to be dissuaded. He hurriedly recited Grace right then and there, and walked over to see the Rav.

The doctor's incredible story left my parents speechless. An open miracle had played itself out before their eyes.

The Rav turned to my parents and said, "Why are you so amazed? Is anything beyond Hashem's ability? Let me tell you what happened to one of the students in my yeshiva, and you will see how great the power of *hashgachah* is.

"The boy had a chronic illness. One day he was overcome with an attack of weakness and collapsed. Unfortunately, there was no one else with him at the time. In his semi-conscious state he urged himself to call for help, knowing that if he didn't, no one else would.

"Painstakingly he crawled to the telephone, pulled it down to the floor, and with his last ounce of strength dialed his doctor's number.

"'Hello?' he pushed himself to say in as strong a voice as possible. 'Is this Dr. Stein's home?'

'You've got the wrong number,' the surprised voice on the other end said. 'This isn't Dr. Stein's home — but he just happens to be here on a house call....'"

No Minyan in Stamford Hill

I WENT TO DAVEN *Minchah* with a minyan in Stamford Hill, a residential neighborhood in London. It was just after Sukkos, and it is generally hard to get a minyan together at that time of year because people do not arrive home from work early enough. Only five people turned up that day. We waited about ten minutes, and then I decided to try to find another minyan. Announcing my intentions, I asked if anyone wanted to ride along with me. One *bachur* accepted.

The next week was the beginning of the new term at my yeshiva in Gateshead, which is about a four-hour drive to the north. I owned a secondhand car, which was a good buy for the little I paid for it, but it was by no means ideal for a long journey. The car began to overheat fairly soon, and I had to stop repeatedly and wait until it cooled down. I realized that the car would probably get me to Gateshead, but I certainly wouldn't arrive in time for *Minchah*. Eventually I stopped at a service station in the middle of nowhere and got out to daven.

I looked for a quiet place to pray and saw a hill a few hundred feet away. I figured that if I went to the other side of the hill, I would have some privacy and not be disturbed. Just as I reached the brow of the hill, however, I heard a voice calling my name from the service station. Who would know my name in this remote place? I wondered.

It turned out to be the *bachur* I had taken with me to find a minyan in Stamford Hill the week before. He was traveling on the Gateshead yeshiva bus, and they had just stopped there to daven *Minchah*. Still, I asked him how he had recognized me from afar. He hadn't — he recognized my car!

Hashem Guides Man's Steps

A FEW YEARS AGO, when my father, z"l, was in the hospital with his final illness, I got an emergency telephone call to come see him, as he had taken a turn for the worse. I was living in a small development town far from the center of the country where the hospital was located, and transportation was difficult. My only way of reaching the hospital was with a car service or a private cab.

For some reason, arranging a ride was even harder than usual that morning and my frantic calls to all the taxi companies met with no success. It seemed that events were conspiring against me, as I began to try the private cab drivers and was met with refusals one after another. By the time I had finished making my calls, there were no more buses leaving our small town either, and I seemed to be in a hopeless situation.

I had never had as much trouble getting out of town before, and it seemed that I had no choice but to ask a favor of some neighbor or aquaintance with a car, for which I was willing to pay, since it was truly an emergency.

Yet a slew of calls still did not turn up anyone who was willing or able to leave town, and it was only a good while later that I finally found a driver who agreed to take up my proposition. At that point, we wasted no time, and in short order we were on the highway to the center of the country. My driver had a cellphone that he used liberally along the way, and from overhearing his conversations (which I could not help but do), I understood that he was a shadchan. In his excitement over some of his suggestions, he spoke loudly and with full particulars, and one would have had to have been either deaf or dumb not to understand what, and whom, he was talking about.

Eventually, he started talking to the father of a certain young lady, who apparently had heard some damaging rumors about a certain "Yishai Yishayahu," the suggested *bachur*. These rumors indicated that Yishai had a particular failing, which was making the young lady's father hesitate. It sounded as if he was thinking of dropping the shidduch altogether.

My heart skipped a beat, for this Yishai was a fellow I knew well. I had tutored him for years and could vouch for the fact that he definitely did not have this supposed failing in the least. There was a reason that people might think so, but anyone who knew him well knew that in his case, the rumor was absolutely baseless.

I hesitated. Should I speak up or not? Should I get involved in other people's business or not? It took only a few seconds to decide that I had better say what I knew; who could tell whether all of my difficulties in getting a ride that morning had not been for the sole purpose of having me hear this particular conversation and help along a shidduch?

When my benefactor clicked off the phone, I hesitantly apologized for having overheard his conversation and told him what I knew to be true about the young man, citing my years of acquaintance with him as evidence.

The eyes of my driver-shadchan lit up. Immediately, he redialed the prospective father-in-law and told him the latest news. And when the father heard that I was the source, he said he would rely on my word alone — since he knew me personally — with complete confidence. Within a few days, there was a *L'chaim* at the father's house and the shidduch was completed with the help of ha-Kadosh Baruch Hu, Who had sent me to the right place to put in my two cents.

As a postscript, I arrived at the hospital to find my father in stable condition. He clung to life for another two weeks before finally passing away. My frantic race to reach him that day had been for "nothing," so to speak.

However, I can't help feeling that both the emergency phone call and the difficulty I had in finding a ride had all been for a different purpose: to put me in touch with that shadchan so that I would get involved in that shidduch and be an agent for good.

May we all hear only good tidings!

A Nod of Approval

ONCE ON AN INTERCITY bus ride toward Jerusalem, I noticed a highly respected *rosh mesivta* and *maggid shiur* arguing with the bus driver. The rabbi was making a request.

"It is now 2:15 P.M. At exactly 3:00 o'clock I have to give a class to some boys, at a yeshiva right near the entrance to Jerusalem. If I go with you all the way to the Central Bus Station and then go back to the yeshiva, I'm afraid that I will be late to the class and I will cause my students to lose valuable time from their Torah study. So could you please stop first at the bus stop right at the entrance to Jerusalem so that I can go straight to the yeshiva and start the class on time?"

The driver, however, answered, "I'm sorry, sir. There are no stops between here and the Central Bus Station."

"But it's on the way. You won't have to do anything other than stop for a moment to let me off," the *rosh mesivta* pleaded. "Listen," he tried a different tactic, "do it for the sake of the Torah, and may this merit help you and protect you. Please."

"Sir," the driver said emphatically, his patience by now worn thin, "will you please be seated."

The *rosh mesivta* went back to his seat, sat down, and in moments was deep in a *sefer*. He had made every effort he could, and whatever would be would be. You could see on his face that he had decided that it would be a waste to spend another moment of thought on the subject.

For my part, I wondered who was right. On the one hand, I understood the driver. He had to follow procedures faithfully, and couldn't make changes for every passenger, no matter how spiritually motivated the request might be. On the other hand, my heart contracted to see the distinguished, honorable rabbi defeated.

But there was no point dwelling on the issue. The driver had stood his ground and the *rosh mesivta* was deep in his *sefer*. The argument was over.

A few minutes later I was witness to the end of the story. If I hadn't seen it myself, I would never have believed it.

At the entrance to Jerusalem, right in front of the bus stop where the rabbi had wanted to get off, the bus crashed into the back of another bus which had stopped short in front of it. With a startlingly loud noise, the windshield of our bus cracked and we braked to a sudden stop.

The driver immediately opened both front and back doors and the passengers, a bit flustered, got off, each heading in his own direction. It was a few minutes before 3:00 P.M. The rabbi gathered his books and strode briskly to the yeshiva to begin his class on time.

Everything Comes from You

"GOD HELPS" is an expression we often use. A well-known scholar protested to me once, "Do you really think God helps? That makes it sound as if you were the one who did everything, and God merely helped you. But Hashem is the One Who accomplishes everything from beginning to end. Occasionally, He will let you do something too.

"The expression, 'God helps,'" the scholar continued, "makes it sound as if I do half and Hashem helps by doing the other half. In Yiddish, as you know, the word for help, *helft*, also means half. Nothing could be further from the truth."

This is true in matters of health, livelihood, and virtually every undertaking on earth. One act leads to another, which leads to another. A person is led step by step but does not always understand at each moment exactly where he is headed. Only the One on High is aware of the overall plan, and He is the One to carry it through to fruition. Only after the fact are we able to piece together the details and point to Hashem's handiwork.

There Are No Chance Meetings

I was once writing a book about a famous Galician Rebbe. I spent hours poring over books and manuscripts to gather as much historical information as possible. It was very important to me to publish a professional, scholarly work, and I was constantly aware of the incredible *siyata diShmaya* that accompanied me throughout my research.

During that period, a huge assembly took place in Jerusalem, attended by tens of thousands of *chareidim*. My friends and I soon lost each other amid the throngs of people. Eventually I found myself standing beside an elderly man who, as it turned out, knew my father. Before the speeches began we struck up a conversation, and I mentioned the book I was working on. I told him I was still checking into a few obscure details.

My father's acquaintance was intrigued, and said he knew a man named Avishai, who had written a book on a related topic. He might be able to help me. He could not recall Avishai's last name, but knew that his brother-in-law was a certain Yonasan Levy. Yonasan Levy happened to be an old friend of mine.

Only someone who has done painstaking research and sifted through piles of material for hours at a time can understand how elated I was to hear this. If I could locate Avishai, he might be able to save me hours of work.

I could not ignore the obvious *hashgachah pratis* that had guided me to stand next to this man, one of the many thousands who had attended the gathering, and had led us into conversation. As a rule, you don't notice who is standing next to you in such a crowd. I thanked the elderly man for the valuable information, and, even more, I thanked the Ribbono shel Olam.

The first thing to do was to contact Yonasan Levy in order to make contact with his brother-in-law, but I hadn't spoken to him for a long time. I do not live in Jerusalem, but since I was there for the assembly, I thought it was only sensible to try to speak to Avishai personally before returning home. While davening *Minchah* with the huge crowd, I offered a private prayer to Hashem that I succeed in my mission in the shortest possible time.

This will no doubt stretch your belief, but after *Ma'ariv*, as the crowd began to disperse, who did I see walking toward me but my friend Yonasan Levy! I ran over to him and called out in disbelief, "Reb Yonasan! You are just the person I wanted to see. Who would have thought I would meet you in this crowd!"

Yonasan was somewhat taken aback by my ebullient welcome, until I told him my story. Naturally, he did not know where Avishai was just then, but he gave me his telephone number.

As I was writing down the number, Yonasan called out, "Avishai! Avishai!" He turned to me and said excitedly, "There he is now. That's Avishai."

To make a long story short, in less than an hour I was seated in Avishai's living room feasting my eyes on a veritable treasure trove of letters, manuscripts, testimonies, old photographs, and other artifacts, which Avishai generously placed at my disposal. Avishai and I amiably reached an agreement regarding the use of his data; he himself was overjoyed to have his collection put to such good use. Together we packed everything up and I left, planning to take the first bus home.

Had I gone ahead and published my book without having seen Avishai's collection, it would have been a mediocre job at best. But Hashem in His great kindness brought me straight to the sources I was lacking without the slightest effort on my part.

I remember thinking at the time that that was the extent of the *hashgachah pratis* I would see that day. I was mistaken. Whereas man's ability to bestow kindness is limited, when ha-Kadosh Baruch Hu decides to shower a person with His blessing, it is boundless.

I walked from Avishai's house into the cool Jerusalem night, my heart singing with gratitude to Hashem. Lugging the large, ungainly cardboard box in my hands, I walked slowly toward the bus stop. Just as I reached it, an acquaintance approached from the other direction.

"Shalom aleichem!" Mr. Bloomstein greeted me warmly. "You're just the person I'm looking for. Actually, I had hoped to see you at the assembly today, but I knew the chances were small. However, when Hashem wills something, it will happen." I couldn't have agreed with him more.

I rested my box on a low wall nearby while Mr. Bloomstein told me why he had been looking for me. Someone had told him about the book I was writing about the Galician Rebbe. His late father-in-law had come from the same town in Galicia and had been a chassid of the Rebbe. He wanted me to mention his father-in-law in the book as a means of honoring his memory. He would be willing to pay for the privilege by helping me finance the book.

Still later that evening, as I sat in Mr. Bloomstein's living room to discuss the publication of the book, I marveled at how much progress I had made on it in one day.

Mr. Bloomstein happened to mention that he had once seen a letter from the Rav of the town I was writing about, in which he mentioned his father-in-law. "I would pay a fortune to get that letter," he said wistfully. I told him I thought I had seen such a letter in the box of paraphernalia Avishai had given me. We rummaged through Avishai's papers, and indeed, we found the letter and it did mention his father-in-law.

Mr. Bloomstein's joy was boundless, and he said he would be happy to finance the entire publication costs. With a flourish, he handed me two signed, blank checks, and instructed me to submit the book to a certain publishing house. I was to pay for publication in two installments with the checks he had given me.

About a year later the book was published, greatly enriched by Avishai's collection of documents and memorabilia. When people praised my work, I was loath to take credit for it, for I knew I had done very little; The Ribbono shel Olam was the One Who deserved the accolades. So I merely repeated to them the words of Avraham Avinu: "Blessed is the God of the world from Whose bounty we have eaten."

I had wanted to write on the title page, "Published by the Master of the universe, blessed is He," just as the Meshech Chochmah had written in his *sefer*, "Written through the will of our Father in Heaven." However, I was told that it might seem presumptuous, since this phrase applied to all works. I did not want to imply that only *my* book had been granted such Heavenly assistance, when in truth Hashem's Hand is evident in any project.

"For everything is from You, Ribbono shel Olam, and from Your Hand do we give to You."

At Just the Right Moment

I AM THE PRINCIPAL of a *cheder* in Jerusalem. During the Ten Days of Repentance, we took the boys on a trip to the holy sites in the Galilee. I had been asked to speak to the boys during the bus ride, and I decided to read them a story about *hashgachah*. The story was about a taxi driver who, through a series of mishaps, prevented his passengers from catching a plane that crashed on takeoff.

It was a good opportunity to explain the idea that every misfortune comes from Heaven through *hashgachah pratis* and one never knows its true purpose. Of course, the boys were very excited by the story (as was our bus driver, who was not yet Torah-observant).

Later, we drove through Kfar Shazur, where Rabbi Shimon Shazuri, Rabbi Yishmael Kohen Gadol, and other Torah giants are buried. Just before we reached the area with the graves, we saw a large vehicle with a flat tire standing in the middle of the road in such a way that our bus could not go through. The boys were very disappointed, but soon they were all telling each other, "It's from *Shamayim*. It's *hashgachah*!" I was happy that my story had made an impression.

We had very little time at our disposal, so we decided not to wait for the flat to be fixed but to turn around and proceed to our next stop instead. This was a Druze village, Kfar Peki'in, where there is a cave that, according to tradition, is the one where Rabbi Shimon bar Yochai learned with his son for thirteen years while he was hiding from the Romans. Rabbi Shimon's famous spring runs through the village, and after stopping at the cave, we climbed down toward the village to see it.

On the way, we told the students about Mrs. Miriam Zinati, an extraordinary woman living in the village who had been fiercely guarding the holy sites there against assorted malicious and bureaucratic threats for decades. We were going to ask her for the keys to the ancient shul we wanted to visit. Someone mentioned that the Zinati family was said to have guarded the holy sites of Peki'in since the time of the destruction of the second Temple.

From the spring, the entire school walked over to the ancient shul to wait for someone to bring the keys. At the shul, however, we found a funeral in progress. A few questions revealed that the deceased was none other than Mrs. Zinati herself. Her bier had been laid in the courtyard of the shul, and a few family members stood around, but there was no minyan to guard her body. Her funeral was due to set out shortly for the cemetery in Nahariya.

We were overwhelmed. We felt that Hashem had brought us there at just the right moment in order to honor Mrs. Zinati properly. Our group included a minyan of *kollel* students, educators, and other school officials. What was more, one hundred *cheder* boys stood there in awe and were soon saying *Tehillim* with fervor.

And so this extraordinary woman, who had lived to an advanced age, merited having a large minyan of Torah-true Jews attend her funeral and say Kaddish for the elevation of her soul, in Peki'in — the town whose sanctity she and her forebears had worked so hard to protect. Alongside stood dozens of children, whose pure, sinless mouths recited *Eishes Chayil* for her from start to finish. Such a group of innocent children does not ordinarily take part in funerals. It was clear that Mrs. Zinati had merited, in her long life and after her death, something that thousands do not. The words of *Eishes Chayil* were fulfilled as these children of Israel "arose and praised her, gave her from the fruits of her hands, and praised her deeds in the gates."

We returned to the bus, and the boys began to review *mishnayos* for the elevation of the soul of Miriam bas Ze'ev. We were astonished at everything that had happened to us. Only now did we realize that if not for the truck that blocked our entrance to Kfar Shazur, we would not have gone to Kfar Peki'in at that precise hour. It was a mishap that had caused us to arrive at exactly the right time, just before the funeral left Peki'in. Our day's adventures made a fine conclusion to the subject we had discussed at the outset of our trip — that everything is directed from Heaven with the greatest exactitude.

The Power of Faith

Blessed is the man who
trusts in God, then God
will be his security.
(Yirmeyahu 17:7)

Saved from the Whirlpool

OUR ELDEST SON Yossi will soon be twenty-eight years old, and he is still single. When we first realized that it was not going to be easy and, as our custom is that the younger children do not get married before the older ones, they would suffer in turn from the delay, my wife and I stopped sleeping at night. Every day we would await "the" phone call, and every night we would stay awake wondering if the next day would bring relief. Someone would promise to give me an answer by the end of the week, and after two weeks of waiting, we would realize that the answer was no. As the years passed, we had many such disappointments.

My entire life had become wrapped up in finding a match for my son. I was nervous and overwrought all the time. I was no longer functioning as a father to my younger children either. I was unable to take an interest in their progress in school or in their general well-being as I used to. Slowly, at home and at work, my mind became occupied by only one thing. Whom to speak to? What to do? Soon even our Shabbos peace was affected, and our Shabbos meals lost the flavor I had once endeavored to give them.

It was the third night of Chanukah. I was sitting alone staring at the flames of the candles, because the whole family had gone to visit my mother and I felt too depressed to go with them. Slowly I felt immense *siyata diShmaya* from Above flow from the candles and envelop me. I told myself: Enough! This cannot go on. I must get a grip on myself. I feel as though I am trapped in a whirlpool, and it is time I pulled myself out of it. At that moment I felt ha-Kadosh Baruch Hu extending to me a powerful support in the form of *bitachon*. From now on, I would have renewed confidence in Him to help us in our time of need.

The issue of shidduchim is not easy, it is true, and can even be quite exhausting, but we must hold ourselves above it and not permit it to drag us down. How? By understanding that it is not we who control things, but rather Someone above us Who controls everything. Ever since that Chanukah, my heart has been full of trust in Hashem, and life has improved for me and for my family.

The following Friday night, after the little ones were asleep and the five older ones were sitting around the table, I decided to air the issue and work it out openly. We discussed the points that I will mention below. Acting upon them has served to strengthen us and reshape our lives.

Gadi and the Steering Wheel

To explain the first point, I told my family about a story I heard from one of the great rabbis of this generation. This *tzaddik* had once been riding on a bus and saw a little boy sitting in the front passenger seat, holding on his knees a plastic dashboard that had a realistic steering wheel with a horn in the middle. His father was the bus driver. The child's eyes were fixed on the road ahead, and as the bus turned right and left, he turned his steering wheel accordingly and "drove" the bus with great success.

Of course, when the bus stopped, he stepped on the "brakes" and even made a pneumatic noise, *pssssss*.... He would occasionally check the back door and call out to the passengers, "You, by the back door, step back, please!" If a car drove too slowly ahead of the bus, the boy would scold, "Hey, you! Don't you see me driving here? You almost caused an accident!"

He worked hard the whole trip, and the passengers were amused at his antics. His father explained, "The boy dreams day and night about being a bus driver and being in charge of a bus and all its passengers. When he used to join me on my runs, I had no peace. He would make me crazy by trying to honk the horn, turn the steering wheel, press the buttons, and signal to other drivers. Then I bought him a steering wheel of his own. Now, when he drives with me, I tell him, 'Gadi, sit next to me, start the motor, and drive the bus.' Gadi does the job beautifully, as you can see, and I can drive in peace."

The rav who told this story saw in it a deep lesson from on High.

"Ha-Kadosh Baruch Hu runs everything," he would say, "but He gives us a steering wheel and tells us, '*Nu*, Gadi, drive the bus!' And we, little children that we are, sweat and struggle to get the bus from one stop to the next. We exhaust ourselves from the effort, while 'upstairs' all the passengers are amused.

"Our livelihood is fixed on Rosh Hashanah, yet we struggle to earn it, and then we work overtime to earn even more. If we think someone is interfering with our earnings, we tell him, 'Hey! Don't you see me driving here? You almost caused an accident!' We are too small-minded to see that our Father is the driver and we are only bidden to wave our arms, and while we are waving them, we mustn't forget that it isn't we who are driving."

"Do you know," I said openly to my older children, "for the past two years, I have been sitting turning my steering wheel and yelling and getting angry and complaining and sweating with effort and making signals. I focused entirely on this or that shadchan who had promised to arrange something for Yossi. If I thought the shadchan's suggestion was not good enough, I would get terribly angry and argue with him. Other times I was deeply upset with others, with their lack of consideration, and with what I considered their small-mindedness. I even felt moved to complain to rashei yeshiva and rabbanim about the attitudes of some parents. In short, I did everything I could to move the bus, but it didn't move.

"This week, while sitting next to the Chanukah candles," I told my family, "I suddenly realized that the bus wasn't moving because Father wasn't moving it. Father will make things move when He sees fit to do so, and all my arm-waving won't help. I might as well save my strength. From the moment I understood that, I let go of the steering wheel, got up, and sat down in one of the ordinary passenger seats. From now on, I will stop struggling. Of course I will not stop doing what I am obligated to do, but I will do it in an entirely different spirit."

Yossi asked me what exactly I meant by that. "I mean that if someone on the road does something to wrong me, I will allow the

Driver *Yisbarach* to yell at him. If things come to a standstill, I won't blame myself or anyone else, since I know that Father made them stop. Therefore, I won't be disappointed if a shadchan fails. In short, I won't rely on powerless human beings anymore, but on *Hashem Elokai.*"

Taking Your Medicine

Next I reminded my family that we can never really understand Hashem's reasons. How can we understand how one couple can be married for years and not have children, while their neighbors next door have a housefull? Can we explain why one sick person recovers, while another only gets worse? Who dares investigate the ways of the Merciful One? Only He knows why my neighbor, my own age, already has grandchildren, while my oldest child is not even engaged yet. We don't understand a thing. All we know is that everything is from Above and everything is for the good.

When a mother gives antibiotics to an older child, I continued, a younger one wails that he wants some. We explain that it is dangerous for him, but he doesn't care. The pill is a pretty shade of pink, and he wants one too. What do you do? You let him cry but you don't give him the pill. What is good for one may be dangerous for another, but little children don't understand that. Some older people also do not understand that what is good for the neighbor upstairs may be dangerous for them. And so they cry and yell, "Abba, I also want some!" But ha-Kadosh Baruch Hu, in His mercy, lets them cry and withholds whatever is not good for them.

Sometimes a child needs medicine that has a bitter taste, and he adamantly refuses to take it. His parents try to persuade him; they explain to him that it is good for him, that it will make him feel better, but he still refuses. In such cases, we just force him to take what is good for him.

I recalled that once or twice we had been sure that ha-Kadosh Baruch Hu was finally bringing our *yeshuah.* Everything had seemed to be on track, but all at once, we started to get vague answers to our queries, and we understood that the other side had backed off. We were deeply disappointed and embittered, and asked ourselves why we had to endure the preliminaries if it was not meant to be.

Our faith should have answered us clearly: That is what our souls needed — to endure that disappointment and take that medicine, even if it was bitter. Those whom Hashem loves, He rebukes. If we know someone cares about us, we are confident they will do us no harm. Surely ha-Kadosh Baruch Hu, Who cares about us more than anyone, would do us no harm. If He did cause us pain, then it must be only because He cares for us. If I don't understand it, it is only because I am a small child.

In sum, not everything that looks good to me is really good, and not everything that seems bad to me is really bad. Ha-Kadosh Baruch Hu Himself, in His mercy, will keep what is bad away from me in any of a thousand ways, despite my foolish protests. And if something is meant for my benefit, for improving my soul, He will put me through it, even against my will. The day will come when I will thank Him for everything.

Some time later, on the yahrtzeit of my father-in-law, z"l, Yossi and I went to the cemetery on Har ha-Menuchos in Jerusalem. My son was still very bitter about his situation, and I tried to console him. We walked among the hundreds of graves, and I stopped alongside one of them and said, "Look at this grave. This man may have been married late in life, and his parents, who are buried alongside him, probably ran around like crazy trying to marry him off. They may have had a lot of bitterness in their lives, but now, everything is clear to them; now they can see that everything was for the best and that their suffering helped to purify their souls."

"Ah, it's easy with hindsight," my son replied, "but the present is so hard sometimes."

I felt for him with all my heart. Wasn't it hard for me too? But all the same, I spoke to him, and the words sank into my heart as well.

"If a person knows, while he is experiencing difficulty, that everything is for the best, then the reward and the purification is much, much greater. Rashi commented on a verse in *Mishlei*: 'If afflictions come upon you, let them be beloved by you.' This refers to the verse, 'My son, do not spurn Hashem's *mussar* and do not reject His rebuke' [3:11]. That is, rebuke and afflictions exist, and we are not consulted regarding them beforehand. But you, my son, do not spurn them, do not reject them. Accept them with love. Know that the continuation of the verse is, 'For those whom Hashem loves, He rebukes.' "

My son, he should live and be well, reminds me of that conversation on Har ha-Menuchos often, and claims that he has drawn much peace of mind from it. It has helped him confront the difficulty of his daily life.

The matter of shidduchim is still in a holding pattern in our house. There are times when nothing is on the horizon, and other times when something seems to be moving or we seem to be reaching a decision, but as of today, nothing has changed, except our attitude. Thanks to the *siyata diShmaya* we have merited, we have stopped feeling that we are the ones holding things back or moving them ahead. Also, we remind ourselves that the difficulties of the past two years are good for us. We are meant to sit and wait.

Of course it is hard, disappointing, worrisome, and even a bit embarrassing. But in whose eyes? In the eyes of mortal man in his world of untruth? One look from Above would clarify for us that ha-Kadosh Baruch Hu chose for us the very best.

Our lives have taught us that we don't know what good is. Ask any unmarried man what is good, and he will answer that it is good to find a wife quickly. If you would ask my son that question now, he would answer, "What is good? What the good Lord decides is good."

I have repeated thousands of times in the past years Rabbeinu Yonah's words on that same verse in *Mishlei*: "A person does not know what is good for him. Hashem Yisbarach knows what will rectify him and benefit him, what is good for him, whether peace or affliction."

Sometimes, when I daven to ha-Kadosh Baruch Hu to heal a sick person, to find a spouse for one who needs one, to give children to those longing for them or a livelihood for those in need of it, I add to myself, "And open our eyes to see that everything is from

You and is for the best." From my personal experience, *bitachon* itself is half the *yeshuah*.

Do Not Overlook What You Have

"Every day, ha-Kadosh Baruch Hu lends me a million dollars," a certain *talmid chacham* used to say. "My friend paid a surgeon ten thousand dollars to perform an eye operation, and I wake up every day with two healthy eyes. I heard about a Jew whose legs were paralyzed, *lo aleinu*, and who needs a full-time companion to assist him, which costs a fortune, and here, I have all of that fortune in my pocket. My legs are healthy, *baruch Hashem*, my hands, ears, mouth, memory, heart, insides — they're all fine, *baruch Hashem*. I have a million dollars — a million dollars!

"At night, Hashem checks to see whether I am worthy of that loan. I am in danger of not receiving that gift again on the morrow. But the next morning, a *mechayeh*! Ha-Kadosh Baruch Hu, in His mercy, grants me that loan again. How can one not be happy?"

That is the third point I discussed with my family that Shabbos evening. After telling them the above story, I reminded my second son, the twenty-five-year old, of something that had happened a few months before. He had come home from yeshiva and I asked him, "How are things?" He answered, *"Baruch Hashem"* with his nose to the ground, as if to say, "Abba, how can things be when you are twenty-five, the oldest one in your class, with an older brother who is still on the shelf?"

As a result of that exchange, I found an opportunity soon after to drive with him to Hadassah Hospital in Jerusalem.

"Let's just walk around the wards," I said.

"What for?" My son probably thought I had lost my senses.

"What for? So that my hale and hearty son, my tall, handsome, bright son, with his 365 and 248 strong, functioning organs and limbs, should answer *'Baruch Hashem'* a little more happily."

That very evening in shul, I read about another case that I could add to the foundation of our newly forming attitude.

A certain person, the father of a large family, living in a very crowded apartment and staggering under heavy debts, sent a letter of desperation to the Lubavitcher Rebbe, zya"a, complaining of his plight and expressing his concern that he and his wife would soon be unable to cope.

The answer, which appeared in one of the volumes of the Rebbe's *Igros*, was as follows:

> I read your letter, and I did not understand even half a word. From between the lines I understood that you have a wife. Do you know that there are people who would be willing to sell everything they own in order to find a spouse? Ha-Kadosh Baruch Hu granted you a wonderful mate and you are complaining?
>
> Furthermore, I see that you have children, and not just one or two but a house blessed with sons and daughters. Heaven help us! Don't you know that there are those crying to Heaven for the blessing of just one child, and you go around blessed by Hashem on all sides and grumble? I am surprised.
>
> Third, you say you have been blessed with a roof over your head. You have shelter from the rain and cover from the sun at a time when thousands wander without a place to rest their heads.
>
> My dear Jew, you have been blessed with all that is good and wonderful, you are full to overflowing with Hashem's blessings; how can you ask for more? First recognize the Creator's kindness to you so far and only afterward hope for further kindness.

One should never forget what one already has, but must rejoice and give thanks for it over and over. When I remember how deeply I had sunk into the whirlpool not so long ago, I think that if not for that grace I received from Above, my family and I would be in serious emotional trouble today. How great is Hashem's kindness to me for having opened the firmament before me and shown me that He is the Mover of all things, that He is the Merciful One, and that everything is for the best. How immense are my thanks to Hashem for having opened my eyes to see all the good that He has granted me, regardless of what is missing. In this way my and my family's lives have peace. For all this I thank Him, and I request that, in the future, everything will continue to be good, for us and for all of Yisrael, forever.

Following His Lead

REB YEHOSHUA, Z"L, believed in Hashem with eternal trust. He was the kind of Jew who lived his life feeling happy that the Almighty runs the universe. He lived in a one-bedroom flat in Tel Aviv with his seven children, and he eked out a meager living buying buttons and threads wholesale and selling them to a few steady customers. He lived in peace and harmony with everyone and everything, trusting Hashem, and he was not disappointed with the results.

Reb Yehoshua was an exceptional person, who even managed to squeeze guests into his *dalet amos*-sized home, where he waited on them hand and foot. He lived his life according to the principle, "I neither guide myself nor run my own life. I am guided by Heaven and my life is run by the One Above."

"Does a man go the way he wants?" he used to say. "Does anyone even ask him? They pull him along from Above. If he wants to go, well and good. If not, he'll be pulled along anyway."

For that reason, Reb Yehoshua always agreed to go in whichever direction Divine Providence led him. He would nod his head in agreement to whatever Heaven sent his way, and this was the source of his peace of mind and equanimity.

Bnei Brak Here We Come

One day, Reb Yehoshua's wife, who shared his strong faith, came to him to discuss her concern over raising their children in the non-religious environment of Tel Aviv.

"The children are growing up and beginning to notice things," she said. "This neighborhood isn't at all good for their spiritual growth. We should really buy an apartment in Bnei Brak and move there."

Because of their meager income, the suggestion seemed about as realistic as their buying a five-star hotel. How on earth could they afford an apartment in Bnei Brak? Reb Yehoshua still didn't know how they would buy bread for breakfast the next day.

But if Heaven had arranged things so that there was a problem with bringing up their children in Tel Aviv, and if a suggestion had arisen to move to Bnei Brak, then Reb Yehoshua would go along with it and be happy. Therefore, he told his wife that as far as he was concerned, there was no problem. "Bnei Brak, here we come," he said.

"What do you mean, where will the money come from?" he could have asked. But where does life come from? Where do children come from? The One Who gives everything to everyone will give the money as well!

And so Reb Yehoshua and his wife fished in their wallets and came up with enough money for bus fare to Bnei Brak. They remembered that someone owed them 1,500 lira, so they collected the money and off they went.

At that time, there was a lot of construction going on in Bnei Brak. They went to see a contractor who was putting up apartment buildings, and soon they were sitting across from him in his office and explaining their situation. They dreamed of buying one of his apartments, they said, so that their children could live in a better environment. They told the contractor that they could give him 1,500 lira as a down payment.

The contractor, a fine Jew, accepted their offer graciously. He took the 1,500 lira, signed them up for a spacious three-bedroom apartment, and explained that because the price was five times the amount that they had just paid, the apartment would be theirs with four more installments.

The words, "four more installments" didn't deter the couple. If anyone had asked them, "Excuse me, but how do you intend to get the 6,000 lira?" Reb Yehoshua would have answered, "Do I have any idea how I got the first 1,500 lira? What do I care about what was or what will be? Ha-Kadosh Baruch Hu runs the world, and if He wants us to buy an apartment in Bnei Brak, He will arrange the next four installments just as He arranged the first one!"

Reb Yehoshua and his wife thanked the kind contractor, left his office and went on their way. Reb Yehoshua continued to buy and sell buttons and trust that with Hashem's help, everything would turn out just fine.

Hashem Arranges the Move

The summer passed, as did the winter, and a year went by. The building they were to move into was nearing completion, and soon it would be standing proudly on Rabbi Akiva Street in Bnei Brak.

But Reb Yehoshua and his wife, the owners of the new apartment, still had no way of paying the next installment. The world ran its usual course: buttons and threads were bought and sold, bread for breakfast found its way to their table, but money for the apartment was still nowhere to be found.

"What are we going to do?" Reb Yehoshua's wife asked him. "We promised to keep up the payments!"

Reb Yehoshua, who always thought of his wife as an emissary of Hashem's *hashgachah*, asked her what she thought they should do.

"What else can we do?" the sensible woman answered. "If we can't pay, we'll have to cancel our contract."

"Cancel the contract?" Reb Yehoshua wondered aloud. "So be it. If that is what Hashem wants at this stage we'll go along with it willingly."

It's not that Reb Yehoshua was a fool or an indecisive person; rather, he was wise enough to have reached the level of *Tamim tihiye im Hashem Elokecha* (*Devarim* 18:13). He walked with Hashem with simplicity, and he followed in the path he saw Hashem leading him, asking no questions about the future, accepting all of the consequences with simplicity, just as Rashi explains the meaning of this verse.

Reb Yehoshua and his wife fished in their wallets again, and again ha-Kadosh Baruch Hu sent them the money for the bus to Bnei Brak. Again they went to the contractor's office. They explained to him that they simply did not have any way to continue paying the installments on the apartment and that they wanted to cancel the contract and take back their 1,500 lira.

The contractor, who was a good-hearted, generous soul, had already figured out what type of people they were. He began to reassure them, telling them not to back out of the deal so fast.

"First of all, I'll let you move in before you've paid up the balance. Second, I won't pressure you to pay. You seem honest and I trust you. I'm sure that as soon as you can, you'll pay every cent of the balance. Third of all, you can change your minds and get your money back whenever you want.

"But listen well to what I'm saying. You're going to get back double. Do you know why? Because the value of the apartment has doubled since you bought it. That means that the 1,500 lira that you've invested is now worth twice that.

"You own valuable property," the contractor concluded. "It would be a pity to give it up just when its value is rising. Don't give up because of the payments. Move in, and Hashem will help you."

The contractor also mentioned offhandedly that their apartment was across the hall from the one he had kept for himself. Apparently, he very much wanted to have neighbors like Reb Yehoshua and his family.

(If anyone ever tells you that contractors can do *chessed*, believe him.)

Once again, Reb Yehoshua felt that Hashem was guiding him. It was possible to move into the apartment without feeling pressured to pay the balance, and the value of the apartment had already doubled. At first it had seemed as if they would have to cancel the contract, but instead, they could move to Bnei Brak after all.

Reb Yehoshua and his wife left the contractor's office in good spirits. These "simple" people believed that Hashem would help them, even though they still had no idea how they would manage to make the rest of the payments. Yet they knew that if Hashem approved of their move, the money would somehow come.

And so, when the building was finally completed, Reb Yehoshua and his wife packed up their things and loaded their possessions onto a truck, while their seven young children jumped up and down in excitement. From a one-bedroom flat in Tel Aviv, they moved into a spacious three-bedroom apartment in Bnei Brak. The children were enrolled in the best schools and their parents couldn't contain their happiness. Reb Yehoshua continued his button business from Bnei Brak as before, trusting Hashem and pursuing his honest livelihood. He filled his days with *chessed* and hard work, and he continued to trust in Hashem and reap the benefits.

How did Reb Yehoshua explain his situation at that time?

"If Hashem wants us to buy an apartment in Bnei Brak, He will arrange for us to be able to pay the contractor in full."

And that must have been what Hashem wanted because He did arrange it.

The Pillowcase-Button Business

Do you remember how when we were little, pillowcases used to have buttons on them? They were fat and round and made of out of metal, and they had thread wound around and around them. Remember?

Well, these were the kinds of buttons that Reb Yehoshua did business in. He could buy them in bulk from the manufacturer, sell them to the retailers, and keep the difference.

That particular button manufacturer was in stiff competition with a kibbutz in southern Israel, which produced identical buttons and sold them all over the country. But since these buttons were not the only kind that the manufacturer produced, he decided to get out of the pillowcase-button business entirely rather than suffer a loss because of his competitors.

One day, when Reb Yehoshua stopped in to buy the buttons, the manufacturer took him aside and told him how tired he was of the competition in the pillowcase-button field, and how the kibbutzniks were doing everything possible to drive him out of the market. He told Reb Yehoshua that he had decided to sell all of the machines in the entire production line for the ridiculous sum of 500 lira.

"Instead of me, a nationwide producer, losing to the competition," the manufacturer explained, "you, Reb Yehoshua, can earn a good living despite the competition. You can produce the buttons yourself and continue to sell them straight to the consumer — the retailers — and earn your keep without a middleman. The competition will not hurt your livelihood in any way."

Reb Yehoshua again saw the Hand of his Father in Heaven. Five hundred lira was a sum he could afford, so the deal appealed to him. Besides, he thought, his bedroom in the new apartment was enormous. He could sleep in another room and turn the bedroom into a factory for pillowcase buttons.

His wife shared his enthusiasm. "One must let himself be led by ha-Kadosh Baruch Hu," she would say, "and not resist or oppose His will." If this is how things turned out, then one had to go along happily.

And so the following week, a truck with a large crane could be seen on Rabbi Akiva Street. The arm of the crane gently lifted eight large machines, one after the other, into the building and slowly placed them in Reb Yehoshua's bedroom.

Passersby smiled to themselves, for good reason: an apartment full of children was being turned into a factory, and a great Yid like Reb Yehoshua was turning into a manufacturer. This was good enough reason for anyone who knew Reb Yehoshua to smile.

When the truck had gone, there in the large room stood eight machines lined up in a row, forming a production line.

"Look here," Reb Yehoshua said to his seven children and their mother. "This is the press. Here is where you put in a sheet of metal, here is where you press down, you lower this handle carefully, and — whoop — the sheet gets full of holes and ten round metal buttons come out of it.

"Here is where you put in spools of threads," Reb Yehoshua said, continuing his demonstration for his new little workers. "You pull here, put your foot on the pedal, and — trrrr — look! The button is covered with threads! Now one potch on the metal circle and we have a perfect button, ready for sale."

And so the introductory lesson concluded, and the children jumped to work with glee. Whoop, trrrr, potch, and press. The children had never had so much fun.

The next day, Reb Yehoshua arrived home with handfuls of raw materials: shiny metal sheets, dozens of spools of thread, boxes and scraps. The factory was in business. The whole family was there, from oldest to youngest, and they all worked enthusiastically at their fascinating new jobs.

They worked for hours, side by side. But unfortunately, although the children had never enjoyed themselves quite so much, by the end of the day, there wasn't a single button that could be sold.

The One Above Laughs

Reb Yehoshua was satisfied. He planned to learn the business slowly but surely, and to sell the buttons and earn an honest keep. He thanked Hashem with all his heart for His great kindness. The family was in high spirits. Its usual optimism had risen to new levels. The children were enthusiastic about the production line, and everything was wonderful.

The next time Reb Yehoshua was at the market all the dealers stopped him to ask about the interesting rumor they had heard — that he had bought the manufacturer's button-production line. They wanted to know his plans for the future and how he intended to sell his buttons. Reb Yehoshua was relaxed and smiling, giving answers that made his listeners' eyes pop out.

"My plant costs me nothing; I don't pay rent. I have seven employees who cost me nothing; I don't owe them salaries. It's a whole factory, a *gantze fabrik*, which God-willing will bring only profits." These and other such answers are what Reb Yehoshua told everyone who asked him about the rumor.

The metal dealers passed the word on to the thread marketers, who passed the rumor on to the machine-oil salesmen, and in the end everyone was soon talking about Reb Yehoshua's amazing success.

And as what usually happens with rumors, this one grew bigger and bigger and spread all over the country. The competition, the button manufacturers on the kibbutz, began to get news from all sides about a certain successful businessman, Reb Yehoshua by name, who had come by a first-rate production line with a free factory and free labor, and who was about to devour them alive. The rumor had it that production was in full force, and that a tremendous marketing plan was about to take over the market.

For lack of any alternative, they decided to send a representative to Reb Yehoshua to try to enter into a partnership with him, or even better to buy his factory at any price. In a tense introduction to the telephone conversation, they expressed their wish to meet with him.

His easygoing answer surprised them. They had expected him to slam down the phone, but instead his response was quite civil. "Meet? Why not? You want to come here? Fine."

And so, they thought, it seems that he might be willing to come to terms, and perhaps even to sell his factory. The representative of the company received a long list of instructions, put on his best suit, practiced the most persuasive arguments he could come up with, and set out for Bnei Brak to meet the renowned Reb Yehoshua.

At first Reb Yehoshua was not willing to consider selling his "factory." "I didn't buy it in order to sell it," he said, but the price that the representative was willing to pay only rose higher.

Reb Yehoshua's wife again came into the picture, and they began to consider their options. "Look, Yehoshua," she whispered, so that the kibbutznik wouldn't hear, "we bought all of this for only 500 lira, and this fellow wants to buy it for a fortune of money. This is Hashem's Hand at work."

"Listen," Reb Yehoshua finally offered his trembling competitor, "I have a debt of 6,000 lira hanging over my head, and I must give this sum right away to the contractor who lives across the hall. If you can pay this debt for me, then I will agree to your deal." In his optimism and perpetual good-heartedness, Reb Yehoshua saw Hashem standing by him once again.

Additional representatives of the kibbutz's company were called to an emergency meeting in Reb Yehoshua's narrow kitchen that same afternoon, where an interim contract was signed as quickly and hurriedly as possible, before the competition could change its mind. That very day, the debt on the apartment was paid in full in one lump sum, to the astonished contractor.

The very next day, another truck with a crane appeared on Rabbi Akiva Street to remove the machines. Again passersby smiled — as did the buyers of Reb Yehoshua's factory.

Of course, Reb Yehoshua continued to smile his whole life. And he continued to prove that "Happy is the man who trusts in [Hashem]" (*Tehillim* 84:13), and "One who trusts in Hashem will be surrounded by acts of kindness" (ibid. 32:10).

Hillel's Peace of Mind

MY NEIGHBOR HILLEL seemed to be an ordinary person — a respected householder, a tradesman, and the father of a large family. He worked all day earning a living. At night he went to a *shiur*. Financially, he had always managed very well, *baruch Hashem*, but of course, when the time came to marry off his children, his needs grew. At that point, when he came under pressure, his special qualities began to shine more brightly and clearly. As his neighbor, I can attest to that.

Emunah and *bitachon*; faith and trust in Hashem. The peace of mind shared by all true believers can be attributed to these qualities. They are not traits that show up on the outside — those who excel in them are usually very reticent about what lies deep in their hearts. And those who know such people well can vouch that they have placed all their burdens on Hashem and carry no excess worries.

Emunah doesn't suddenly rise up in times of trouble. When a person is in the midst of his suffering, he is not really in the proper frame of mind for working on his character or changing his basic life views. Hillel instilled the trait of *bitachon* in his home in small ways. If a pitcher would fall and break, for instance, he would say, "That's okay. It's all from Heaven." If there was a power outage, he taught his children to say, "It's all for the best. Everything is from Above." And if someone was not feeling well, *chas ve-shalom*, he would accept it, saying, "This is how it was meant to be." Hashem's Name was constantly on Hillel's lips, and because of this, he spread a shining light throughout his home.

Once, when both of our families were on our way to shul, my young son told Hillel's son that he wanted to run fast to get there in time to get one of the new *siddurim*. Hillel's son responded, "If you are meant to get one, you'll get one anyway. No one will take it from you." He was too young to understand what he was saying, but it was clear that he was quoting a refrain he had often heard at home.

At that moment I envied Hillel his powerful *emunah* and *bitachon*. It pained me to realize how much more spiritual my life would be if my faith were as strong as his. In my opinion, this kind of jealousy is a good thing, and I am not ashamed of it. It provides me with the drive and inspiration to improve myself.

On the surface, Hillel and I were quite similar, but underneath, how great the differences were! We lived across the hall from each other, which is why I was so aware of his peace of mind and calm approach to everything.

The story I am about to tell happened to Hillel twenty-five years ago, but I was privy to every part of it. From the very beginning, I was sure that Heaven would deal kindly with my neighbor, because he was a man who placed such great confidence in his Creator. Hillel was on such a high level of *bitachon* that, like others on that level, he merited to see wonders. I was uniquely placed to witness the whole story.

The Noam Elimelech says, "If a person trusts Hashem with a believing heart, his livelihood will be provided for him with no pain or servitude." I considered Hillel one of those who the Noam Elimelech said would see every sort of miracle and wonder, for he already saw every penny of his income as a miracle and wonder.

A Baby Cannot Wait

In the course of time, Hillel was privileged to marry off one child after another, but in the process, he accumulated an enormous amount of debts. He was weighed down by mortgage payments for his children's apartments, he had borrowed money for wedding expenses, and he ended up owing tens of thousands of dollars. The repayment dates were looming, but he had no idea where the money would come from.

By nature, Hillel was just the opposite of a debtor. Circumstances and necessity had brought him to his current state, but he refused to let it continue. I know a bit about the problem because I had also incurred debts in marrying off my own children, although *baruch Hashem* not on the same scale as Hillel.

My neighbor told me he was concerned about his situation because it was unintentional; he had expected to manage differently, but things had not worked out the way he had imagined. "I need some strengthening in my faith," he told me. "I have not the smallest doubt that everything is from Heaven and that everything can be resolved completely in an instant, but who am I to decide? Maybe I am required to do something. Maybe Hashem wants me to sell my apartment."

Hillel told me that before doing anything, he intended to speak to a well-known Rav of his acquaintance to ask his advice, hear *da'as Torah,* and strengthen his *emunah.*

"*B'ezras Hashem*, Heaven will direct me on the true path," he said. "After all, nothing stops Hashem from rescuing people — in a big way or a small one. I know this distress is Heaven's design down to the last detail; perhaps it is all to atone for my sins."

Even a man of complete faith has difficult moments. Every hero has moments of weakness; no one is exempt from trials and times when the way is not clear. But there is an enormous difference between one who collapses from weakness and falls helpless under the strain, and one who knows how to collect himself and restore his sense of balance after the difficult moment has passed.

"Man's spirit sustains his illness," King Solomon said. Hillel had a "man's spirit," and it sustained him through his "illness."

In the course of our conversation about his difficulties, I acquired a precious pearl of wisdom from Hillel. "A baby cries in the middle of the night, and his mother gets up to make him a bottle. While she's preparing it, the baby continues to cry. Why should he cry? The food is practically ready — he'll receive it in a moment. But a baby is a baby and doesn't understand. He wants to see it for himself or, rather, taste it for himself, without delay. So he cries. Of course, if he were smarter, he'd wait without crying.

"That's how it is with shidduchim, too. When a young man is waiting for his intended bride to turn up, he fumes in frustration. Doesn't he know that in Heaven the match is being made and it will soon be ready? But he has no confidence that it will work out, and he isn't comforted. He wants to see his salvation with his own eyes, now, this minute.

"That's how things are with me right now," Hillel concluded. "I have no doubt that my deliverance will come. My bottle is already prepared for me somewhere. But I am a baby, and I want to see it now, right away. I have a choice: I can cry; no one will stop me. But if I were a little smarter, I would wait patiently until the bottle is brought to me."

The Rav's Advice

A few days later, Hillel told me that he had gone to seek the Rav's advice. The Rav listened to the whole story from start to finish, asking many detailed questions about Hillel's income and expenditures. He agreed that Hillel had no way at all to pay off all his debts.

"But before you do anything," the Rav advised, "do some *hishtadlus*, make some effort, take only a small step to attain your large sum of money. When a person does his share, ha-Kadosh Baruch Hu does His. You just have to prepare a large enough vessel to receive the infinite bounty of Heaven. And this large receptacle is *hishtadlus*, a step in the right direction, mixed with *emunah*."

Hillel told the Rav he had no idea how to raise the money. The Rav repeated his advice and said no more. Yet Hillel somehow felt strengthened. He left the Rav's home encouraged, and hopeful that

Hashem would grant him the wisdom to think of something.

Less than two months remained until the date that most of his debts came due. Hillel still did not know what to do. But he trusted in Hashem, and he was not disappointed. Hillel's *emunah* and *bitachon* never left him for a moment, so why should it be surprising that he was granted a miraculous kindness from Heaven?

Heaven's Kindness

At the time Hillel was pondering his course of action, a fire broke out in one of the buildings in the neighborhood. It was the will of Heaven that no one was hurt, but it was also the will of Heaven that one family was left destitute.

A small neighborhood committee was established to help the family, and Hillel was a member of it. One of the neighbors suggested that they contact some well-known philanthropists abroad, tell them what had happened, and ask them to contribute. A few large donations would bring in more money than hundreds of small gifts. One person was appointed to make up a list of possible wealthy patrons and another was assigned the task of finding someone to send abroad to solicit the money, and the meeting was adjourned.

At the next meeting, a list was presented of about twenty wealthy people from the United States and Canada, people who customarily donated large sums to religious institutions in Israel. When Hillel glanced at the list of philanthropists, one name in particular stood out: Chaim Benson. Quietly, he asked for more information about this wealthy gentleman. The compiler of the list answered, "He used to live in Eretz Yisrael but moved to the United States, where he went into business and became successful. He changed his name from Bruk to Benson. But in all honesty, I must tell you that he is not in the same financial class as most of the others."

"Chaim Bruk," Hillel repeated in wonder. "Years ago I knew a Chaim Bruk. We studied together in yeshiva. Is his father's name Aharon?"

"Yes, I think so," the neighbor responded.

The participants at the meeting decided to write letters to the men on the list, seeking their help in aiding the destitute family. The neighborhood Rav was asked to travel to the United States soon after the letters were sent out, in order to collect the funds in person.

In the meantime, Hillel thoughtfully made his way home. That evening he sat down to write a letter to his childhood friend, Chaim Bruk — that is, Chaim Benson. Perhaps this was meant to be his *hishtadlus.*

Dear Chaim — may you live and be well,

I wonder if you remember your childhood friend Hillel Katz. An acquaintance mentioned your name to me recently. You may also remember that our dear fathers, *z"l,* were good friends. I am presuming on our old friendship to write this letter.

Recently, unwillingly and unintentionally, I have fallen into debts totaling over ten thousand dollars. I incurred the debts because, *baruch Hashem,* I married off seven of my children within a few years. Unfortunately, most of the debts are coming due in a few weeks, and I have no idea how to raise the money.

Naturally, although I have the greatest confidence that Hashem will provide for me now as He always has, I asked Rav L., whom you may remember, for advice. He told me to take some action on my own, small though it might be, toward finding a solution.

I have no idea what kind of *hishtadlus* might be appropriate for attaining such a large amount of money. I believe that ha-Kadosh Baruch Hu is the Master of Funds, that He hears my sighs, and that He can surely solve my problem one way or another — but I still must do my *hishtadlus.*

With your permission, therefore, I would like to fulfill my obligation to do some *hishtadlus* with this letter. Perhaps you, as a successful businessman in the United States, can give me some business advice, some idea of how to go about finding enough *parnasah* to cover my debts. As strange as this letter must seem to you, it seems ten times stranger to write it. However, each of us must do his part the best he can, and we do not know the effect our actions may eventually have.

I sincerely hope you will be a Heavenly messenger to help me in my time of need with some good advice.

Sincerely,
Hillel Katz

Hillel called the list organizer to ascertain Chaim's address, and went to the post office the next day to mail the letter. *Hishtadlus* is only doing your part. It doesn't matter how it is done or to whom it is directed. The hearts of both the rich and the poor are ruled in Heaven. Hillel was content. He had done his part.

Heaven's Messenger

Two weeks later, Hillel Katz received the following letter in the mail from Chaim Benson:

Dear Mr. Katz,

I received your letter exactly on the day of my father's *sheloshim*. I was very moved to receive a letter from Eretz Yisrael, where my father, z"l, is buried, a land so close to my heart on such a day, but so far from me physically. I read your letter, and your trouble touched my heart. I am sorry that I don't remember your name among my childhood friends, and I didn't know of the friendship between our fathers at all. However, if it existed, it should bear fruit, particularly since I learned of it on the thirtieth day after his passing.

I do know your Rav, however, whose name you mentioned in your letter. I have spoken to him, and he told me all about you. I cannot send any business your way, but in the merit of all your outstanding character traits that the Rav mentioned, and in memory of my father, Meir Ariel ben Dov, please accept this check. When you go to the Kosel to daven, please mention him.

I will be happy for the opportunity to make your acquaintance as a forgotten childhood friend, and as the son of a friend of my late father's.

Chaim Benson

Attached was a check for ten thousand dollars.

Hillel was shamefully embarrassed. There had been a terrible mistake. This Chaim Benson was not the Chaim Bruk he knew from school. His father, Meir Ariel, was not Aharon Bruk of Meah Shearim, Jerusalem, who had passed away a decade or more before. It had been one big mistake. This Chaim was not his childhood friend. Their parents had most likely never met each other. So the check actually did not belong to him at all.

Unhappily, he went to ask Rav L.'s advice. The Rav was astonished. "Someone from the United States called me and asked about you, but I thought it was about a shidduch. I spoke to him very enthusiastically. I didn't imagine what lay behind it." After thinking about it for a minute, the Rav telephoned Chaim Benson, told him the whole story, and asked what Hillel should do with the check.

Chaim laughed out loud. "Why, let Mr. Katz keep the check, of course," he said. "This is a story from Heaven!" he concluded, still laughing. It was clear that he could easily spare the ten thousand dollars. "Do you know what we'll do? Let Mr. Katz visit my father's grave every year on his yahrtzeit, and I will feel amply compensated.

"Please understand, Rav L. I say Kaddish for my father, z"l, but my business won't always permit me to say it at his grave in Israel. During my father's later years, I hardly visited him, and I wasn't even at his funeral. It is worth everything to me to invest this sum in a *chessed* in my father's memory, and to ask in exchange that a chapter of *Tehillim* be said at his grave on his yahrtzeit. My father would surely be happy that such a good and worthy person is visiting his grave."

"I'm sure he's even happier that he has a son who so generously helps out his fellow Jews," Rav L. concluded the conversation.

Hillel sent Chaim Benson a letter of deepest gratitude, and was able to pay his debts on time. He visited Mr. Benson's grave every year thereafter with a minyan of Jews that included me. More than anything else that happened, though, I was impressed with the lesson I learned from Hillel at the beginning of his troubles: Most people are like babies who cannot control their impatience and who cry for their bottle. But one who knows that it is being prepared for him doesn't cry. One who believes that his bottle is being prepared for him has peace of mind. He increases his *hishtadlus*, to be sure, but he knows he will get the bottle in the end, even if it is the result of a fire, a list, and a mistake.

Miraculous Recovery

WO DAYS AFTER our son was born, the hospital pediatrician came to report a "minor" problem.

"Your newborn suffers from poor muscle tone," he said. "That is, his muscles are not fully developed, and we will have to look into it further."

My wife and I were not too concerned on hearing this, because we had been told something similar about our older daughter and *baruch Hashem*, she had developed completely normally. We were under the impression that it was a fairly common problem that corrected itself in time.

We were mistaken. As the months passed and our baby grew, his muscular control appeared to be growing worse. He could not support himself at all, and was first able to hold up his head at an age when most babies begin to sit up. In addition, his joints were extraordinarily flexible, and his arms and legs could be turned in directions that normally are impossible. Still, we were not too alarmed about it.

The doctors at the local mother-and-child clinic, however, did a good job of frightening us by declaring that his slow motor development together with the joint problems indicated mental retardation. Our pediatrician assured us that the poor muscle tone and loose joints were not related; the muscle condition required treatment, but the loose joints were not a serious problem. In any case, it had been the latter that had frightened the clinic doctors into an incorrect diagnosis.

Since our baby was a happy and alert child, followed everything with his eyes, played with his toys, and showed an ability to concentrate, it was clear to us that he had no mental problem but only a muscular one. We would have been content to wait and see how things developed, if not for our caregiver's neighbor's baby.

Our baby went to daycare every day, and the caregiver's neighbor noticed that our child had the same difficulty as her own child, who until today — he is in his teens — is unable to sit up without being strapped to a wheelchair for support. When she saw our baby she called us immediately, and urged us to take him for physical therapy without delay. She insisted that early intervention was essential.

Our son was six months old. Since our pediatrician agreed with the neighbor's recommendation, we called the Child Development Institute of our health fund to make an appointment, which they were ready to give us ... in another six months. We knew we were losing precious time; at six months of age much more could be done than at one year.

With the help of our pediatrician, we were given an appointment for an evaluation in another two months. The specialist told us that the name of our son's condition is hypotonia, meaning "lax muscles." His reflexes were also slow. This is caused by some sort of short circuit in the brain, whereby impulses to the muscles are interrupted — although there is no impairment of either the child's muscles or his mental faculties. The only course of treatment possible is exercise and physical therapy.

The waiting list for physical therapy was very long. Private treatment was expensive. We were in a quandary, for we were told over and over again not to waste any time in beginning therapy.

At such a time, the only thing to do is ask the opinion of someone steeped in Torah. We went to our Rebbe, *shlita*, to ask his advice.

Go to the Righteous Ones to Ask

I carefully wrote out a request to present to the Rebbe: "My little son, eight months old, suffers from lax muscles, hypotonia. The doctors are of the opinion that we must start physical therapy right

away, the sooner the better. They say that every passing day increases the risks for the future. It's already late. But we cannot get
an early appointment at our clinic. What should we do?"

The Rebbe received me graciously. He read what I had written
with great care. Then, after a brief moment, he answered, "Wait two
more months." He stretched out his hand for a farewell handshake
and nodded his head benevolently.

I hesitated to leave. I wanted to be absolutely sure. "And then,
should we try the treatment at the health fund clinic or look for private treatment?" I asked.

The Rebbe was quiet for a moment. Then he said, "By then
you'll see."

I left the Rebbe's room, and someone else entered. Whole
worlds passed through that room, one after another.

At home, the whole family had been saying *Tehillim* and waiting to hear what the Rebbe had said. I told them firmly and unequivocally, "We are not to do anything for two months. No
physiotherapy without instructions from the Rebbe."

I felt as though we were the tranquil eye in the midst of the roil-
ing storm. Friends, acquaintances, physicians, and the caregiver's
neighbor were amazed. They told us repeatedly that immediate
treatment was necessary and that we were taking a great risk in
waiting. We shouldn't even wait for our appointment at the clinic,
but engage a private therapist.

A Shock in More Ways Than One

Emunas chachamim is not so easy to carry out, but we were determined to follow the advice of our Rebbe, no matter what anyone
else said. We maintained our normal schedules.

Two weeks after I had spoken to the Rebbe we were on our way
to take the baby to his caregiver. The stairs of her house were long,
steep, and narrow, and she lived on the third floor. To save time, I
picked up the stroller with the baby strapped into it, and started up
the stairs.

To this day I have no idea how it happened, but halfway up, my flexible, lax-muscled son suddenly slipped or jumped out of the straps and started rolling down the stairs.

For a second or two I stood there with the empty stroller in my arms. As quickly as I could, I put it down on the landing so it could not roll down on top of the baby. I heard him bumping against each step as he fell. When I finally reached him, he was lying inert at the bottom of the staircase, bruised and swollen.

I checked to see that he was breathing; then I stroked him gently and spoke to him. A gigantic weight lifted off of me when he started to cry. Picking him up carefully, I took him outside and my wife flagged a taxi to take us to the nearest emergency room. In fear and trembling I prayed, Ribbono shel Olam, this child has suffered so much. Please have mercy on him.

We were admitted immediately, and the medical staff conducted an extensive examination, with all kinds of tests. Amazingly, they found no fractures or internal bleeding, but said that he had a severe concussion.

A full CAT scan showed that everything was normal. I asked the neurologist hesitantly if there was any sign of brain damage on the scan. The doctor checked again, studied it carefully, and answered decisively that the brain was in perfect shape.

The neurologist listened with great interest to our account of the baby's medical history. Then he checked the baby's reflexes. We stood aside, ready to bear whatever Hashem had decreed for us. To our mutual astonishment, he found the reflexes responding normally. After several hours of observation it was clear that all was well, and we were sent home with the great gift we had received from ha-Kadosh Baruch Hu.

The Concussion

From that day on, our baby began to turn over in his crib. Our son's muscles grew stronger from day to day. We saw it with our own eyes. His strange twisting stopped completely, and as if in a dream, we watched his quick, astonishing progress.

We accepted this improvement quietly, placing our full trust in

Hashem. By the end of the week the baby was able to get up on his hands and knees and rock back and forth. The following week he began to crawl — and quickly. Soon he was sitting up by himself. It was as if he wanted to catch up on everything at once.

With the passing weeks, a dramatic change came over our son's life and ours. It dawned on us that the short circuit in his brain between the message center and his muscles must have been restored. The concussion was a trauma that had turned into a blessing. We had not done a thing; ha-Kadosh Baruch Hu had fixed the short circuit.

Those days were an emotional time of spiritual uplift. We clearly saw Hashem's Hand with our own eyes.

Every stage in our son's development, every step he takes, is accompanied by great excitement, and our immense thanksgiving cannot be expressed in words alone. Now that our son is three, and a healthy, charming child, we recognize the enormity of the miracle that happened to us, and we raise a paean of thanks to Hashem for it.

We can only hope to tell people of Hashem's greatness and glory in our own small way by publicizing as widely as possible the immense reward for pure trust in Hashem and His *tzaddikim*.

A Jew of Old Jerusalem

I WANT TO TELL YOU the story of a real old-time *Yerushalmi* Jew of your grandfather's, or perhaps your great-grandfather's, generation. His name was Mendel Gefner, and he typified the unsung and unknown, simple men of faith and moral courage who lived in Jerusalem not so long ago. You may even be one of the lucky people who were privileged to know or even be descended from one of them.

Mendel's warmhearted, many-faceted personality deserves a full biography, but for now, we will tell you about one or two events in his life, and perhaps we can all benefit from the sparks of *emunah* and *bitachon* he radiated throughout his life on earth.

He was a happy person, a chassid who trusted Hashem and re-lied totally on the wealth of kindness showered upon us by the King of the universe. As you know, one who trusts Hashem is sur-rounded by kindness all day long.

His family was large, *baruch Hashem*. Ha-Kadosh Baruch Hu cre-ated many souls for him to care for, and though his means were less than ample, he raised them all happily and cheerfully, giving thanks to the blessed Creator of all living things.

What was his occupation? He was completely preoccupied with the delights of the holy Torah, which he studied with great but hidden genius. And he busied himself constantly with mighty deeds of Torah and *chessed*: He organized minyanim to daven for help from the Almighty during times of trouble — of which there were not a few in the Jerusalem of fifty, sixty, and seventy years ago. He found time to hold long, deep conversations with the righ-teous men of his generation, who would send him on various mis-sions for the spiritual rectification of the generation.

He lived a long life full of activities of eternal significance that kept him occupied from morning till night. And yet he had *parnasah;* Mendel was a child of wealth. He was the pampered son of a very rich Father, a Father Who was a powerful figure with the key to a great treasure: the key to *parnasah*. His Father was the King of kings, ha-Kadosh Baruch Hu, Who owns all silver and gold and disburses it to man.

So why should Mendel worry about making a living? He did what he had to do to earn a livelihood, and ha-Kadosh Baruch Hu provided for him from on High. He labored in Torah, and his *parnasah* was delivered to him straight from Heaven. As King Solo-mon said (*Mishlei* 1:22): *Birkas Hashem hi ta'ashir,* Hashem's blessing makes one wealthy, which the commentators explain means, "There is no need to weary oneself in order to become rich; the blessing of Hashem suffices. With this blessing, there is no need to suffer and toil overlong to increase one's wealth, since whatever blessing is due is sufficient."

"I am jealous of you, Reb Mendel," one of the great rabbis of Jerusalem once told him privately. "You will be a very wealthy man, and enormous sums will pass through your hands." Mendel looked at him uncomprehendingly. What enormous sums? Why should he have them? What was his interlocutor talking about? What was he trying to say?

"Mendel," the rav continued in language Mendel could understand, "you have been blessed with a large family, b'li ayin ha-ra, and ha-Kadosh Baruch Hu will undoubtedly send you the large sums you will need to marry them off honorably. Marrying off a child takes a great deal of money. Make a calculation, Mendel, and you will see that Heaven will yet send enormous sums through your hands."

The great man's words came to pass. Mendel merited receiving blessing and a satisfactory livelihood from the generous, full Hand of Hashem. He managed to find coins in his pocket, baruch Hashem, and was able to marry off his children honorably. He was as far from being wealthy as it was possible to be, but he never needed to seek favors. His Father took care of him, for He is a merciful King, may He be blessed.

Gefner's New Store

The Gefner family had moved from the old city of Jerusalem because life there had become too precarious, and had gone to live in Meah Shearim, then a relatively new neighborhood. Mrs. Gefner was a righteous woman. She stood in their new meat and live-poultry store in the shuk, the marketplace, of Meah Shearim. Her lips murmured verses of Tehillim as she asked ha-Kadosh Baruch Hu to send customers, lots of them, to come and buy chickens in honor of Shabbos — and, she added quietly, to pay for them. Gefner's new store was not yet well-known in town. But, she thought to herself, is anything too hard for Hashem? He can do anything. He had planted the "olive shoots" that sat around her table,* and He would help her feed them.

The crowing of the live chickens did not distract her from the

* See Tehillim 128:3.

wonderful sound of Mendel's learning coming from the two small rooms behind the store, the sweet sing-song of his Torah study that filled her home. This was the acme of her entire existence. She would do anything to allow him to learn Torah in peace and security. Soon he would join her in the store, taking a short break from his learning and holy toil to do a bit of *hishtadlus* for his livelihood.

The chickens squawked, but her thoughts turned to her children, the delight of her life. As she thought her thoughts and waited for customers, something was happening in the square in front of her store. A man was carrying in crates and crates of live chickens and setting up a stand right in front of the entrance to her store! She was so shocked she couldn't speak.

Soon the man began to hawk his wares in a voice that echoed all over the shuk: "Chickens for Shabbos! Rock-bottom prices! Live chickens *lichvod Shabbos*! Cheapest in town!"

Mrs. Gefner thought he would soon move on and tried to ignore him, but the man stood there hour after hour and sold chickens to whomever passed by. "Just look at that," she complained to Mendel. "Here we sit with all our chickens clucking away for naught, and he stands practically in front of our door selling away!"

Reb Mendel was calm. "No one can do anything unless it is so decreed Above. A person's sustenance is allotted him. Whatever he is supposed to receive he will get. No one can keep from us whatever has been apportioned us by Heaven."

"But who ever heard of such a thing?" his wife complained quietly. "To stand in the doorway of a chicken store and sell chickens? Someone should tell him he is doing a bad thing. They should tell him to go and sell his chickens somewhere else. After all, ours is a new store and isn't known yet."

"Don't worry," Mendel reassured her with a smile. "Everyone has his own portion, and no one can touch what has been prepared for another. Ha-Kadosh Baruch Hu feeds and supports every insect and every creature, every man and every beast, every chicken and every chicken-seller."

"So what will happen? Is he going to stand here every day?" She wanted to understand and share in this font of calming *bitachon* that she had acquired with her marriage.

"Let him stand there every day. So what?" Mendel said. "Is he the one who supports us? Do our customers support us? Ha-Kadosh Baruch Hu Above supports us from His largesse."

The man came back the next day and the next, but Mrs. Gefner remained calm.

The Famous Chicken

Meah Shearim was in an uproar. Everyone was talking about it. "Eight eggs at once!" "Gefner's chicken laid eight eggs at once!" "Let's go see the wonder chicken in Gefner's new store!"

The Gefners put the famous chicken on a high shelf in the store with her eight eggs resting under her in a circle, and everyone feasted their eyes. Word spread quickly, and the phrase "Gefner's new store" flew from mouth to mouth. Children begged their parents to let them buy the Shabbos chicken at Gefner's. The children wanted to see the chicken with the incredible clutch of eggs, and so did their mothers. "Where is Gefner's new store?" all the shopkeepers in the shuk heard again and again. *"Vu is Gefner's yatke?"*

And once Jerusalemites had made their acquaintance with Gefner's store, once they had met Reb Mendel and Mrs. Gefner and seen their special chicken and bought a chicken or two *lichvod Shabbos,* they gave themselves the same pleasure every week. Gefner's *yatke* soon had a steady clientele, and one could see the fulfillment of the promise to those who rely upon Hashem to provide.

Wedding Plans

It was one of Reb Mendel's greatest hours. He had merited to arrange a match for his pious daughter with a great *talmid chacham,* the son of the great *gaon* Reb Chaim Yaakov Klapholtz, *zt"l,* one of the true giants of Torah. Reb Chaim Yaakov's home was as poor as could be, but it was filled with happiness and delight. Reb Chaim Yaakov sat at home most of the time, learning Torah in holiness and purity. What could be more fitting than an engagement between his family and the family of Mendel Gefner?

Now these two worthy figures sat opposite each other. On the rickety table before them lay a piece of paper inscribed with the words: Engagement Contract. These two felt privileged to be writing an engagement contract. They were brothers, Reb Chaim Yaakov and Reb Mendel. In essence they were both sons of the same rich Father, *Yisbarach*. That is why they were both so relaxed and cheerful as they spoke about the wedding expenses. They would promise and their Father would pay.

"I'll pay half and you'll pay half," Reb Chaim Yaakov declared, in a sonorous but refined voice, "as is customary in Jerusalem."

"Hear me, my righteous *mechutan*," said Reb Mendel, taking Reb Chaim Yaakov's hand in his. "Please take on only one-third of the expenses of the wedding and let me pay for two-thirds. That is my wish and surely you will respect it. Please do not burden yourself with more than one-third. It will be my privilege."

A broad smile spread over Reb Chaim Yaakov's glowing face. "Look here, Reb Mendel. I cannot in truth even promise one-third. So what do I base my commitment on? If you count my money or assets, I don't have even a sixth of the expenses. But do you know what I'll do? I will commit myself to pay one third of the wedding expenses, and ha-Kadosh Baruch Hu will help; it is for me to promise and for Hashem to pay from His treasure troves of silver and gold.

"But since we are already talking about *His* treasures," continued Reb Chaim Yaakov, "why shouldn't I commit myself to a half? What difference does a half or a third make to our Father in Heaven?"

The Me'or Einayim asks in his commentary on *parashas Va'eschanan*: Where does blessing reside? The answer is: In that which is hidden from the eye, in the hidden stores Above. One who relies on that hidden treasure is the one in whom blessing resides. One who places his trust in his business prowess reduces the blessing from Above, and it is questionable whether his business will be judged deserving of bounty. But one who sees his business as an empty receptacle designed only to receive Divine bounty, one who relies on the true Source of bounty, on the vast treasure Above, he is the one who earns his livelihood in plenty.

The source of livelihood of those unique people who do as much *hishtadlus* as they can and rely completely on the One Above is never clearly revealed. It comes steadily and generously from the unseen Higher Source that they trust and rely on.

Reb Chaim Yaakov and Reb Mendel signed the engagement contract, with each side promising to pay half, based on their accounts in Heaven's bank. We are happy to report that each of them later was able to pay his half, thanks to ha-Kadosh Baruch Hu's generous Hand, and they continued to enjoy the infinite wealth of the Heavenly treasure trove throughout their lives.

He Is the Happy One

One day, back at the *yatke* — where chickens were the occupation but hearts were focused on Hashem — a chicken supplier arrived at the store and asked to be paid. Reb Mendel owed him for dozens of chickens that the dealer had supplied, and now the man needed cash. "Two pounds and seventy-five shillings," he demanded, in Mandate currency.

Reb Mendel did not happen to have much cash on hand in the store that day; even one pound was not a minor sum of money in those days. *Baruch Hashem*, Reb Mendel had plenty of expenses, and even if he had satisfied all the Gefner family's needs, that didn't mean that he had provided the Shabbos *challos* for his widowed neighbor yet. In any case, he searched all his pockets and couldn't find a penny.

"Do you have other stores in the vicinity that you need to visit?" Reb Mendel asked the wealthy merchant. "Please go to them first, and when you're finished come back. *B'ezras Hashem* you'll get your money."

The merchant complied with Reb Mendel's request. What did it matter to him if he was paid sooner or later, as long as he was paid that day? Reb Mendel turned to the customer who had just come in. But Mrs. Gefner could not contain herself. "Where are you going to get the money from? What did you gain with the delay? The man will soon come back, and we don't have a penny to pay him!"

Reb Mendel pointed upward. "Doesn't Hashem know that I have to pay the dealer two pounds and seventy-five shillings? He has always provided the money to pay the supplier, and He'll do so now, too."

"But how, Mendel, how? We have nothing here! Maybe we should go out and look for the money somehow?"

"How?" Reb Mendel replied, while subduing a fat chicken that had started to flap its wings wildly. "I don't know and it's none of my business." The chicken started cackling furiously as it tried to reach one more crumb on top of its crate. "The One Who cares for the needs of this noisemaker will take care of me too. I am alive, am I not? The One Who provides life will also provide a living."

"Who is happy? One who does not rely on his intelligence to succeed, but relies only on the mercies of Heaven," as Rabbeinu Yonah comments on *Mishlei*, "and who, even when his mind tells him he will find no way to succeed, does succeed on the strength of his trust in Hashem — he is happy."

Another customer entered the store. "Shalom, Reb Mendel! I think it has been some time since I last paid up my account. The truth is, I just didn't have the money. Now, *baruch Hashem*, I can pay you. Will you please add up my bill?"

Reb Mendel checked the client's account and added up his bill. The sum before his eyes hardly astonished him, as he knew Hashem would see to it that he was taken care of. "Two pounds and seventy-five shillings," he said, a smile of happiness and gratitude spreading across his face. Mrs. Gefner's gasped in astonishment. Ha-Kadosh Baruch Hu was taking the money out of the customer's pocket and putting it directly into that of the chicken supplier. They had had nothing to do with it. Ha-Kadosh Baruch Hu had again indeed taken care of all their needs.

In the Place Where
Ba'alei Teshuvah Stand...

*Our Sages say that even the
righteous cannot reach the
lofty place of ba'alei teshuvah
— penitents and those who
return to Jewish observance.
(Berachos 34b)*

A Good Word

I LOVE TO TALK TO nonreligious Jews I meet here and there, on buses, waiting in line at the clinic. When I sit down next to someone who is obviously not observant, I do not feel that I am bound to influence him to change his mind, and I certainly do not expect to persuade him to become a *ba'al teshuvah* on the spot.

In my experience, all sorts of subjects come up in conversation in this manner, with neither side feeling any pressure. I simply state my opinion freely and naturally, supporting it with my faith and *emunah*, of course, with respect for his point of view, and try to find whatever points we might have in common.

I usually find that, since the conversation is not geared to persuading anyone of anything but rather to discuss and explain, my ideas are often considered. Sometimes, I admit, I am rewarded with a cold shoulder, but I never stop trying.

This is the approach I took when I sat down next to Lior Avital on a bus one day. "Hello," I said, "my name is Shlomo and I'm from Shikun Tehillah. We have a long ride ahead of us, and we may as well spend it in pleasant conversation. We are fellow Jews, after all."

Lior was a nice fellow from Kibbutz Nof. We spoke about the government, unemployment, the economy, politics, and the weather. Somehow, during the conversation, he elicited the information that I was privileged to be the father of eleven wonderful children, *kein yirbu*.

Lior was amazed, and asked how I was able to manage with so many children. For his part, he said, he could not see himself dedicating his life to raising children. At that point I explained my beliefs to him a bit more fully, and I told him that all the difficulties entailed in raising eleven children did not add up to one-tenth of the pleasure and satisfaction they brought.

"One's heart grows to encompass all this; one's soul fills to overflowing with fountains of warmth. To be the agent of nurturing eleven worlds, is there a greater privilege than that?" I asked. Then I changed the subject.

About ten years after that meeting, I was in Monsey, New York, on my way to a family *simchah*. My taxi driver was a bearded Jew. When I tried to explain where I wanted to go in broken English, he replied in Hebrew, "You can speak to me in *lashon kodesh*, if you like. I come from Eretz Yisrael."

Naturally we began to converse, and briefly exchanged biographical information. When he heard that I lived in Shikun Tehillah, he said quietly that he had become a *ba'al teshuvah* because of a Jew who came from Shikun Tehillah. I was curious to know who had been the one to help him, thinking that I probably knew the person. The driver said he did not remember the man's name, but he knew he was the father of eleven children. The driver's name was Lior Avital. Instantly my conversation on a bus in Eretz Yisrael from ten years before flashed through my mind.

It was a most moving meeting. Lior told me that our conversation had been so easygoing, so natural, that my words remained in his head. He had thought a great deal about what I'd said, and began to consider his Jewishness in a new light. He had gone on to question his own way of life, to ask questions, and to seek answers. He was now, as I could see, an observer of Torah and mitzvos.

But that is not the end of the story. I returned to Eretz Yisrael and, other than mentioning the incident to a few people, thought no more about it. On Election Day, however, I was chairman of the election committee working at the voting station at Kibbutz Nof, and I recalled that Lior came from there. When the elder Mr. Avital came in to vote, I immediately saw the resemblance and took time out to speak to him.

He told me that not only had Lior returned to his roots, but all three of his brothers had followed in his footsteps. Lior was already the father of five children, *kein yirbu*, and had merited enjoying the pleasure and satisfaction of being Heaven's agent in raising children to Torah, marriage, and good deeds.

Everyday Miracles

T THE LEV L'ACHIM office in Jerusalem, the secretary went down the list of phone numbers as he went about arranging home visits to people who might need strengthening in *Yiddishkeit*. It was a job he enjoyed. Home visits were very effective. At home people were usually relaxed and receptive. The volunteers were skilled and experienced in their work, and their efforts were often crowned with blessing.

The Reuvenis were the first family on his list who had expressed interest in a home visit. He dialed and dialed again, but encountered only a busy signal. Next were the Shimonis. A long ring. Another long ring. And another. No one home. Back to the Reuvenis, and then again to the Shimonis. No luck on either call. The secretary made a mark beside each name and went on to George Levi. One ring and — an answer!

After the exchange of a few words, Mr. Levi expressed immediate interest and said he would be delighted to have the volunteers come over that night. The secretary called the volunteers on the spot, gave them Mr. Levi's exact address, and wished them much success in sanctifying Hashem's Name and bringing another family back to their Father in Heaven.

It was a chilly evening as the volunteers strode down the dark street, seeking the correct address. Suddenly, a face appeared in the gloom.

"Are you from Lev l'Achim?" the man asked. "I'm the person you're looking for."

They shook hands, and George Levi invited them into his home. The warm reception encouraged the volunteers, who found that Mr. Levi was more than ready to hear what they had to say. They all sat down around his dining-room table, and the conversation flowed freely.

George Levi was a new immigrant from France who had already begun investigating *Yiddishkeit*. He had enrolled himself in an excellent yeshiva for *ba'alei teshuvah*, which had a class starting the following evening.

"To tell you the truth," Levi admitted, "I was very hesitant about attending the yeshiva. My evil inclination wasn't making it very easy. All sorts of doubts and considerations have constantly been running through my head — to go or not to go, to change direction in life or to stay the way I am, to commit myself or not to commit myself.

"The difficulty of deciding was putting me under a lot of stress. Just this morning I prayed to the Ribbono shel Olam, 'If this yeshiva is good for me, send me a sign from Heaven that I should go.' I decided that if I didn't get any sign, I would take a different direction in life. And then, just then, the phone rang with the call from your office saying you wanted to come over tonight. I couldn't ask for a clearer sign than that!"

The astonished volunteers registered the fact that they had been sent for just this purpose as messengers from Heaven, and they did their job well. They were able to communicate the importance and beauty of *Yiddishkeit* to George Levi, and they quoted a saying of the *tzaddikim*: "It is hard for a Jew to act like a Jew, but it is even harder for him to act like a gentile." They encouraged him, and gave him the strength to take the immense step that would allow him to really start living. It goes without saying that George went off to the yeshiva the next day, and is now in the advanced stages of returning to Judaism.

"It just goes to show you how one who wants to purify himself is helped," the secretary responded excitedly when he heard the story. "This line was busy, that line didn't answer, and I merely proceeded to the next number, having no idea that at the other end of the line was a man for whom that phone call would tip the scales and affect the rest of his life."

A "Childish" Mistake

TAMIR WAS VERY FIRM and secure in his decision to become a *ba'al teshuvah*, but his brother Amos was still vacillating. He believed and didn't believe, wanted but didn't dare, was afraid to try yet afraid to fail. Tamir would reassure him over and over, but Amos was too scared to take the plunge. At a certain point, they decided to go to Rabbi Chaim Kanievsky, *shlita*, in Bnei Brak, and ask him about Amos's doubts and concerns.

"Merciful Father," Tamir davened all the way there, "be with me, for Your own sake. I had the privilege of seeing Your light. Please give Amos the merit of seeing the meaning of life too. May this be a favorable time before You for him to make the right decision and do *teshuvah*."

The taxi made its way through the crowded streets of Bnei Brak to the corner of Chazon Ish and Admor MiGur streets and stopped for the brothers to ask directions.

"Excuse me, little boy. Where is Rabbi Chaim Kanievsky's house?"

"Get out here," the boy said, "and go straight down this street till you get to Meltzer Street. Ha-Rav Kanievsky lives across the street from the Wagshall wedding hall, I think."

They paid the driver, got out, and started walking. It is hard to imagine what these kibbutzniks thought about busy, crowded, bubbling Bnei Brak: the flocks of yelling children, the buildings crowded one on top of the other, the sounds of learning from all the shuls and study halls, the announcements plastered on every bare wall, the crowds, the modestly dressed women, and the bustle.

They were approaching Meltzer Street when suddenly two boys came running up the street after them, huffing and puffing for all they were worth.

"Excuse me," one of them said, out of breath. "Are you the ones from the taxi who asked directions?"

The brothers confirmed that yes, they were indeed.

"I'm so sorry, really sorry. I made a mistake. After you left, just to be sure, I asked my friend where Rav Kanievsky lives, and he told me that I had sent you the wrong way. You're completely in the wrong place."

Amos couldn't help smiling. Imagine one of the kibbutz children going out of his way like this, he thought. Not likely. There was something about the tenor of this whole incident that he had never before encountered.

The boy begged them to let him take them where they needed to go, all the way to the door. "I'll just call my parents and tell them I'll be a little late," he said. "I know exactly where the Rav lives now."

The second boy tugged at his friend's sleeve and whispered loudly, "I think you have to pay for their taxi."

The first boy began to apologize even harder. "Of course, I'll happily pay for a taxi for you to get there. After all, I made the mistake. I haven't got any money, but if you come home with me — it's not far — my parents will pay for you to take another taxi. I should never have sounded so sure of myself when I didn't really know where the Rav lives."

Amos's eyes filled with tears. He took hold of Tamir's arm and said, "We don't have to go to a Rav, Tamir. Let's go home. I want to do *teshuvah*. If this little boy is an example of what it's all about, I am going to go all the way."

A little touch of *hashgachah pratis* and a whole lot of *kiddush Hashem,* and a good measure of *chessed* propelled Amos into the warm embrace of his heritage.

The Four Cubits
of Halachah

*Our Sages stress the importance of
performing mitzvos by telling us
that from the day the second Temple
was destroyed, Hashem now dwells
within the boundaries of Jewish Law.*
(Berachos 8a)

Saved by Halachah

RABBI COHEN WAS flying home from New York. He had attended the wedding of one of his former pupils, which had afforded him great pleasure. He had also been able to see many members of his family. All in all, it had been a satisfactory trip.

The stewardesses began to walk down the aisles, checking off each passenger's name against a list of food requests: the standard menu with a choice of chicken or beef entree, vegetarian, kosher, and "special kosher" — by which the airlines mean glatt kosher food. A stewardess courteously asked the young man seated next to Rabbi Cohen which menu he had requested. The young man, obviously not Jewish, said, "Standard menu, please, with beef." Rabbi Cohen had ordered "special kosher."

Soon the stewardesses returned with the food trolleys and distributed the trays among the passengers. The young man received his standard tray and immediately began to eat. Rabbi Cohen's tray was covered in plastic wrap and had a mashgiach's seal on the closure. He opened the seal on his tray and removed the wrapping to see what there was to eat. The meal was a deli sandwich, some vegetables, and an extra roll, and other than the wrappings and the seal, his tray looked remarkably similar to his seatmate's. The young man, noticing this, asked Rabbi Cohen what was so special about the kosher meals. Rabbi Cohen told him that Jews were commanded to be careful about what they ate, and that eating forbidden food had a negative influence on the soul. The young man seemed satisfied with this brief answer and continued eating.

Rabbi Cohen got up to wash his hands before eating the bread. But as he made his way to the sink, he suddenly remembered the halachah forbidding one to eat meat that has been left unattended. (The Shach states that it is forbidden to eat meat that has been left unattended even if it bears an identifying sign.)

Rabbi Cohen washed his hands, returned to his seat, and said the blessing on the roll. He then ate only the roll and some vegetables. He was happy that he had been given the opportunity to observe a halachah that is not so frequently encountered.

Rabbi Cohen's seatmate, though, was puzzled. "Why aren't you eating?" he asked.

"I guess I'm not that hungry," the rabbi replied casually.

But his fellow passenger was not to be put off. "Just a few minutes ago we were both wondering out loud when they would bring dinner. Why did you suddenly change your mind about being hungry?"

Faced with the stranger's sincere curiosity, Rabbi Cohen felt it would be impolite not to answer.

"As a Jew, I'm not allowed to eat meat that has been left unwatched," he explained simply, assuming this would end all discussion.

But what his seatmate said next was totally unexpected. "Great is the Jewish God! How He watches over you!

"Now let me tell you something. When you left your seat, my curiosity got the better of me. I've always wanted to taste kosher meat, so I ate yours. Then I realized that you would be left without any meat, so I replaced what I had taken with the meat from my tray."

A Minyan in Antwerp

YEHUDAH HAD JUST driven onto the main highway between Brussels and Antwerp, when he detected a slight wobble in the steering mechanism. He wanted to pull over to the side of the road and stop, but his friend Michael, who was sitting in the passenger seat, urged him to continue driving.

"Hashem will help," Michael said. "We haven't davened *Minchah* yet, and if we keep going we will get to Antwerp in time to daven with a minyan."

Yehudah reluctantly continued driving, hoping that the condition was not dangerous. The wobble in the steering, however, grew steadily worse until Yehudah decided to drive onto the shoulder of the road and stop the car. As he turned the wheel to the right, they heard a loud bang and the car swerved badly. The right front tire had had a blowout.

Having no tools to change the tire and not being a member of an auto service club, Yehudah and his friend were stranded on the highway, far from an exit, with no help in sight. Nor did they see a roadside telephone nearby. Had Yehudah stopped when he had first sensed that something was amiss, they at least would have been closer to the entrance ramp, and they might have walked back to the city to call for help.

"Well, we had good intentions, anyway," Michael said. "We wanted to daven *Minchah* with a minyan. You'll see, Hashem won't desert us."

But Michael suggested that, in any case, they had better daven right there at the side of the road before sunset overtook them, for now they had neither car nor minyan.

Just then a tow truck from an auto service company pulled up next to their car. A mechanic stepped down briskly and asked what the problem was. Quickly and efficiently, he pulled out his tools and changed the tire. Yehudah and Michael were speechless at the appearance of this messenger from Heaven who had come to help them out of their predicament.

As he gathered his tools and prepared to climb into his truck, the mechanic told Yehudah that they were lucky he had received their call just before he left the garage. Puzzled, Yehudah said that he had not called him. The mechanic replied that he had been summoned to repair a car that was stuck on that same highway, and the car model was just the same as Yehudah's. He said that when he had seen them pulled over at the side of the road, he assumed they were the ones who called in.

"Well, the person who really made that call is probably stuck some distance ahead of you, so I had better get moving and find him," the mechanic said.

The pair were soon safely on their way, and to Michael's great satisfaction, they arrived in Antwerp in time to daven *Minchah* with a minyan.

Nothing But the Truth

ONLY THE TRUTH," Abba always used to tell us. "Remember, stick to the truth. Not only will you never lose by telling the truth, but you will never gain from lying. No matter how much you think you have profited from a lie, it's not true profit. The truth brings its own reward."

I once had the privilege of seeing my father put his views into practice to the tune of a forty-thousand-shekel loss, and I'll never forget the lesson I learned.

That evening Abba parked his car in the Givat Shaul neighborhood of Jerusalem, which is near the entrance to the city. We had arranged to meet his brother there, in order for the three of us to travel together to a wedding in Bnei Brak in my uncle's car. After the wedding we returned to Jerusalem, and my uncle dropped us off in Givat Shaul. We headed toward our own car to drive home.

Our car was not where we had left it. Although it was doubtful that we both had erred, we looked further along the street. No car. We were obviously victims of a popular Jerusalem crime: car theft. It was just as obvious that it was the will of Heaven that my father suffer this loss, but we were understandably extremely annoyed. Even though it was not a new model, the car was still worth about forty thousand shekels.

We started walking, in hopes of finding a cab. Abba was quiet and uncomplaining.

"Oh, well," I tried to console him, "you really needed a new car anyway. Now you'll be able to collect the insurance money and buy a new one."

Abba shook his head. "I'm afraid not," he said. "My policy specifies that when there is no extra security lock on the steering wheel, in addition to the alarm system, the car is not covered. I never got around to buying a steering wheel lock for the car, so I can't make a claim."

"But you've been paying the premiums for such a long time," I protested. "You've paid so much money. Now you deserve to get it back. It's mostly your own money anyway," I reasoned.

"Insurance companies are not interested in philosophy or logic," my father said. "A contract is a contract. I paid them knowing all their conditions. It's my fault that I didn't heed one of the conditions. So they are not obligated to pay me. And that's that."

"Come on, Abba. Who will ever know whether you had the lock on or not? If they ask you, you can just say that everything was the way it was supposed to be."

"The Torah says that it's forbidden to lie," Abba said curtly.

I tried one more tack. "The insurance company is so big. What does one more payout mean to them?"

"That's true," Abba replied, "but I personally, as a Jew, am forbidden to lie. Even if it means losing forty thousand shekels."

The next day, Abba filed a report of the theft with the insurance company. In the short interview that ensued they asked him about the steering wheel lock, and he did not lie.

Abba didn't receive a penny from the company, but he was proud of the fact that he had withstood temptation, that he belonged indeed to a nation apart, a nation that clings to the truth of the Torah.

I suppose the reader is now hoping to hear how Abba was paid back in the end. He did not have a windfall of forty thousand shekels, and for that reason I hesitated to write this story. However, I think it shows that a measure of greatness resides in every Jew, and even though the halachah requires this behavior of us all, it is still an impressive story. The uncompromising straightforwardness a Jew adopts in order not to violate a prohibition of the holy Torah is worthy of being held up to the light.

By the Sweat of Your Brow

(Bereishis 3:19)

Leibel the Scribe

Every person is affected by two concepts: decreed and allotted. It is decreed that he work. Every Rosh Hashanah he is allotted a particular sum of money for his livelihood. On the one hand, if he doesn't work as much as was decreed that he work, he won't receive his allotment. On the other hand, there is no real connection between what is decreed and what is allotted. He will work as much as was decreed, yet he will receive only what he was allotted and no more.

What is "decreed" is the hishtadlus, effort, every person must invest; emunah, faith, represents what is "allotted." For ordinary human beings, emunah without hishtadlus will not bring a livelihood. However, believing that one's hishtadlus has intrinsic power is a serious mistake. The correct way to live is to carry out your part with consistency, in accordance with the decree of "earning your bread by the sweat of your brow." At the same time, you must believe that your livelihood comes from what you were allotted and is not the result of your efforts. Wise is he who knows that there is no connection between hishtadlus and parnasah, and foolish is one who assumes that there is indeed a connection between the two.

Stories about ordinary people who distributed large sums of money to tzedakah and didn't lose out (and even profited), or whose emunah was so strong they were unfazed by competition, are more than just a series of events that occurred to these particular people. These stories describe a way of thinking that guides these people's lives. It is this way of thinking, this outlook on life, that enables the heroes of these stories to act in the manner that they did.

It is important to internalize this message before you read about Leibel the scribe.

*L*EIBEL WAS ONE OF THE best scribes around. Pious and God-fearing, his work was a joy to behold. He toiled over every word, every letter, every ornamental "crown." He wrote at an unhurried pace, slowly completing line after line, each one clear and beautiful.

Leibel's *parashiyos* were in great demand. Rumor had it that even great rabbis ordered from him. In order to receive one of Leibel's *parashiyos*, however, one had to be prepared to wait a long time. Aside from the fact that his work progressed slowly, Leibel did not spend many hours a day writing. He didn't like to work under pressure; he hated to be hurried. The line of customers waiting for his goods was long indeed, but Leibel had all the time in the world. As far as he was concerned, anyone in a hurry was welcome to order from any of a hundred other scribes. He never asked anyone to order from him; whoever wanted to had to wait.

Leibel would sit down with the parchment and his quill at nine in the morning, after davening and studying the *daf yomi*. He'd write for four hours, until 1:00 P.M. He would then take his meal, rest a bit, daven *Minchah*, and continue on to the *beis midrash* near his home, where his study partner sat waiting for him.

Leibel's study partner was a friend who held a position teaching Gemara to teenage boys in a yeshiva, and he was a perfect match for Leibel. For three wonderful hours every day, the two studied diligently, swaying over open Gemaras and forgetting everything else in the world. Sometimes they got so carried away that they would lose track of time and look up from their Gemaras long after the three-hour time span had passed. These were Leibel's "Gan Eden hours."

After *Ma'ariv*, Leibel's young son would come to the *beis midrash*. Leibel chatted with him about what was going on in *cheder* and reviewed the daily material with him. In this manner, he kept tabs on his son's progress and formed an idea of how attentively he listened in class. He did the same with all his children, even the older ones, who are today all outstanding Torah scholars.

At approximately eight o'clock, Leibel would go home, spend a pleasant hour with his children, and take part in whatever they were doing. At nine-thirty, he received his friend Shachna, the local grocery store owner, who was a scholar in his own right. The two had a regular study session in *Tur* and *Shulchan Aruch*. They generally studied until eleven, at which time Leibel accepted potential customers interested in ordering *parashiyos*. On quiet evenings when no one showed up, Leibel would continue studying with Shachna until midnight.

Leibel's children knew their father was immensely fond of this evening study session. They could recall only rare occasions on which it had been canceled during the many years the two had been studying together. Leibel didn't attend many weddings. He even celebrated his own children's engagements within the framework of his schedule, wrapping up the festivities before 9:30 P.M.

At 6:30 A.M., before leaving for *Shacharis*, he would sit with a cup of coffee, studying *Chumash* with Rashi for a quarter of an hour. After his morning prayers, he'd devote approximately three-quarters of an hour to the daily *daf*.

Leibel stuck to this schedule for years. Steady as a timepiece, he was faithful to his agenda, allowing nothing to interrupt his prescribed routine.

His was a good home. Leibel's eight children were quiet and well-behaved, like himself. He radiated a special something that affected his entire family.

What about *parnasah*? They managed. Leibel's *parashiyos* earned enough to support his family with the basics, not much more. His wife complained that the house was full of old furniture that needed to be replaced; she often asked him to spend a bit more time writing each day. But Leibel didn't want to give up so much as a moment of the time he'd allotted for studying Torah.

When the children came of age, Leibel's wife complained that many a good match was rejected for the sole reason that Leibel couldn't afford to give much. "Couldn't you spend a little time writing in the afternoon? In the evening? Instead of sitting with your afternoon *chavrusa* for three and a half hours, instead of studying with Shachna until the middle of the night, why can't you write another *parashah* in that time? Why not earn another few hundred dollars? Our financial situation would be so much easier that way," she cajoled her husband.

But Leibel felt that compromising on his learning time would be the greatest loss of all.

"At the beginning of the year, ha-Kadosh Baruch Hu designated the barrel of wine from which I would drink all year," he explained. "The spout on the bottom of the barrel is represented by the four hours I work each morning. What is it you want me to do? Would you like me to attach an additional spout to the barrel by working more hours during the afternoon and evening? Why, that way, the wine inside the barrel will run out even faster, and I'll have to make do with less later on. An additional spout won't give me any more wine."

This is how Leibel expressed his *emunah,* his conviction that he would get precisely what he was destined to get; additional work hours, he felt sure, would not add to or detract from that amount in any way.

Leibel's eldest son relates, "When my friends used to tell me that their dental work cost a fortune, I noticed that nothing of the sort ever occurred in my family. Somehow, we never needed dental work. I thought to myself that apparently some people spent too much time working. They probably earned too much money, money that had to be taken away from them somehow. Ha-Kadosh Baruch Hu therefore sent them to the dentist, who relieved them of any 'extra' money they were not destined to have. I discussed this idea with my mother, who agreed with my observation that our family did somehow manage to avoid spending money on unforeseen emergencies."

"When I became engaged," relates Leibel's second son, "my father discussed his way of thinking with me at great length. It seemed to me that he felt obliged to explain and apologize for the fact that my wedding was to be celebrated in a very modest manner, nothing like the fancy affairs my friends enjoyed. He said, 'Look, my son, ha-Kadosh Baruch Hu has the ability to give and give and give without limits. But He wants us to do our part. I fulfill the obligation of *hishtadlus* by working four hours each morning.

Baruch Hashem, that's enough for us to get by. *Baruch Hashem,* none of us has ever suffered from hunger or lacked any basic necessities.

"'After working four hours each day, I feel both physically and spiritually unable to continue writing. I love to study Torah; my study sessions constitute an integral part of my life. For this reason, I was always at peace with my decision to limit my day's work to four hours. Now that I've reached the stage where I must begin marrying off my children, expenses are naturally higher. We therefore purchase only modest gifts and avoid extras as far as the wedding is concerned.'

"It hurt me that my father felt he had to justify himself. All of us children loved him dearly, and his Torah study was far more precious to us than a fancy wedding. I told him I was happy with the modest state of affairs and assured him that I too would try to live my life in a similar fashion. I thanked him for teaching me the *middah* of *histapkus,* making do with little. I saw that I had taken a load off his heart by demonstrating my understanding and willingness to accept.

"After my marriage, I was fortunate to arrange three private tutoring sessions with children and yeshiva students. The income from these sessions, in addition to my *kollel* stipend, made it possible for me to pay my rent and other monthly expenses. My brothers, each in turn, did the same. We considered it our privilege to take this financial burden off our father's shoulders."

Everything seemed to be going just fine, until Chaim Ovadiah, Leibel's sixth child, came of age. Chaim Ovadiah was physically handicapped from birth, and his condition affected his ability to learn as well. Although the boy had always managed very well among his peers, his handicap put him at a distinct disadvantage when it came to shidduchim. Chaim Ovadiah was a bright and sensitive boy; he needed a girl with the same qualities.

At one point, an interesting suggestion came up. The girl, in addition to being adopted, suffered from a very slight handicap. Leibel and his wife heard favorable information about her, and the match appealed to them.

However, the girl's adoptive father was only willing to proceed with the shidduch on one condition: he insisted that the groom's side promise thirty thousand dollars toward an apartment. As was the norm in Leibel's circles, the girl's father wanted to see his adopted daughter settled in an apartment of her own. He was willing to pay his part; the rest he demanded from the other side. Leibel discussed the situation with his rebbe, who instructed him to agree to the terms and proceed with the shidduch. Chaim Ovadiah soon became engaged, and Leibel's joy knew no bounds.

"A few days after the engagement party," relates Leibel's son, "I visited my parents. My mother was ecstatic, but she was concerned about raising the money they had promised. Understandably, she begged my father to put in a few more hours of work each day, and, as usual, my father wouldn't hear of it. His emotional calm was astounding. 'The sum of money I need is beyond what I can earn even if I work additional hours,' he said with a smile. 'I need special help from Heaven in any case. So why worry? Ha-Kadosh Baruch Hu has no problem delivering thirty thousand dollars to my doorstep; for Him, even so astronomical a sum is no harder to arrange than ten dollars. True, He wants me to do my part by putting in some effort. So — I'll add a bit to my *hishtadlus*, and everything will work out....'

"Ima's eyes sparkled with joy. Finally, my father was talking about adding to his *hishtadlus*; she had finally convinced him to put in some more hours of work each day. My father, however, went on to explain what he viewed as additional *hishtadlus*: 'I have decided to begin rising one hour earlier each morning. That way, I can daven with an earlier minyan and begin working one hour earlier each day. I'll add to my 'toil by the sweat of my brow' and Hashem will add to our 'bread.'

"My mother was disappointed or, more aptly, worried. 'What good is one extra hour when we need to come up with thirty thousand dollars, in addition to our ordinary household expenses? Why can't you trim your study sessions a bit? You yourself said there's such a thing as *hishtadlus*. But putting in only one extra hour of work a day is not sufficient *hishtadlus!*'

"But Abba was firm in his decision. 'No reasonable amount of effort will help me earn the sum of money I need. I take that to mean that I must do my little bit and Hashem will do His part. If I was designated to earn thirty thousand extra dollars this year, I'll get the money. If not, I won't, no matter what. Why kill myself working overtime? I'm ready to do what I must in order to receive from Heaven the amount of money I was allotted.'

"Ima knew the words to Abba's explanations by heart. Abba continued spending his afternoons delving deep into complex concepts in Gemara along with his study partner. As always, my little brother came to spend an hour learning with my father after *cheder*. He spent the evening with the family, and Shachna's nightly visits continued as well. In short, my father's schedule remained exactly the same, except for the fact that he awoke and left the house one hour earlier than usual. This was his *hishtadlus,* and he hoped for the best.

"His tranquility was a lesson in *emunah.* He seemed like a person with not a care in the world. He was not in the least worried. He did what he had to and trusted Heaven to send him what was designated to be his. He avoided taking a loan, since he had a year to come up with the money. He decided to give his *hishtadlus* a year's chance and see what would come of it. 'Who knows?' he said. 'Perhaps by the end of the year I'll have the entire sum. Why should I take a loan? If we don't have the money by then, we'll think about it when the time comes.'

"One day, a wealthy man from the United States approached Abba and asked him to write a *sefer Torah.* He wanted to donate a Torah to a large shul in the city where he lived.

"How did he get to Abba? It's a long story: A member of the man's immediate family began suffering from a particular misfortune, and he was advised to have a scribe check his tefillin. When he got to the scribe's house, he noticed a few other pairs of tefillin on the scribe's desk.

"'Look,' said the scribe to the wealthy man, pointing to a particular pair of tefillin. 'I've never seen such beautiful *parashiyos.* They were written by Reb Leibel from Eretz Yisrael. It's said that he wrote *parashiyos* for the Rebbe of Ploni.'

"The affluent man knew as much about *parashiyos* as the scribe knew about the stock market, but he trusted the scribe's opinion. He duly whistled in appreciation and noted my father's name.

"When the wealthy man merited salvation from the misfortune that had stricken a member of his family, he traveled to Eretz Yisrael to offer his gratitude and praise to Hashem. During his trip, it suddenly occurred to him that it would be a fitting sign of his gratitude to donate a *sefer Torah* to his shul. Recalling the name of the scribe who had written the *parashiyos* that had so overwhelmed his local scribe with their beauty, the man began asking around. He was told to forget about his idea: Reb Leibel wrote only *parashiyos*, not *sifrei Torah*, and even then the line was long.

"The man decided not to give up so easily. He made his way to our house, put down fifteen thousand dollars in cash and said, 'See here, Reb Leibel. I am not limited in time, and I have lots of money. I want a *sefer Torah*, and I want one written by you. I'm prepared to pay thirty thousand dollars (at the time, a more than generous sum to pay for writing a *sefer Torah*). I'm leaving this as a deposit, and I'd like a signed pledge in exchange.'"

Leibel was not one to be blinded by money. This wasn't the first time he'd heard such talk, but most people were in a hurry. As soon as they heard how long it would take him to produce what they wanted, they went elsewhere. Money? This money, like all other money, came from ha-Kadosh Baruch Hu's treasure house.

"Look," Leibel told him, "my time is taken until the end of the year. I've already promised people *parashiyos*, and I can't go back on my word. I write slowly, and I don't spend many hours a day writing...."

The wealthy man was not to be put off. "I don't mind if you start writing next year. It's not urgent. In another three and a half years, God willing, my eldest son will celebrate his bar mitzvah. I would like to dedicate the *sefer Torah* on that day. If you can guarantee that it will be ready by then, that's okay with me. I belong to a very large shul in America, and a *sefer Torah* written by a scribe of your caliber will truly be appreciated."

"Father was not surprised," continued Leibel's son. "What was designated for him he received. He tried a little, and Hashem helped. 'I'll be here in Eretz Yisrael toward the end of the year again,' said the wealthy man as he left. 'I'll bring another fifteen thousand dollars with me on my next visit.'

"This happened at eleven o'clock at night, just after my father's learning session with Shachna. The following morning, Abba rose as usual, at the hour he'd by now grown accustomed to. At 1:00 P.M., he got up from his work. He studied with his afternoon *chavrusa*, learned with my little brother, and met with Shachna in the evening. In short, nothing changed; his routine continued uninterrupted, steady as always."

Chance Meetings

A S A FUNDRAISER for an important and worthy cause, I am often privileged to witness incredible examples of *hashgachah pratis*. On a recent trip to the United States, I constantly saw the Hand of Hashem guiding my steps. Here are but two examples of this continuous supervision.

As soon as I arrived in New York, I made an appointment to meet with a well-known philanthropist who lives in Flatbush — a section of Brooklyn about an hour's subway ride from where I was staying in Manhattan. The day before the scheduled appointment, the philanthropist phoned and left a message on the answering machine in the apartment, saying that some urgent business forced him to cancel our meeting. I do not know why, but I did not listen to my telephone messages that morning as I usually do, and I set out for Flatbush ignorant of the cancelation.

When I arrived at the man's home after a long ride on the subway, his secretary told me that the appointment had been canceled and I had come that long way in vain. Naturally disappointed, I left his home and began walking along the streets of Flatbush with no special destination in mind.

As I walked along, I met an acquaintance and stopped to talk with him. That conversation turned out to be a turning point in my visit. Had I listened to the recorded message that morning and stayed in Manhattan that day, I never would have received the valuable information I heard during that chance encounter in Flatbush. (Though no doubt ha-Kadosh Baruch Hu would have arranged for the information to reach my ears in some other wondrous way if He wanted me to hear it.)

Another such incident had occurred even before I left Eretz Yisrael. I had gone to the cemetery at Har ha-Menuchos in Jerusalem to pray at the grave of the Belzer Rebbe, zt"l, for the success of my trip. I also visited the graves of my parents, who are buried nearby. As I passed by a prominent, commemorative stone standing in a section off to the side, I felt an inexplicable urge to see what was engraved on the stone. It was the grave of ha-Rav Reuven Yosef Kadmonstein, av beis din of Maon Kodesh in Jerusalem.

It was a name I recognized. Rav Kadmonstein had been a well-known personage in Jerusalem before his passing. I lit a candle, picked up a small stone lying nearby, and placed it on the stone over the grave, according to custom. Then I recited some Tehillim beside the grave. No prayer is ever said in vain. Every prayer accomplishes something, every prayer has the potential to bring about the fulfillment of a request.

I went home to prepare for my trip. While I was packing that night, a neighbor came by and asked if I would take a package of books with me to the United States. He had recently published a biography of the late, renowned mashgiach of Yeshivas Toras Chaim in America, and he wanted me to take a few copies of the book to show the people I would meet abroad. I agreed to do it for him as a personal favor, even though I had not intended to spend my time in America marketing books.

After a hectic day of last-minute errands, I finally sat down in my assigned seat on the plane and breathed a sigh of relief. I sat there...and sat there. For some reason the plane was not taking off. Its doors were still open.

Finally a passenger came huffing and puffing onto the plane

and hurried to his seat — which just "happened" to be the empty one next to mine. Throwing his things into the overhead storage compartment, he sat down and tried to catch his breath. The doors closed, and the plane began taxiing down the runway.

"It's a miracle I caught the plane," the latecomer said to me. "I was late getting to the airport, and I was sure I had missed my flight. In fact, when I reached the check-in counter there was no one there but the airline workers. One of them told me that if I hurried I might catch the plane because it had been delayed a few minutes for technical reasons. It seems as if the technical problems were arranged just so that I would not miss my flight."

My seat companion explained that he traveled to the United States frequently and knew many people in the different religious communities there. When he introduced himself as Tuvia Kadmonstein, I was taken aback. "Was your father by any chance the Rav Kadmonstein associated with Maon Kodesh?" I asked. He was.

"Less than twenty-four hours ago," I marveled, "I lit a candle and recited *Tehillim* at your father's grave!" I told him of my visit to Har ha-Menuchos the day before and the inexplicable impulse that had led me to pray at his father's grave. Tuvia was overcome by emotion and could hardly speak.

Although we had never met before, we both felt that a warm bond had been forged between us. In appreciation, Tuvia gave me much helpful advice about fundraising in the United States, a subject in which he was knowledgeable.

Near the end of our flight, I took out a copy of my neighbor's book about the *mashgiach* of Yeshivas Toras Chaim and leafed through it. Tuvia asked me what I was reading and looked at the cover with interest. He said he knew some affluent people who proudly claimed to be students of the *mashgiach*.

"They will surely be thrilled to know about this book," Tuvia said, and he gave me their names and addresses. I could hardly believe my good fortune in being provided with an instant key to the hearts of some prospective donors.

My mission was more successful than I could have hoped. My

"chance" meeting with Tuvia Kadmonstein after my "chance" visit to his father's grave were directly responsible for the success of my venture.

When I repeated this story to some friends, one of their children asked me if I would go back to Har ha-Menuchos and pray at someone's grave before my next fundraising trip.

"No," I answered. "People, books, graves — whatever we think is associated with our good fortune — are merely messengers. Neither things nor people determine the success of our undertakings. Hashem causes His blessings to be delivered by His emissaries. The Ribbono shel Olam plans our every step and directs our destiny."

Work Ethics

MENASHE AND NACHMAN, both in their early forties, are good friends, and work together in the same branch of Microwagon, a large firm with offices all over Israel. Nachman's father, z"l, held a senior position in the company for many years. Upon his retirement, he helped his son land a job with the prestigious firm.

After a number of years at Microwagon, Nachman recommended his friend Menashe, who was duly hired. The two have been working together for fifteen years now, and both are very successful in their work. The company manufactures an excellent product that is sold all over the world. As company employees, Menashe and Nachman reap the benefits of the firm's success.

When Nachman, and Menashe in turn, first joined the company, it was managed by an observant Jew. At a certain point, however, the company was sold to a businessman named Jay Ellicant. Menashe and Nachman quickly learned two things: one, that Ellicant was completely nonreligious; and two, that he was a nice man who treated them just as kindly and fairly as he did all his other (nonreligious) employees. Ellicant acknowledged and appreciated his employees' integrity, accuracy, and work ethics. He never initiated debates or arguments over issues concerning religion or the sort of life a Jew ought to lead.

The trouble began when an outdoor musical performance was scheduled to be held in an arena in the heart of Tel Aviv and a large advertisement campaign was initiated to publicize it. Such an event inevitably involves a large measure of *chillul Hashem* and more than a little lack of *kevod ha-Torah*. The sponsor of the ignominious event was to be none other than the Microwagon firm. Menashe and Nachman felt uneasy about the whole thing, but they decided that for the time being they would not get involved.

It wasn't long before a great storm of protest broke out. Many of the most prominent rabbis in Israel cried out against the looming disaster, doing everything in their power to minimize the extent of the *chillul Hashem*. They enlisted the help of community leaders, rabbis, and Knesset members, asking anyone with even a little bit of clout to speak to the organizers of the event.

Ordinary people worry only about their daily concerns such as making a living and their family problems, but the giants of our generation feel the pain of the *Shechinah* in exile. The *gedolim* instructed the religious community to concentrate all their efforts on preventing the large-scale desecration of Hashem's Name. The community's protest received a lot of publicity. The event and the opposition to it became *the* topic of the day.

Microwagon had many clients among the Orthodox community. These manufacturers immediately informed Mr. Ellicant that they would not continue to purchase his product as long as he was the sponsor of such an offensive event. Nachman and Menashe, as employees of Microwagon, also came under attack.

The organizers of the huge event remained indifferent to the impassioned pleas of the Orthodox public. Much hard work had already gone into it, and they said there was no way they would consider making any changes in the program.

The delegation of religious leaders therefore decided to tackle the problem from a different angle. They asked for an appointment with the sponsor. Mr. Ellicant thought he should first have a word with his loyal employees, Menashe and Nachman. Perhaps they would be able to explain to him what the rabbis wanted.

Menashe and Nachman were taken aback when their boss called them into his office to discuss the situation. The meeting with Mr. Ellicant put them in a tight spot — they now had no choice but to clearly and firmly tell Mr. Ellicant to his face how they felt about the event, even though it might jeopardize their jobs.

As the older of the two, Menashe was the first to respond. "Although it's true that we work under one roof and there is certainly no dispute between us," he began, his heart pleading with Heaven to put the right words in his mouth, "you must know that we live in two entirely different worlds.

"In your eyes, Mr. Ellicant, the most important thing at the moment is to advertise the name of our company. In your world, an opportunity to put Microwagon on center stage is a goal that probably justifies any means.

"For us, however, there are other goals in life. True, we've been earning our livelihood in this office for many years, but as you may remember, when you considered keeping the factory open on Shabbos, both Nachman and I stated unequivocally that we would not be able to continue working in the office if you would do so.

"You see, although earning a living is very important to us, it is not something we would pay *any* price for. As important as Microwagon's success and growth is to all of us, there are some things that have to come first. In that case, it was Shabbos. That is my response in this case, too."

"Do you mean to say that if you were in my place, you would let such a great advertising opportunity slip through your fingers just because some rabbis do not approve of the event you are sponsoring?" asked Mr. Ellicant.

"I would do so," replied Menashe, "not because it doesn't find favor in the eyes of the rabbis, but because it doesn't find favor in the eyes of the King of kings, in Whom I believe with all my heart and soul. The rabbis are simply obeying His word."

"Well, I think that no man has the right to tell anyone else how to run his affairs or to prevent him from getting ahead. Why shouldn't I sponsor the performance? If some people do not agree, they do not have to attend. So why the fuss?"

"Let me try to explain," Menashe said. "If your brother were to make an unintentionally disparaging remark in public about your father, wouldn't you want to defend your father's honor and persuade your brother to think twice before he speaks? You see, these men feel true anguish at the thought of such a large-scale defamation of holy things. They feel they must protest their brothers' unwitting humiliation of our good and benevolent Father, Who is always so kind to us all."

Ellicant was not convinced. In fact, he had by now adopted a fairly hostile, defensive stance.

Menashe had hoped to discuss the issue calmly with Mr. Ellicant and explain his point of view, but he saw that his boss was beginning to regard him as an enemy. I suppose I had better say no more and avoid more arguments, he thought to himself. The two workers left the office.

Nachman reproved Menashe for having argued with Mr. Ellicant. "Of course, there's no way we can support his decision," he maintained, "but you should have evaded the issue somehow. After all, we're not trying to get him to change his way of life. The important thing is to preserve the pleasant relationship we've always enjoyed with him."

Menashe disagreed. "What's *most* important is that I do everything in my power to prevent him from causing a *chillul Hashem*, even at the risk of ruining our good relationship. I'm not ashamed of my belief in Hashem; I'm proud of it, and I like to say so out loud. If Mr. Ellicant sees that even an ordinary Orthodox Jew supports the decisions of our great rabbis, he is bound to change his opinion about this."

The men returned to work. Menashe was distressed more by the fact that Nachman disagreed with the way he had handled the situation, than by his disagreement with Mr. Ellicant.

After his conversation with Nachman and Menashe, Mr. Ellicant refused to meet with the delegation. The rabbis contacted the two employees, and asked them to speak to their boss. Of course, they said the subject had already been raised and Mr. Ellicant was determined to sponsor the event.

The next day, a well-known rabbi called Menashe and suggested that it would be helpful to the cause if he and his friend were to place a notice in the newspapers. They should disclaim their connection to the sponsorship of the event and decry the large-scale desecration of Hashem's Name sure to occur. In his opinion, the rabbi said, it was necessary to counter the media reports that "even Microwagon's religious employees" were supporting the event.

Menashe decided to inform his boss before placing the notice, in the hope that he would withdraw his sponsorship. Ellicant's reply was terse: "Such a step is unacceptable. My decision to sponsor the event is final."

Nachman was afraid to go ahead with their announcement. "We will surely be fired," he fretted. "How can we cut off the branch we are sitting on?"

Menashe, no less concerned about the loss of his job, attempted to explain to Nachman (and to himself as well) the reasons to go ahead. "The branch we are sitting on is not held up by Microwagon. Our support is from Heaven. If the *gedolim* have instructed us to announce our opposition, we must heed their words."

"But I have worked here so many years, and my father before me. I am afraid to do something I will live to regret," Nachman replied.

The two argued for a long time but Nachman remained reluctant. Menashe felt that Nachman's agreement was essential. Finally, he came up with a suggestion.

"Let's go ask the Rav!"

"But the great man cares only about avoiding *chillul Hashem*," Nachman hedged. "He is not concerned about my source of livelihood. What if he says we must go ahead and place the ad? And what if, as a result, we do indeed get fired?"

"Then we'll lose our jobs for the sake of Heaven," declared Menashe resolutely. "All the newspapers will report that Ellicant's Orthodox employees preferred to risk their jobs rather than continue working for a firm that suppports *chillul Hashem*."

They rode to the Rav's house together. Two friends, two hearts. Two hearts? *Yisrael ein lahem ela lev echad le'Avihem she'ba-Shamayim*, "The people of Israel have but one heart, and that belongs to their Father in Heaven" — except that the *yetzer ha-ra* had taken residence in Nachman's heart, pestering him with a host of troublesome questions and doubts.

The Rav received them warmly. He asked them to be seated and sat down opposite them to hear about their problem. The Rav inquired about Nachman's family and other matters not pertaining to his livelihood. Finally, the Rav said that for the sake of Hashem's honor, it was imperative that they publicly declare their opposition to their company's sponsorship of such a disgraceful event.

"It is important that we grant God's will at least as much consideration as we grant our own interests and desires," said the Rav. "If a *chillul Hashem* comes from the firm for which you work, there is no way Hashem's blessing will rest upon it. Even if business continues to boom, a devout Jew has no interest in taking part in success achieved through such means. You ask about the future. Hashem will surely not abandon you."

The next day, their notice appeared in all the major newspapers, clearly stating their opposition to company policy on this issue.

When Mr. Ellicant arrived at work that morning, he stopped at Menashe's desk. Nachman was there too. He looked them in the eye and said, "Let me be frank. I've never encountered such a problem with any of my employees, and I don't intend to ever have such trouble again. There is no way I can overlook this."

"We are truly sorry it came to this," said Menashe, "but we had no choice. We, too, felt we could not overlook it." They parted in silence. There was nothing else to say.

Nachman and Menashe simply did not show up the next day for work, nor the day after. It was soon widely known that Microwagon's two Orthodox employees had left their jobs in order not to be counted among those who profane the Name of Heaven. The ripples of this *kiddush Hashem* spread far and wide.

That same week, it occurred to Mr. Ellicant that he might be accused of firing his employees for religious differences, but he really had no objections to their continuing to work for him. He therefore sent a letter to Menashe and Nachman, stating that he had not fired them and would like them to return to work. "After all," read the letter, "we have worked together for so many years, I am sure we can agree upon a new code of work ethics."

"Dear Sir," Menashe responded immediately, "although we hold you in great esteem, we honor our Creator more. We cannot in conscience return to work for you unless you publicly state your regret at having sponsored such an indecorous event.

"We thank you for your fairness, and we hope you will open your eyes and recognize your own intrinsic worth as a Jew. There are some things a Jew simply does not do, neither for honor nor for money."

Such a media furor ensued that an international business magazine featured an article about what had happened. The writer obviously took an irreligious stance in describing the opposition to the public performance and made much of the fact that it took place in spite of all the opposition. He even mentioned the two religious workers who had resigned rather than support their employer's position against a rabbinical ruling. He quoted the employer's words: "We had many nice years together, but work ethics are ethics, too, and one cannot make light of them, not even during a period of difficulty."

Nachman commented bitterly, "Who will ever hire us after such adverse publicity?"

Once again, Menashe acted as a voice of reason, calming Nachman's fears: "It wasn't Mr. Ellicant who provided us with our livelihood in the past; it's not any potential boss who will provide it in the future. Ha-Kadosh Baruch Hu is the only One Who stipulates how much we earn. If it is His will, then we will both find excellent jobs. Let us cast our burdens upon Him, and He will surely provide for us. No one can prevent us from receiving what is destined for us in Heaven."

A visitor to Eretz Israel from England "happened" to see the article in the business magazine. He was perusing its job-wanted ads, for he wanted to hire local staff to manage his business in Israel. He was particularly interested in finding a couple of honest, trustworthy, experienced men to hire as co-managers. He was due to return to England in two days' time, but still hadn't found anyone to run his business for him.

Leafing through the magazine in his hotel room, he came across the article about Microwagon's sponsorship of a huge musical extravaganza that had taken place recently, and he was most interested in the writer's quote about ethics.

He had no trouble tracing the phone numbers of Nachman and Menashe. He phoned Nachman, introduced himself, and made an appointment to meet with him and his friend regarding a business proposition. The interview resulted in the offer of jobs to both men. The Englishman wanted two responsible workers, and Menashe insisted on a contract that stipulated that the business would not infringe or cause them to infringe on any halachah or rabbinical ruling. The Englishman agreed, and the contract, including the stipulation, was duly signed.

Nachman could hardly believe their good fortune: a handsome salary, more than he had earned at Microwagon, and the astounding *hashgachah* surrounding the events. One thing puzzled him, however. How did the Englishman hear about them?

"I happened to read about what transpired between you and your former company, Microwagon," he said. "What really impressed me about the whole episode was the way your boss, who ought to have been your staunchest enemy, spoke openly about the many good years you put in working for him. He said you had a strong set of work ethics that he could not make light of, even during a difficult time for his company. Well, 'work ethics' was just about the most important thing I was looking for in an employee, and that is not such an easy thing to find."

Menashe and Nachman were astonished. That is not what Mr. Ellicant had said! They had read the magazine article themselves, and they had thought their boss's words had been hostile and disparaging. "We had many nice years together," Mr. Ellicant had supposedly said, "but work ethics are ethics, too, and one cannot make light of them, not even during a period of difficulty."

They interpreted Mr. Ellicant's words as meaning that despite the fact that they had had many nice years together, he was disappointed that his employees had made light of work ethics, which, in his opinion, ought to be honored even during times of difficulty. The English businessman had understood that Ellicant was admitting that, even during a difficult time for his company, he could not make light of the fact that his workers had always had a fine set of work ethics.

"Do you see?" Menashe asked Nachman. "The branches we're sitting on have nothing to do with either Ellicant or Microwagon. We're sitting on branches supported by Heaven. If we cut one branch, we'll land on another."

"The *gedolei ha-dor* issue their instructions according to *da'as Torah*," Nachman said with newfound conviction, "but the ordinary Jew sometimes thinks he knows better. After all, he's the one in business while the Rav sits and studies in the *beis midrash*. With his limited mind, he cannot grasp how it is that the Rav can issue rulings related to business matters, and he does not know that his only chance for success depends upon having the blessing of Torah on his work."

Fired? So What?

IRED. "Whoever understands the complete meaning of the word," Shia says, "can understand how I felt that day. Unease, humiliation, anger, but more than anything, concern for the future. How would I live from now on?"

Shia was an excellent teacher in a *cheder*. For reasons unknown to him, he was given notice at the end of the school year that he would not be on the staff any longer. Shia was shocked. His heart was broken, and he found it difficult to look people in the eye. One day he had a class full of happy children to teach, and the next day he was unemployed.

Just as he was feeling he had reached the lowest point in his life, he met his good friend Moshe. Moshe perceived his downcast state, and inquired with concern about the cause of it. Miserably, Shia told him he had just been fired.

"So," said Moshe in response, "your faucet was removed, and you are about to have a new one installed."

"What did you say?" Shia asked. "Are you offering me a job as a plumber?"

Moshe smiled at Shia's confusion and told him the following story.

A simple fellow from the provinces once went to visit a friend who had become a wealthy man and now lived in the city. In those days, most people drew their water from the neighborhood well. Not too many people had installed plumbing in their homes, and a faucet, through which water flowed directly into one's kitchen, was an unknown device. No one else in the city, as a matter of fact, except the rich man in our story, had such a magical contraption in his home.

The simple man was speechless with wonder when his friend, the rich man, demonstrated how the faucet worked. Unbelievable! With his own eyes he saw how a twist of the round handle on the wall caused a gush of water to come pouring out of a long, narrow tube of metal underneath it.

"Do you mean to tell me that you don't have to go to the well to draw water anymore?" the countryman asked. "No more buckets and ropes? Just like that, you can have as much water as you want, coming directly into your own house?"

He left the rich man's house determined to do whatever it took to acquire just such a faucet for his own home in the country. It would be the wonder of the whole town! He sold some of his possessions, pawned a few others, and borrowed money from friends and acquaintances. He traveled to an even larger city, sought out a metalwork shop, and with shining eyes purchased a faucet with a tap above it, just as he had seen in the rich man's house. What a pleasure! As soon as he got home, he would place his newly ac-

quired treasure on the kitchen shelf, turn the knob and then, wonder of wonders, he would have running water right in his own
home.

When he arrived home, the simple countryman invited all his
friends and neighbors to come and see the magical device he had
acquired. "My dear friends," he announced to the impressive as-
semblage, "I have good news for all of you. I hereby declare an end
to sore backs from carrying heavy buckets, and blisters from pulling
on ropes. From now on, we need not even worry about the amount
of rainfall."

He paused for a moment to let the full import of his words sink
in. Then, dramatically raising the faucet in his hand for everyone to
see, he explained, "This piece of metal is a faucet, and it signifies the
end of all our troubles. I shall now place this wonderful device here
on my table and turn the handle. You will then see a stream of water gush out before your very eyes."

Everyone instinctively stepped back. After all, nobody wanted
to get soaked. The water carriers trembled in fear of losing their
livelihood, but they too waited eagerly to see an abundance of water flow from their friend's contraption.

The countryman placed a large basin under the strange-looking
"faucet" to collect the flood of water he expected to flow forth. Oh
yes, he was wise enough to be careful with this wonderful tool; he
didn't want the water damaging his furniture.

With a great flourish, the ignoramus began turning the knob.
He turned it faster and faster until it could turn no more. Nothing
happened. He tried turning the second knob. Nothing happened.
Angry now, he forcefully twisted both knobs in both directions
again and again. He banged the faucet with his fist, but not a drop
of water came out.

The villagers were acutely disappointed and began to murmur.
"What kind of a joke is this? Are you trying to make fools out of us?
Do you think we have nothing better to do than stand here watching you play with a bent pipe?" They stomped out of his house in
anger, made their way to the local well, and drank thirstily before
going about their business.

"Ha, ha!" laughed the man at the metalwork shop when the ignorant countryman came to complain about the defective merchandise. "Did you really expect water to flow from this faucet? It's just a hollow pipe."

"But I saw just such a pipe in my friend's house," wailed the simple man, "and I saw with my own eyes how a stream of water gushed out."

"The water is coming from the reservoir," explained the metal worker. "A faucet has to be connected to a source of water by pipes that bring the water from the source. Then, when you turn the knob on the faucet, the water will run in your house. A faucet is no good without a source of water."

"So it is with *parnasah*," said Moshe. "One's livelihood comes from Heaven. Your job is to connect the faucet. Why are you so glum?" he asked Shia. "Is it because your faucet was disconnected? That's not the worst thing in the world. You have to remember that you only lost your job, not the Source of your livelihood. Ha-Kadosh Baruch Hu will find a way to send what is coming to you. He will send you a different source of water to which you can connect your faucet."

And that is what happened to Shia. He found a new reservoir of water for his faucet. "*Baruch Hashem*," he says, "I make a comfortable living, and I never forget that it isn't the faucet that provides me with water, but the Source Above."

Jobs Do Not Grow on Trees

I HAVE BEEN WORKING as a highway engineer for many years. At first, I was employed by one of the largest engineering companies in Israel, and, thank God, I was very successful in my work. From time to time, it occurred to me that I might do well to open my own private engineering company, but I was hesitant to take such a bold step.

Of course, the potential earnings for an independent engineer were far greater than those of an employee. However, there was also a risk involved. What if I would not get any jobs? I must note that in my chosen career as a highway engineer, jobs do not grow on trees, as the saying goes. You have to develop connections with the right people. I feared I did not have the necessary connections to bring me potential customers, so it seemed unrealistic to break off and start out on my own, tempting as the prospect might have seemed.

About sixteen years ago, the volume of work in the office I had worked in for so many years began steadily decreasing. Hardly any new orders were coming in. It is a fact of life that every so often promising new engineering companies spring up and take over the market, leaving the older companies no choice but to submit to the way of the world. The office I worked in faced reality and began to fold. One by one, all the employees received notification that their services were no longer required.

I too received such a notice. One day, my boss called me aside. He thanked me warmly for the many wonderful years we had worked together. He then sadly informed me that the office was about to close, and I would therefore be forced to leave. He handed me a check for my final month's wages, and ended our meeting with a firm handshake and best wishes for the future.

Against my will, I suddenly found myself self-employed. I was deeply worried.

Check in hand, I returned to my office. Placing the check in my briefcase, I began to empty my desk. I cleaned out my drawers, disposing of various unimportant scraps of paper and placing pencils, pens, and erasers on the manager's desk. Next I cleared the shelves, and my office soon appeared empty and barren, a reflection of the way I felt.

Nevertheless, I sat in my chair until four o'clock in the afternoon, the end of the usual workday, as if someone would have docked my salary for leaving earlier. I stared out the window and then up at the ceiling, where a lone spider wove its threads. Finally, I rose and left my office, locking the door behind me. I went out onto the busy street, where everyone except me seemed to be going somewhere purposefully. Intending to deposit my check, I walked slowly down Ibn Gavirol Street toward the bank where I kept my account. Just ahead of me, I spotted a group of elderly retirees strolling leisurely down the street, probably heading to the local health clinic. I caught up with them and paced alongside, feeling we had much in common. I passed a row of public telephones and paused for a moment. I felt like phoning someone, but I couldn't think who.

As I approached the bank, I opened my briefcase to take out the check. I couldn't find it! I riffled through the contents of my briefcase, opened one zipper after another, checked all the pockets — in vain. The check was gone! I clearly remembered having placed it in my briefcase, but it just wasn't there now.

I turned around and made my way back down the street in an even blacker mood than before. At least this gave me something to do, I thought bitterly.

I reached the building I thought I had left forever. I went upstairs to what had once been my office, entered what had once been my room, and approached what had once been my desk. I opened drawer after drawer, searching for the check, but they were all empty.

I now turned my attention to my briefcase to give it a more thorough search than I had been able to do on the street. I dumped its contents on my desk and searched every compartment, going through every scrap of paper. Oh! There it was, in plain view, right on top of everything else. I glanced up. The spider was still there, mocking me.

What a ridiculous situation! I had walked the entire length of Ibn Gavirol Street twice, only to find the check exactly where it was supposed to be — in my briefcase. A scornful voice inside me taunted, "You're doing rather well as an self-employed engineer, aren't you?"

Where to now? The bank, of course. I put the check in my pocket, closed my briefcase, and set off once again.

On my way out, I noticed an acquaintance talking on a public telephone. He motioned for me to stop and wait until he finished his call. I was in no particular hurry, so I stopped and leaned against the wall. The cardboard figure propped up next to the Lotto booth smiled at me. "Laugh all the way to the bank," read the caption. What a joke!

"What a coincidence that you just passed by," my friend said as he hung up the phone. "A friend of mine, the owner of a large business, called me yesterday to ask if I know a good engineer whom he could trust with a big project he wants to undertake. At the time I just couldn't think of anyone, but as you passed just now I remembered that you're an engineer. Would you be able to take on an engineering project now?"

Dear God in Heaven, I whispered, my various thoughts whirling through my brain as my heart pounded furiously, I did not remember You in my pain, and yet here You are, openly revealing Your Presence. My friend couldn't think of anyone to recommend. He suddenly saw me…just like that. Ribbono shel Olam, it was You Who hid that check from me, You Who sent me back to the office to look for it, You Who made sure I passed by the public telephones just as my friend stopped to make a phone call.

"Yes," I told my friend, "I am interested in undertaking such a project."

I was ashamed that I had allowed myself to sink into such a state of depression during the past few hours. Had I actually been so foolish as to think the job I had held until now was the only way I might earn a living, and that without it I would have no income? How could I have forgotten just Who is the Main Supervisor in charge of all jobs, the One Who could take away one job and send another in its stead?

I felt like the fool who, upon finding the ATM machine at the bank temporarily out of order, bangs his head against the wall and wails in anguish over the money he has lost. Imbecile! I would tell him. What are you crying about? Go into the bank and withdraw as much money as you want! And if the bank is closed, well, tomorrow it will be open. Your money is ready and waiting for you inside. If you can't take it out today, you'll get it tomorrow. The broken ATM machine doesn't signify the loss of your fortune.

My reaction to the loss of my job was similar. Accustomed as I was to receiving a regular salary from one employer for so many years, I was devastated when it was taken from me. I fell prey to feelings of helplessness, and sank into a black mood.

But why should I have been so sad? Whatever was prepared for me was ready. Whatever Heaven had decreed for me I would get. The bank was closed today? It would be open tomorrow!

A broken teller machine does not necessarily mean that I have no more money.

A mere couple of hours after I lost one job, I had a new one. It was decided in Heaven that I experience a brief period of heartbreak and worry in the form of a seemingly pointless stroll on Ibn Gavirol Street. Just when it seemed my situation could not possibly get any bleaker, salvation came. The apparent loss of my check caused me to pass that public telephone just in time to meet Hashem's messenger.

That was my first project as an independent engineer, and it helped me jump-start the business I have been running for the past fifteen years. All the time I had worked for someone else, I had been dreaming of breaking off and starting out on my own, but I had been afraid to do so. Heaven took away my job and thereby helped me become independent.

This incident taught me a guiding rule in life: Hashem gives and Hashem takes. Man must not rely on any one thing as if his living depends on that alone. It is not one's job that provides one with a living — it is Hashem. *Hu notein lechem le-chol basar...*, "He gives bread to all flesh, for His mercy is eternal and in His great goodness nothing has ever been lacking nor will it be." Sometimes a person finds himself switching one type of income for another. Heaven moves him along in any case, but isn't it a shame to wallow in feelings of self-pity in the interim?

That's Life, My Friend

WHEN I WAS ENGAGED, I once got a ride home from a family wedding with a cousin who had been working as an insurance agent for two years. We got to talking, and he related that he had joined the Rimini Insurance Agency shortly after his wedding. He bought a car, learned the job, and immediately threw himself into selling Rimini's insurance plans.

From the course of our conversation, I understood that he was devoting endless hours to the job. He left the house early in the morning and returned late at night. His employer prepared a packed schedule for him each day, dispatching him to meetings and conferences all over Israel. This hectic schedule never slacked off. He was on the road two hours after Shabbos, and returned home just barely two hours before the next Shabbos. He dominated our conversation, speaking of bonuses, premiums and profits, of cost-analysis and coverage, of marketing and expenses.

"What are you aiming for?" I asked. "What is it you want to achieve? What is the point of all this nonstop hard work?"

"My goal," he responded loftily, "is to conquer the world with attractive insurance plans. We have heavy competition from other insurance companies. In order to succeed, we need to sign up thousands — no, tens of thousands — of people. My job as an agent is to sell the plans to as many people as possible, to open file after file, to recruit customers in every town and city in Israel. In order to do this, I must visit hundreds of homes all over the country. The profits, in the end, benefit everybody."

Inexperienced as I was, I still didn't get it. "Listen," I objected, "you are telling me all about Rimini's profits, its goals and its aims. What I want to know is, what do *you* get out of all this? What are you sacrificing your life for?"

"What do *I* get out of it?" my cousin echoed. "Why, every policy I sell affords me a nice monthly percentage. For each fifty insurance policies I sell, I go up a grade in prestige and earnings. And the more policies I sell, the higher the percentage I earn on any policies

I sell in the future."

"Ah," I said, "I'm beginning to understand. Your interest in their business is due to *your* profits. Rimini's success doesn't really interest you as much as your own monthly salary, is that right?"

"Well, of course." My cousin sounded impatient and annoyed. "The whole point is the potential for profit. Do you think it's such a simple matter? Agents who work hard and do well receive a steady monthly check of five figures. It's not really a salary; it's the percentages earned from policies sold. If I succeed in recruiting additional agents for the company, I get a percentage of the policies *they* sell, too. That way I can scale the pyramid and receive percentages from work done by those under me. To sum it all up, insurance is a field that offers great potential for serious profits."

"How much are you earning per month right now?" I asked. I was still a *bachur*; I was unaware that this wasn't really a socially acceptable question. My cousin, however, did not seem to mind, and responded readily. (Perhaps he was hoping to recruit me as an insurance agent.) "Three thousand shekels," he said, somewhat apologetically. "But that's a beginner's salary," he hurried to add. "After all, I've only been working for two years now. I hope to be getting a raise shortly."

Compared to the average *kollel* stipend, I thought three thousand shekels a month was a rather handsome salary, especially in light of the fact that my cousin was a young man with only one child. His wife also had a job. I therefore could not understand why he was driving himself so hard. "What is your end goal?" I asked foolishly. "How high a salary are you aiming for?"

"How high a salary?" he asked incredulously and laughed. "The higher the better. I want to earn big, to climb ever higher, to get all the benefits. I want to *earn*, my friend, to earn and earn."

I didn't let up. I truly wanted to understand. "But how much do you need to earn? At what point do you stop?"

"First of all, I want to live well, in comfort and style. I want to have an easy and pleasant life. True, I do live well right now. If I were to take only the present into account, I suppose I would continue working on a low flame. I'd work normal hours. But I'm looking beyond the present; I need to invest now for the future. I want to marry off my children in style, without having to go into debt. Maybe I'll be able to leave Ashdod and buy my own apartment in Jerusalem. If I have money, I'll be able to invest it and purchase property. In short, I want to ensure that I'll always have a comfortable salary and live well."

"In other words," I said, "you are burning on the front burner now for the sake of your future. You earn enough to live comfortably, but you spend your days on the road. You are not at ease, you are never home, you do not really 'live' now, because you want to live well in the future."

My cousin was hurt. "Why do you say I'm not really living now? I'm being very logical. Instead of taking it easy today and getting stuck on a salary of three thousand shekels, I'm mature enough to think about the future. Why do you say that is not living?"

"I always thought," I explained, "that living means enjoying life, living calmly. Being home with your family, having time to do all the things you would really like to do. Forgive me, but returning home two hours before Shabbos and running out again two hours after Shabbos — what kind of a life is that? That's not really living.

"We are on our way home from a family wedding. If you would really be living, you would have allowed yourself to enjoy the company of your family, rejoice with your uncle, the father of the bride, sit comfortably at the meal, and stay for the dancing. But you showed up for the last half hour, said 'Mazal tov' to everyone as required, and left immediately. What kind of life is that?"

"That's life, my friend," my cousin said resolutely. "That's how it is when you are in business. I think I am living very well. I chose this way of life, and I have a goal: to earn more and more. That is why I live the way I do. You think I'm burning too high a flame now; I feel I'd be 'burning' my future if I didn't live this way now. I would not be able to marry off children on a salary of three thousand shekels a month. If I rest on my laurels today, if I dance at weddings and enjoy catered meals in the company of my family, the day will come when I will be saddled with debts. Today I work like a horse, but I will be able to live well in the future."

I respected his opinion. After all, I was an inexperienced *bachur* and he was already the father of a child. I was not yet earning a livelihood, and he was an insurance agent with the prestigious Rimini agency. However, I disagreed with him on one thing. He said, "That's life," while I thought to myself, *That's no life*. The present is too precious to fritter away on nebulous plans for the future. I would rather live on a low standard — with a salary that allows me to get by — with peace of mind, than work day and night in a frenzied effort to reach that great day when I might be able to afford an apartment in Jerusalem and whatever else I imagine goes with it.

At the time, I did not have enough self-confidence to be sure I was right. Deep in my heart I could not accept his theory, but I knew I was as yet untested. It was just a few months before my marriage, and the topic of livelihood interested me greatly. I sought someone I respected with whom I could talk the matter over. I decided to discuss my thoughts with our mutual grandfather, a simple but most intelligent Jew.

Saba himself had worked throughout his life, and was in fact still doing some part-time work. However, he worked limited hours and kept to an organized schedule. He designated a certain number of hours a day for Torah study and never deviated from it. He always appeared calm and unhurried. The next time I visited my grandfather, I described the life a "friend" of mine was living, and asked him what he thought about it.

"What is he talking about?" Saba asked angrily. "Why is he pushing himself so hard? For the future? I wish him a long, healthy life, but who promised him he would reach the future? How can a Jew allow himself to say, 'I'm working today so that I'll have an easy life twenty years from now'? Did the prophet Eliyahu reveal himself to this friend of yours and guarantee him another twenty years of life? Can anyone be certain that if he works hard today he will surely have it easy twenty years from now? How can anyone dare presume he knows what might occur during the next twenty years?"

"But most people do live that long," I ventured to say.

"Yes, that's true. It is always sensible to have some sort of savings plan for the future, if possible. I'm not denying that, but one should not ruin his life to do it. These are years in which you will be, *b'ezras Hashem*, raising a family. When, if not now, will you be a father to your children and a husband to your wife? You will arrive at your life in another twenty years and discover you haven't got a life at all."

My grandfather was indignant at the idea, but tried to maintain his level tone of voice. "Do you think that when he reaches the peak he is aiming for now, he will stop? Does he truly believe that when his salary reaches twenty thousand shekels a month he will slacken off and go to the *beis midrash* to study the *daf yomi*? I doubt it. He will probably be so accustomed to a whirlwind lifestyle that he will find he is incapable of relaxing his grip for even a moment. He is not only burning his present; he is burning his whole life. Some people sacrifice their lives in order to live well at some point in the future, only to find they never get to live at all. Why is it these people do not stop to consider that if a calm, enjoyable life is so wonderful, it might be worth living that way right now?

"The future? Marrying off children? Yes, it is a concern, but Hashem helps. Look, my beard is already white, and I've merited to marry off all my children. The same God Who sees to it that you have three thousand shekels a month when that is all you need sees to it that you will have more if you need it in later years. But there's nothing more pointless than living such a harried, frenzied life. Your friend does not enjoy the three thousand shekels he is earning right now because he is too busy preparing for what he will need later. A Jew does not live that way.

"You are right," Saba told me. "You are one hundred percent right. It's important to live right now. If you live right today, you will live right in the future too, with God's help. Hashem will send you an honorable livelihood. Do whatever you need to do in order to live a good life today. Think about yourself, your home, your family. Leave all worries about your future needs to ha-Kadosh Baruch Hu, Who will always see to your present needs.

"Remember what Reb Eliezer ha-Gadol said: 'Whoever has what he needs now and says, "What shall I eat tomorrow?" is lacking in *emunah'* [*Sotah* 48b].

"Listen to me," Saba concluded. "I have experience in these matters. I have seen many people toil and struggle in order to put aside a nest egg for the future, but they never lived a life. There were those who did not live long enough, and there were others who merited long lives, *baruch Hashem*, but what kind of lives did they live? Maybe they did have fat wallets, but their hearts were as dry as tinder wood. They had no time for emotions or feelings; they were automatons, work machines. By contrast, I know many a man who made do on a skimpy salary but enjoyed every minute of his life. Sensitive people with good hearts, sterling character traits, people who found sweetness in a page of Gemara, in a Shabbos or *Yom Tov* spent with the family."

"But, Saba," I objected, "the world is like that. Everything revolves around money."

I was convinced of the truth in his words, but I wanted to hear more.

"The world is *not* like that," Saba corrected me. "There are many hardworking Jews who realize that work does not constitute one's entire life. Their lives are filled with spirituality and joy, not work and more work. Besides, even if you were to prove to me that the majority of people in this world believe that work makes up one's whole life, I would confidently tell you that in this case, the majority is dead wrong. The media, the advertisements, the hoopla and to-do — all these give people the false impression that earning lots of money is the most important thing in life.

"That's not life," said Saba, pointing to the people rushing past his window with worried frowns on their faces. "*Nachas*, peace and quiet, peace of mind — *that's* life, my friend. Whoever thinks otherwise is mistaken."

I was overjoyed to hear Saba's view. As I said, I was to be married a few months later, so I paid close attention to his words and heeded his advice. I prayed with all my heart that I'd have the sense to avoid making the same mistake my cousin did. I promised myself that I would make every effort not to forfeit my own life.

Not All Profits Are Financial

MY NAME IS SAMMY and I own a small restaurant in Israel. I spend most of my time there grilling steaks, shnitzels, and chicken, and chopping lots of vegetables for salads. I am not an especially talented writer, so I hope my story will interest you. As my mother always said, "When you speak from the heart, everyone will understand," and my story comes straight from my heart. In any case, the important thing is the message I want to pass on.

I was not always in the restaurant business. I was a mover for many years, transporting households for people all over the country. Unfortunately, money problems overtook me, and I had to look for a different way to earn a living.

For years I lived in an apartment in a housing project. But I wanted to build myself a private home and live like a lot of my friends, so I borrowed money from family and friends. Before I knew it, I was knee-deep in debt. My overdraft at the bank kept increasing, and soon I owed money to most of my relatives and not a few friends. I barely was able to pay everyday expenses for my family. It was just too much for me to handle, and I didn't know what to do.

In the meantime, my house was basically built. All the walls were up, but I had no money left to pay for hooking up the necessary utilities — gas, water and electricity. The inspectors had also found some flaws in the building, but I could not pay to fix them and receive the required approval. So I had a house that had put me in debt, and I couldn't even move in. We continued to live in our tiny apartment.

That's when I quit my moving business. I borrowed some more and bought a little restaurant. At least I would have a steady income; people have to eat. The restaurant was located along a main road, and there was no competition nearby. Many hungry drivers were happy to stop to eat a hot meal on the road. It didn't take me long to get the hang of running a restaurant, and the job suited me to a T. Not only that, but the restaurant was successful, and it was soon bringing in a tidy amount every week.

I had to work very hard for the money, though. My hours were from early morning till late at night, six days a week. But all I cared about then was making money. I wanted to earn as much as I could and pay back my debts. The bank manager realized that I had started to earn a few hundred shekels a week, and he allowed me to carry an overdraft until I could start paying it off. I kept to a really tight budget and used every extra shekel to cover my debts.

My hope was that I would get those debts under control and then maybe have enough money to fix the building flaws, get the final approval, connect the utilities, and move into my new house.

Unfortunately, all this pressure about money knocked every other thought out of my head. I was only concerned with making more and more money. Even though I now had enough for my daily expenses, I had no peace of mind. My debts were still mostly unpaid, and I had the feeling that no matter how hard I worked, I would never climb out of the pit I was in.

I am ashamed to admit it, and may Hashem forgive me, but in the midst of my confusion I decided to keep the restaurant open seven days a week. I did not want to miss out on an extra day's earnings. Every shekel was important to me, and the cash intake on Shabbos was triple that of a weekday.

Somewhere in the deepest part of my conscience I didn't feel good about this. I knew I was a Jew and that it's not good for a Jew to work on Shabbos, but the thought of that enormous bottom line was *my* bottom line. And so I spread the word in the area that the restaurant would be open on Shabbos and that we were serving cholent and other Shabbos foods on Shabbos itself.

It happens that the restaurant is near a religious neighborhood. The religious community had never patronized the restaurant, so it didn't occur to me that I might be causing them any trouble by staying open on Shabbos. If some people don't like it, they don't have to eat here, I thought. That is why I was astonished to see three religious young men with beards and *peyos*, wearing black coats and hats, entering the restaurant one day.

I am not the type to get into fights, but I felt my muscles flexing instinctively, and I was sure that in a minute we would be exchanging blows. But one of the men smiled at me and said pleasantly, "We'd like to talk with you when you have a few minutes, Sammy."

Talk with me? Talks are what they have in Madrid and Oslo. I sell liver in barbeque sauce and veal with garlic slivers and onion rings. The shwarma was starting to smoke and had to be seasoned, and the trout had to go into the broiler. What would I have to say to those religious guys?

I didn't say anything, so the fellow asked, "When would it be convenient for you to have a few words with us?" Convenient? I was only interested in people coming in to eat and paying for their meals. I had to work; I needed money.

"You have a very nice restaurant," said another. He smiled at me, and I don't know why, but I smiled back.

"Will tonight be good for you, Sammy?" asked the first one.

The smile was still on my lips. "All right. Come tonight," I answered.

They left, and I was rather pleased. I had expected a confrontation, but they had been so nice.

They returned that evening, all three of them. My son took over the counter, and I sat down with them at a table outside.

"Is that your son?" one of them asked softly. "What's his name? He looks just like you. Does he have any brothers?"

"His name is Oded. And yes, he has two brothers, Elad and Tzachi."

"And how would you feel if Oded were getting married and instead of coming to the wedding, Elad decided to spend the evening playing basketball? Would you mind?" asked the second fellow.

"Mind? Of course I would mind!" I was bewildered. What was he talking about? "At a family wedding, the whole family should be there. That's no time to play basketball," I said.

"So answer honestly, Sammy. If Tzachi would go and try to persuade Elad to leave the basketball court and come to the wedding, would you think he was interfering in other people's business, or would you think that he was doing his family duty?"

"His duty, of course," I said. It wasn't so hard to talk about weddings for a change instead of taking food orders. "It would be the right thing to do to bring his brother to the wedding. You can play ball any time. Weddings don't happen so often."

"That's just the way it is here, Sammy," he continued. "My name is Menachem, by the way. Nice to meet you," he added, pressing my hand warmly. "And my friends are Yehudah and Akiva. We have a brothers' duty, to tell you about a wedding in the family."

"I don't cater weddings," I said, confused.

"You are my dear brother, Sammy," Menachem continued, "and I feel that I must persuade you to leave your restaurant and join the Jewish family on the day our Father in Heaven celebrates His Shabbos."

Menachem's message suddenly became clear as day. The word *Shabbos* cut straight to my heart. But I didn't feel as if Menachem was using a knife; his soft words were wrapped in silk. "Shabbos is a day of blessing for the Creator of the world and a day of rest and joy for Jews. Whoever sits around the Shabbos table has a treasure to enjoy. You are missing out, Sammy. On such a 'wedding day' you should not be 'playing ball' in your restaurant and grilling meat."

"I'm not playing around," I said bitterly. "I have so many debts that I can't see how I can give up my Shabbos earnings. Believe me, the minute I've gotten rid of the overdraft I'll close on Shabbos. I never used to work on Shabbos, and I don't really approve of it. My father was a good Jew. But my money troubles don't give me any choice. If the bank manager sees that I've started to bring in less money, he'll send collectors to impound all my property."

I went inside, took out my ledgers and showed the trio what I meant. The profit from the previous two or three Sabbaths was really a lot of money. There was no way I could pass it up. The wedding story was fine, but this was real life. They seemed to be nice fellows, but they just didn't know what they were talking about.

"Maybe we can help you," Yehudah said. "After all, no matter how much you make on one or two Sabbaths, you aren't going to get out of the red in one shot. On the other hand, we know it's hard for you to give up good money. So maybe we can help you come up with an idea. Maybe we can figure out how you can appease the bank manager without trampling on Shabbos."

Akiva put his hand on my shoulder. "Sammy, we know that deep down you believe that success comes from Heaven. You can earn three thousand shekels today and have to spend it tomorrow on urgent repairs or an unexpected family emergency, and in the end you don't have the three thousand shekels. You don't need only money, you need, as we all need, a blessing on your money that it will be used on what you want and not on things you don't want."

I nodded my head in sudden recollection. "You know, just a few months ago, when we had those heavy storms, I had to spend an unexpected few thousand shekels to reroof the restaurant and fix all the damages to the building. That sure was money with no blessing."

"You see?" Akiva said. "The One Who made the rain fall could have made sure that there would be no damage at all. But sometimes when there are painful earnings there are painful expenses too. Shabbos is the source of all blessing. Those who keep it see the blessing, and those who violate it push the blessing away. Sometimes you see it only a while later, but sometimes you can see it right away."

I agreed with them — theoretically. Everything they said was true, but I was sure that my business would have to stay open on Shabbos at least until my earnings doubled.

Yehudah said, "Wait a moment. What are we talking about — around four thousand shekels a week, which is about sixteen thousand shekels for four Sabbaths. Maybe we could get you a loan for that amount with a generous repayment schedule. Would you close on Shabbos then? If you went to the bank manager with a lump sum like that, he would see that you're not neglecting your overdraft, and he would be lenient with you."

All their words spun around in my head. What *would* he say? What would *I* say? For years I hadn't had time to say anything; I just worked around the clock. Now someone else was thinking of me and trying to make things easier. What could I say?

We began to make calculations. I told them about my unfinished house and the official approval form, and about my small apartment and my life that was no life. I saw in their eyes that they felt sorry for me and that they really wanted to help me with all their hearts. At the same time, I knew they were most anxious that I stop working on Shabbos and stop giving pain to the Creator.

We arrived at a figure. They would raise 32,000 shekels for me, a sum that equaled about eight working Sabbaths. I would give them postdated checks according to the schedule they laid out for me, which was a very comfortable way of repaying them. In exchange, I would not open the restaurant on Shabbos for the next two months. For those two months, the sign on my restaurant would read, "This restaurant is closed on Shabbos."

What would happen afterward? "*Hashem ya'azor*, Hashem will help," they said. "Whoever took care of things until now will take care of them later. The holy Shabbos will protect you and help you."

They came back with the money, and I gave them my checks. The bank manager said he appreciated my efforts, and his words gave me hope for a better future. On Friday afternoon, I closed the store, went home, and the Shabbos rest began. No work, no customers, no frying or cooking, no profits and no losses. Just *Shabbos kodesh*, a clear head, rest and relaxation. I took a deep breath of freedom. I began to enjoy my children a little. I felt that I was calming down. When I opened the restaurant again on Saturday night, I was a different man.

My connection to those young men got warmer. Under their influence, Shabbos for me became holier and filled with a new light. Each Shabbos I felt more closely connected to my Jewishness, and the beauty of the Shabbos Queen began to shine a little in my house.

After about three weeks of closing my restaurant on Shabbos, I decided to reapply for official approval for my house, even though I hadn't done a thing to repair the defects. Yet, I thought, who knows? Shabbos is a source of blessing, and I now had a small share in keeping Shabbos.

I submitted a new application. The inspectors came. They checked the house, saw the faults, and to my utter amazement, they approved with no reservations. I was stunned. I didn't understand how it had happened. I called the municipality to check that there was no mistake. The words of the clerk at city hall bowled me over: "Don't worry, Sammy. Your house is completely approved, and you can take the form you received to the bank, get a mortgage, connect the utilities, and move in."

With the form in hand, I went straight to the bank manager. The good impression my large deposit had made was reflected on his face. He approved a mortgage for three hundred thousand shekels. The utility companies signed all the contracts and installed the connections right away. Soon after, my family and I moved into the new house, and my life improved noticeably. With the mortgage, I was able to pay back much of the money I had borrowed to build the house.

As for actual profits, I must honestly say that the restaurant earns just the same as it did before I started opening on Shabbos. I am repaying the loan to the young men on schedule, and my other debts are getting paid off slowly but surely, but I don't see anything extra coming in.

But I think I have learned something very important, and this is my main message: Money isn't everything. I was living a life without blessing. I worked hard, always trying to pay off my debts at a snail's pace. I lived in a tiny, cramped apartment, knowing that I had a large house that I couldn't use and feeling inadequate. Now, maybe I earn less because I keep Shabbos, but suddenly I have started seeing blessing. I feel as if I have stepped from the shadow into the light, and I feel happy and fulfilled.

My head always used to ache with calculations: How long would it take to pay off my debts? When could I fix the cracks in the walls of my new house and get the approval form so that I could move in? How many shekels for this and how many for that? Just thinking about it made me miserable, and I couldn't stop thinking about it.

Yet my dreams of moving in came true that same year. In my rosiest imagining, I never expected that the bank would approve such a large mortgage or that things would move so fast. But that is just what happened. From the day I began closing the restaurant on Shabbos, blessing has followed me. My life is much calmer even during the week now — and all the more so on Shabbos. I take time now to be a father to my children, and I take time to savor the sweetness of life.

When blessing, not money, becomes the important thing in life, your heart can be light. And to receive this blessing, one must come close to the source of blesssing — *Shabbos kodesh*. That's what happened to me when I stopped working on Shabbos.

Splitting the Sea

*Our Sages say that the making
of a match is as difficult
as splitting the Red Sea.
(Sanhedrin 22a)*

The Power of Shemiras ha-Lashon

A S PARENTS WHO have gone through many difficult periods in raising our children, we would like to tell you about a tried-and-true *segulah* that has the power to arouse Heavenly mercy and speed the arrival of personal Divine assistance.

We first heard about the method from a family who had tried absolutely everything else and whose prayers were finally answered after they used this particular *segulah*. As simple human beings, we do not and cannot understand the ways of Heaven, but we learned a lesson from that family, applied it to our own situation, and were also answered favorably. The *segulah*, briefly, is to arrange forty consecutive, entire days of *shemiras ha-lashon*, complete abstinence from evil speech, in the merit of whoever needs help from Above.

How We Apportioned the Hours

At first, some of us wanted to take on full days of guarding our tongues, but we quickly discovered that *Tafasta meruba lo tafasta*, "If you take on too much, you won't accomplish anything" (*Rosh Hashanah* 4b). These things have to be done gradually, in moderation. In order to achieve round-the-clock pure speech, you need to solicit the help of others and divide up the day among you. Ideally, each person should take on the hours that are personally most convenient and promise to be the most risk-free. We know of several cases, ours included, where a twenty-four-hour watch that was kept for forty days, or 960 consecutive hours, helped the person in need.

Our family divided up the twenty-four-hour period among eleven people, each of us committing to one time period for forty days in the merit of our daughter, who had been waiting for her match for many years.

Reuven's commitment was to refrain from speaking or hearing *lashon ha-ra* during the hours when he could guarantee that he could fulfill it — from 11:00 P.M. until 7:00 A.M. — for forty days straight. He decided to make sure to always be in bed during those hours, as it says in the verse, "Do not sin...be upon your beds and be silent..." (*Tehillim* 4:5).

Shimon, who always davens at seven o'clock, committed himself to avoiding *lashon ha-ra* from 7:00 A.M. to 8:30 A.M. for forty days. He put a note in his tefillin bag to remind himself to be careful.

Levi, who teaches in the morning, is in class every day from 8:30 A.M. to 11:00 A.M. without a break, so he committed himself to forty days of abstaining from *lashon ha-ra* during those hours. Since he was concerned that he might occasionally lapse while engaged in conversations with other teachers or with pupils, he asked his wife, who is usually home alone at those hours, to take on those same hours herself. That way, between the two of them, those two and a half hours would be covered.

Yosef, a scribe who works alone in his room in the morning, took on his stint of *shemiras ha-lashon* from 11:00 A.M. to 1:30 P.M. He gave over the merit of forty days of those two and a half *lashon ha-ra*-free hours to finding a match for his cousin.

Grandma chose from 1:30 to 4:00 P.M., when she usually takes a nap and the phone is off the hook. But just in case she forgot, Grandpa accepted the same hours. As a reminder, they set their alarm clock to ring every day at 1:30 P.M.

Yehudah, who gives a class from 4:00 P.M. to 5:30 P.M. in shul every day, chose that hour and a half. Zevulun, who attends a *daf yomi* class from 5:30 P.M. to 7:00 P.M., picked that hour and a half of Torah learning for his watch, for as we know, learning Torah wards off sin. His wife, who is usually busy with the children from 7:00 P.M. to 8:00 P.M., chose that hour for herself.

It was difficult to find someone to cover the hours from 8:00 P.M. to 11:00 P.M. — three hours when phone calls are cheaper and phone lines are loaded in Eretz Yisrael from Dan to Beersheva. Naftali committed himself to one hour, between 8:00 P.M. and 9:00

P.M., and he decided that for the next forty days he would disconnect the telephone at that time; there would be no phone calls and
that was that. When he saw that he was forgetting, he set his cellular phone to ring at eight o'clock every evening, and the ring reminded him to disconnect the phone.

His wife was brave enough to undertake the hour from 9:00
P.M. to 10:00 P.M. She decided that for forty days she would not answer the doorbell during that hour. She wasn't embarrassed to explain the reason to a neighbor, who had begun to wonder why she
wasn't answering the door in the evenings. The neighbor was so
impressed that she also decided to keep *shemiras ha-lashon* during
that hour herself.

Binyamin, who committed himself to guarding his tongue from
10:00 P.M. to 11:00 P.M., decided to start learning a new *sefer* at just
that hour for forty days. In that way, he would be sure that, with
Hashem's help, he would be protected from sin. As a result of this
commitment he chose to leave early from a friend's wedding, for
fear that he would forget himself and say something improper. He
apologized to his friend in advance, and the friend understood perfectly and had no complaints.

In this way, we had a group of eleven relatives — brothers, sisters, spouses and cousins — who banded together around the clock
for forty days to assist our daughter in finding a shidduch.

A Few Tips

1. It is a good idea to keep a note in your pocket that says, "I have
   committed myself to guard my tongue from this hour to that
   hour. Please assist me that I not fail." This note is a supplication
   to Hashem and a reminder. It is very helpful to have such a note
   to show to a friend who starts saying the wrong sorts of things
   during "your" hours. Don't be embarrassed. Be proud and fly
   your flag of service to Hashem.
2. During your hours, you can set up all sorts of tricks to help yourself, such as not answering the phone (what was voice-mail in-
   vented for?), not answering the door, learning, or finding some

other gainful occupation.

3. It is a good idea for everyone to find a partner to be on guard during the same hours; that way, even if, *chas ve-shalom*, the first person fails, there is a chance that the hours will be guarded by the other person.

4. The main commitment is not to speak *lashon ha-ra* at all and to make every effort not to hear it as well. If for some reason, someone around you starts speaking it, get up and leave. If you can't do that, ask them clearly to stop, so that you won't be guilty. If that doesn't work, at least try to find some positive way to view the person about whom you have just heard gossip. Tell yourself that you probably would have done the same thing, and that you won't judge anyone until you have stood in his shoes. And then believe these things with all your heart.

5. Be particularly careful on Friday and Shabbos, when your schedule is different. In spite of the difficulties, your commitment must be kept faithfully.

The Benefits of Dividing the Hours

When a group of people is committed seriously to *shemiras ha-lashon* for specified times, there is no doubt that it affects them positively the rest of the day. The mitzvah remains engraved in their hearts. The purity that guarding their tongues provides is absorbed deep into their souls. Anyone who has the merit of two "clean" hours a day knows this very well.

Furthermore, it affects the entire neighborhood. People around you know that during those hours, they have to keep themselves from speaking *lashon ha-ra* near you, and the great harm done by this grave sin is being prevented in your environs.

Moreover, in general, serious people continue guarding their tongues even after the forty days are over, having seen what good their commitment has done them. As ha-Rav Yehudah Segal, *zt"l*, used to say, "There is no family in the world whose affairs do not take a turn for the better when they commit themselves to improving their observance of *shemiras ha-lashon*."

Our Own Story

We first tried this *segulah* when we had not been able to find the right shidduch for our oldest daughter. As is the custom in our family, the younger children do not get married until the older ones do, and therefore her brother, who was only a bit younger, was also getting older as he waited for her. While we were keeping the forty-day watch the first time, a certain shidduch began to take shape. We began to exult and thank Hashem with all our hearts.

As we are a *chassidishe* family, all the research and arrangements are made before the couple actually meet. Thus, on the thirty-eighth day, we reached the final stages of settling the match, and the other side promised to give us their final answer in two days' time — the fortieth day. We were astounded. How the eleven of us would rejoice at receiving the good news exactly on the fortieth day and know that our efforts had been rewarded!

However, on the fortieth day we were told, "Everything seems fine. We like everything about the match. We have no complaints at all. But our hearts tell us that this is just not the right one for us." Their answer hit us like a clap of thunder. Just on that very day! We saw it as a clear sign from Above that the forty days had not been fulfilled properly. One of us must have been lax. We don't understand the ways of Heaven, but that was how we read the message.

We called all eleven of the relatives involved and told them what had happened. It turns out that some of them had just about forgotten the whole thing. We immediately decided to start over with renewed determination. The Sages say that no one succeeds in Torah unless he first makes a mistake. We applied this lesson to ourselves and resolved to try harder this time. We began again, and after just a few days, a suggested match began to move along nicely. On the twenty-eighth day, we had the merit to finalize the shidduch for our eldest daughter.

Our group of relatives decided to continue with the project so that, in the merit of guarding our tongues, we might help our older son become engaged, too. We started anew with the same distribution of hours, and though there were challenges along the way, *Ha-ba le-taher mesayin oso*, "One who comes to purify himself is as-

sisted in doing so" (*Shabbos* 104a), and we were guided. Ten days after we had started, things started moving. On the thirtieth day of
the new cycle, just a few weeks after our daughter's engagement,
we had the privilege of seeing our son become a groom.

Since then, we have recommended this *segulah* to everyone we
know, and we are ready to join any group that needs our help.
Baruch Hashem, we have seen miracles take place, but only when the
commitment was taken seriously and kept faithfully. We personally know dozens of people who will attest to this.

Sometimes a Hint Comes from Above

One case in which we participated in someone else's commitment
to forty days of *shemiras ha-lashon*, also toward finding a shidduch,
revealed to us a most unusual chain of *hashgachah pratis*.

In the midst of the forty-day effort to abstain from *lashon ha-ra*, a
certain match started to take shape. Someone had suggested the
daughter of Mr. Green to the mother of Nachum. That evening,
Nachum's father went to consult with his Rebbe, while his mother
sat at home keeping her hour's *shemiras ha-lashon* watch. In order to
strengthen her resolve, she picked up a recently published booklet
about *shemiras ha-lashon* and began leafing through it.

The author of the booklet cited various *halachos* pertaining to
lashon ha-ra and gave examples. One of the examples began as follows: "Nachum told his friend that he was unofficially engaged."
The mother's heart skipped a beat when she read those words. The
hint was clear as day, but she was too rational to get excited by a coincidence like that. Still, she took it as strong support from Above.

She kept reading the booklet. Soon she came upon another il-
lustration of a halachah: "The Green family was about to conclude
the engagement of their daughter." Who could tell? Maybe at that
very moment the Rebbe was giving her husband a positive answer.
Two minutes later her husband called to tell her that the Rebbe
gave his blessing to the shidduch.

This seemed to be a clear hint from Heaven that there was a direct connection between guarding one's tongue and being helped

to find a shidduch. The next day, Nachum's engagement to the Green's daughter was concluded to the joy of all concerned.

May Hashem help us all to merit success in guarding our speech, and may we enjoy many complete, joyous occasions. We would like to suggest that groups of girls, boys, and young people, as well as adults, be organized to commit themselves to *shemiras ha-lashon* through this forty-day *segulah*, for the merit of friends, relatives, or acquaintances in need of a *yeshuah*. The merit of their pure speech would stand by them, and they would see Hashem's deliverance with their own eyes.

Check Out Your Sources

SOMETIMES EVERYTHING IS perfectly matched. The groom suits the bride's family; the bride is just what the groom's family is looking for. Everything is perfect and could lead to a perfect engagement... but the advice coming from other people is less than perfect. Experienced shadchanim have learned this lesson, at times at the expense of a shidduch that was meant to be.

A girl's parents naturally will seek information about a prospective groom from their own sons or sons-in-law. Who would know the girl and her home better than a brother or a brother-in-law? If he knows the boy as well, he should be a perfect source of information, right?

Not always.

The young fellow being consulted is not always smart enough to be objective, and it has happened that a personal falling out between him and the prospective groom has blinded him to the true qualities of the boy. So when he's asked, he makes a face and says confidently, "Abba, it's not for you!"

Some young men have an inflated idea of their responsibility in giving an opinion on a prospective shidduch. They seem to feel that their sister deserves an absolutely perfect mate, and it is hard indeed to find someone who is absolutely perfect. Any boy who falls short of such demanding requirements is rejected immediately. A father is inclined to trust his son's judgment, reasoning that, after all, he knows both sides well, and so if his son rejects someone, then surely there is nothing to talk about. But it is not always so. The couple might have everything in their favor except for the advisor.

My friend Shimon had consulted a shadchan for his daughter. The shadchan verified his information about the girl and decided that she was a solid, average, nice girl with ordinary intelligence and good *middos*, and nothing could be said against her — the kind of fine Jewish girl who has kept the Jewish People going for thousands of years. And so the shadchan suggested to Shimon the names of solid, fine Jewish boys, the same type of boys, as a matter of fact, that he had previously suggested to him and who were now Shimon's sons-in-law.

But for some reason, Shimon kept refusing his suggestions, one after the other. The shadchan couldn't figure it out. Months passed, the girl grew older, and he did not have a clue about all these rejections.

Then Shimon's son got married. Shimon confessed to the shadchan that his son had known all the candidates and classified them all as "mediocre merchandise." Shimon asked the shadchan to raise his standards.

All was now clear. The girl's brother had ruined every offer. In his opinion, this time his father deserved the ultimate *bachur*, the scholar of the generation.

Shortly after this, the shadchan was able to suggest a really good match to Shimon, and Shimon thought it sounded good. His heart told him that it was suitable in every respect. The other side, in this case, said he would have to wait, that they were not considering shidduchim at all at that point.

Shimon decided he would be patient and wait for them. It seemed so perfect to him. He had not the slightest doubt that this was the shidduch meant for his daughter, and he believed the delay was just a matter of time. Chances are that his "expert advisor," the young married son, told him that this was the thing to do.

Shimon waited faithfully for the promised response. Whenever anyone would inquire or offer other suggestions, he would give the same answer: "We are in the middle of something." Months passed, months in which many *L'chaims* were drunk in other homes, but Shimon still waited.

Truly, there is a time for all things. When the time came, the other side decided it was time to make a move toward finding their son a shidduch. But they had forgotten all about Shimon. Someone made them a serious offer, they liked it, and within a few days their dear son, Shimon's desired son-in-law, was engaged to a girl from a distinguished family in the same town.

Shimon's world collapsed that morning when he opened the paper and looked at the engagement column. He could hardly have looked different if he had been looking at an obituary notice on the other side of the page. The other family had concluded a shidduch with someone else! And he had rejected dozens of suggestions in the meantime, leaving his daughter one of the last of her group to become engaged. A cloud of bitterness filled his mind.

That evening, Shimon went to see his friend, the shadchan. The look of agony on his face said it all. The shadchan sat there quietly and listened to Shimon's anguished plaint. He understood that deep down Shimon was angrier at himself than at the other family.

But Shimon was filled with trust in Hashem through and through. Quickly enough he recovered his aplomb, admitting that everything was from Above, that it was meant to be. He said the past was past and he would look to the future.

The shadchan realized that his friend was now extremely anxious to find a match for his daughter and would be willing to hear his recommendations without further delay. He consulted his list and was reminded of an excellent prospect, Gershon Levy, a *ben Torah* with good *middos*, not bad looking but a bit on the heavy side and slightly older.

Upon hearing the boy's name, Shimon's eyes lit up. "I know his father very well. He's a wonderful man. We will definitely consider his son!" Shimon paid no attention to the two minor drawbacks the shadchan had mentioned.

The shidduch was concluded in no time at all. It progressed from one stage to the next as quickly as could be. Shimon inquired about the prospective groom, and was delighted with everything he heard. The Levy family were thrilled to find a family who saw beyond their dear son's appearance to the shining light within him. By the end of the week, the matter was settled between the two families, and they drank a *L'chaim* to the new shidduch. Both sides were happy; everything was fine.

Now, as things go, it is certainly possible that Shimon might not have even considered an older boy in the first place had not ha-Kadosh Baruch Hu arranged for him to have waited so long and to have been so deeply disappointed. Because of his bitter experience, Shimon was prepared to consider a wonderful older boy. The main point of this story, however, has yet to be told.

The day after the families drank the *L'chaim*, Shimon called the shadchan to convey the good news. Almost as an afterthought, Shimon asked him for a favor.

"My married son lives a few houses away from you," he said to the shadchan. "Would you please go over and tell him we made a shidduch last night? His telephone has not yet been installed."

The shadchan was astonished that the married son didn't know anything about the matter, and Shimon explained how this had come about. After his deep disappointment, he had felt emotionally drained. The suggestion of the older boy had seemed so promising from the first minute, and he had wanted it so wholeheartedly, that although he had always consulted with his son before, this time he just hadn't. He had asked around and had heard good things, but he didn't ask his son. And then things had moved along so quickly that he simply hadn't gotten the chance to tell his son about it.

That evening, the shadchan found himself reluctant to go and tell the son, and so he postponed the task. The next day, after the announcement had already appeared in the papers, he met the married son on his way to shul.

This not-yet-twenty-two-year old had been waiting in a fury. As the shadchan came near, he challenged angrily, "Did you suggest that overweight guy for my sister? And an *'alter bachur'* at that?

What have you done to my family? What kind of goods have you sold us? You should be ashamed! If I had known anything about it, I would have made sure my father wouldn't have done anything so stupid!"

The shadchan reeled from the undeserved attack, but did not answer. He knew in his heart that all the parties to the shidduch were delighted. The older boy was a treasure after Shimon's own heart. Shimon thanked Hashem for everything he had suffered, since it had brought him to this shidduch. Hashem had saved him from talking to his son beforehand, and who knows how long his daughter might have remained single had he done so?

Hashem's Many Messengers

F THE SUBJECT IS shidduchim, there is no end to stories of *hashgachah pratis*. Everyone who has ever gotten married can attest to the fact that a person's heart is in Hashem's Hands, and when the right time comes, everything falls into place.

A particularly interesting story of a shidduch occurred not long ago, through the agency of a most unusual emissary. As one of the members of the family tells it:

A lonely, broken woman was fated to bear the burden of a sick child along with her other troubles. His treatment kept him in hospitals for long stretches at a time, and she was left alone at his bedside day and night.

A group of seminary girls noticed the woman and her child on their *chessed* rounds at the hospital, and were touched by her loneliness in her battle for her child's life. They volunteered to sit at his bedside so that she could go home to rest.

As things go, most of the girls slowly lost interest and turned to other cases, but one of the volunteers continued faithfully to help the lonely woman. This girl had become extremely attached to the child and his mother. She would come day and night to help in every way she could with all her heart and soul. This she did until the child's treatment required that he be moved to a hospital in a different city.

In the new city, the lonely woman found kindness as well, in the form of a warm, generous woman, a true *ba'alas chessed*, the mother of a large family, who used to visit the nearby hospital to feed the sick who could not tend to themselves. On one of her visits she came upon the woman and her child, and after hearing the woman's tale of troubles and tribulations, invited her to her home and from then on, took a personal interest in her case.

In the course of one of their long conversations, which took place at all hours of the day when the lonely woman used to visit the *ba'alas chessed*'s house, the hostess mentioned that she had a son, an exceptional student studying in yeshiva, who was coming of age. No sooner had she heard this, than the mother of the sick child suggested the wonderful girl who had been so kind and had helped her so much in the previous hospital.

Although she wasn't sure of the girl's last name, and couldn't find it written anywhere on the myriad slips of paper in her purse, she knew so much else about her and her special family from their long acquaintance that the suggestion began to sound more and more reasonable.

Still, it seemed odd that a stranger, and one from a different background at that, should be the one to suggest a shidduch to this woman's family. However, there is much to the power of persuasion, and a quick investigation was made — only to reveal that the girl was from the same chassidic circle as the family in question!

The end of the story is a happy one. The lonely, broken woman merited to make a fine match between two prominent families. It was truly *invei ha-gefen be'invei ha-gefen*, and the matchmaker earned a place of honor at the *simchah* that followed. This did so much for her broken spirits, and so restored her faith in herself, that she found renewed strength to deal with her crises.

And so, as with Rivkah Imeinu, one deed of *chessed* led to another to found a *bayis ne'eman be'Yisrael*.

Yankel

YANKEL DIDN'T LOOK twenty-six, but that's how old he was. And he was still single.

Why do you suppose Yankel was still a bachelor? There are a few possible answers. Some people are willing to pass up a heart of gold and a sterling character if a boy's appearance doesn't fit their prefigured criteria. They reject a boy who is charming and kindhearted because he is too tall or too short or has a small physical imperfection.

If a boy's looks are not enough to thwart his prospects, then it might be his lifestyle. Yankel was an energetic, dynamic fellow, who loved to keep busy. It was hard for him to sit and learn from morning till night. When he discovered this inclination in his early teens, he discussed it openly with his mashgiach. *Baruch Hashem,* he learned well all day, he explained, but he wanted to spend the evenings helping out in the yeshiva office.

The mashgiach was an intelligent, understanding person, who knew Yankel well and appreciated his sincere intentions. He knew that the boy was a good person and that he learned well during the day. The rebbes loved him; he was a good student and a charming person. Besides, he knew how to fix the air conditioner when it broke down in the middle of a class, and always noticed when the teacher needed a cup of coffee. So the mashgiach asssented to Yankel's request, and even encouraged him to work in the office in the evenings.

Yankel ended up spending a great deal of time in the administrator's office: typing, photocopying, and even stuffing envelopes when necessary. The rosh yeshiva also took advantage of his skills on occasion. All in all, Yankel felt that the time he took off from learning in the evenings contributed greatly to his ability to sit and learn properly during the day.

Yankel's father knew about all this and understood his son's needs. He took pleasure in the mashgiach's praise and repeated the compliments to Yankel with pride.

Yankel's mother, however, was filled with doubts. She claimed that the "good" boys spent their time in the *beis midrash* and did not hang around the office. Her husband maintained that even though there is nothing more important than learning in the *beis midrash*, a boy who merely sits there without learning might actually be better off using that time to help others. As for shidduchim, it was too early to think about that. To the credit of his wise Jewish mother, she never criticized Yankel.

As the years passed, Yankel's occupation became a fact of life. For three out of his four years in *mesivta*, Yankel's evenings were spent working in the office. A few months after starting *yeshiva gedolah*, Yankel was given responsibility for the yeshiva's *gemach*, the free-loan fund. Soon he was conducting the loan fund's business with people over the telephone and signing letters, order forms, and receipts in his own name.

With all of this, Yankel never neglected his learning. The mashgichim all sang his praises, for he conducted the *gemach*'s business in such a way that it never interfered with his study periods at the yeshiva. He felt he was utilizing his time to the maximum, and every minute of useful activity gave him great peace of mind.

As time went on, Yankel realized he was writing a lot of *gemach* checks to newlywed grooms, while he remained with the younger single students in the yeshiva.

This was what Yankel's mother had feared all along. Letting Yankel work on the side had been a terrible mistake, she said, and the facts proved it. His father did not agree; he thought that Yankel was a mature and well-balanced young man, and that any delay in shidduchim was the work of Providence. When the right day came, the issue of Yankel's work would be resolved for the best.

Yankel himself had no regrets. He had had ten good years in yeshiva. In the depths of his heart he might have felt a twinge of doubt, but his father's *emunah* was so strong that it carried him forward, as it had all along.

Now Yankel was twenty-six. A man named Naftali Domberg called him, offering him a well-paying job in the United States for the summer as assistant administrator of a large summer camp. They needed a young man who was both a *yerei Shamayim* and capable. The mashgiach had recommended him.

Yankel's mother objected strenuously, and was determined to keep her son at home. She felt he could not exploit his marriage opportunities by working in America, and that was what truly mattered.

With the greatest courtesy and respect, Yankel told his mother that anyone who didn't want him as a son-in-law because of his dynamic, busy nature he would not want as a father-in-law. "I have to be who I am," he said. "I don't like playacting, and I don't want to put on a show and do things that are against my nature just to get married. If everything comes from Heaven, then a solution from Heaven will be found for me also." His father agreed.

After receiving his mother's full consent and that of his rav, Yankel packed up his things and flew off to America without second thoughts. A person has to know himself, his strengths and weaknesses, he felt. That is the only way to lead a healthy, balanced life.

"A person should be embarrassed to sin," his mashgiach used to say. "There is no greater shame. But anything that is not a sin, and that a person is sure is what Hashem requires of him, he should do with joy and determination."

When Yankel arrived in the United States, exhausted and overwhelmed, he discovered after going through customs that his passport had disappeared. He searched through all his bags, but could not find it.

He searched and searched, but at a certain point, he decided that he would have to leave the airport without his passport and get help later on. He hesitated to call Naftali Domberg for a ride from the airport, as it was already late at night. He saw a religious Jew and decided to ask him how to find the address that he had written on a slip of paper. The stranger actually knew Naftali Domberg, whose name appeared on the paper, and he offered to take Yankel there himself, as it was on his way.

The helpful stranger introduced himself as Gershon Strasser, and explained to Yankel that he had been at the airport to see his son off to Eretz Yisrael. As they drove along and conversed, they soon discovered that Reb Gershon was a childhood friend of Yankel's uncle. How small the Jewish world is!

When they arrived at the Domberg home, they found it dark and locked. On the door was a small note: "Yaakov, when you arrive, ring the bell until I wake up to open the door. Naftali Domberg."

In a hushed consultation, Gershon proposed that rather than waking Reb Domberg in the middle of the night, Yankel should come and stay at his home, which was only fifteen minutes away. They left a note on the door with Gershon's address and telephone number.

While Yankel davened *Ma'ariv* in a corner of their living room, Mrs. Strasser was visited with an inspiration. As Yankel partook of the tea and cake his hostess offered, her idea took shape.

Yankel managed to sleep for a few hours, but Mr. and Mrs. Strasser didn't sleep a wink. They both had the strange feeling that Yankel would be a perfect match for their daughter, and was destined to become their long-awaited son-in-law.

While Yankel was still sleeping, Gershon Strasser was already out and about, traveling to the shul near Naftali Domberg's house to ask him for information about the boy.

Naftali conveyed to Gershon all the positive information he had received from Yankel's mashgiach. Gershon begged Naftali to serve as the go-between and suggest the match to Yankel's parents. By the end of that week, Yankel became the chosen son-in-law of Reb Gershon Strasser.

There is one more detail that is important in its own way: The very next morning after his arrival in the United States, when Yankel was about to leave the Strasser home, he dug into his bag for a clean handkerchief, and what did he see resting on the bottom of his bag? His passport, of course. It had accomplished its purpose.

And that is how Yankel found what he had been missing....

Who Can Understand?

INCHAS, A NEWLY MARRIED young man, was alone at home when the phone rang.

"Hello, Pinchas!" The voice was familiar, but Pinchas could not place it.

"Hello," he answered. "Who is this?"

The caller seemed to have plenty of time. "Don't you recognize my voice? Guess who it is."

"I really don't know. Please tell me who this is," Pinchas answered politely.

"This is your best friend!"

My best friend? I have a lot of friends, Pinchas thought, and several of them might consider themselves my best friend.

For some reason, it occurred to him that the speaker sounded like his friend Shammai Kahana, a young man he had known when they had studied together in Yeshivas Chatzeros ha-Torah. Shammai had lived next door to his family at the time, and they would usually get together to study during *bein ha-zemanim*. It was hard to say that they had been "best friends," but still, that must be who was calling him.

"Shammai'ke," he said fondly, picturing the smiling face of his friend, "how are you?"

Instead of answering, "No, this is not Shammai'ke," the voice responded unexpectedly and with a strange urgency, "Which Shammai'ke?"

"Shammai Kahana from Yeshivas Chatzeros ha-Torah," Pinchas answered, totally confused. Who could it be? The voice sounded like Shammai's and even the kidding around was Shammai's style.

"You *did* say Shammai Kahana from Chatzeros? I am in shock, young man, in total shock. This is Yeshayahu Tourker, and I tell you I cannot believe this."

Pinchas smiled. Of course. It was Yeshayahu Tourker, his father-in-law's good friend and jovial seatmate in shul. He never missed an opportunity to bring a smile to someone's face. Pinchas had only been married for two months, and Yeshayahu already claimed him as a "best" friend. But why was he in shock?

"Do you have any idea how incredible this is?" Yeshayahu was totally serious now. "This is absolutely amazing."

Pinchas couldn't wait to hear the explanation.

"First I have to tell you that my daughter is now of marriageable age, and we are in the midst of seeking a good shidduch for her. We have recently had several young men suggested to us, and two of them seem very suitable. One fellow studies at the yeshiva you studied in before you were married, and that is why I called you just now. But the second young man just happens to be someone called Shammai Kahana who learns at Yeshivas Chatzeros ha-Torah! I've heard good things about both of them, but I wanted to ask someone I can rely on to fill me in on their backgrounds. I called you first to get information on the other boy, never dreaming you knew Shammai!"

Pinchas was amazed. "It's true," he admitted, "Shammai Kahana still learns in Chatzeros ha-Torah, but since he lives near my parents, we still meet during *bein ha-zemanim*."

Mr. Tourker was prepared to start the conversation over from the beginning. "And so, Pinchas, my best and most esteemed and wonderful friend, if this is how *hashgachah* has arranged things, that I should confuse you and cause you to think that I am your friend Shammai'ke, then all I have to do now is ask you to tell me about your 'best friend' Shammai Kahana."

Pinchas recalled the *gemara* that teaches us that a woman is designated for a man by Hashem. He sensed that *hashgachah* was leading him to get involved in this match, so he enthusiastically began to relate all the good things he could remember about his friend Shammai, from when they were just kids and from when they had learned together in yeshiva.

Soon afterward, Shammai got engaged to Yeshayahu Tourker's daughter. Another match made in Heaven, apparently brought about by a simple, inconsequential mistake.

As King David said, "Who can understand mistakes?" (*Tehillim* 19:13).

THE PARABLE OF THE JEWEL

In the Book of Bereishis (37:1), Rashi tells a parable about what a person does when he drops a precious jewel on the ground. He will sift through stones, dirt, and sand until he finds it. When he does, he throws away all the other stones he has picked up and keeps only the jewel.

Who knows how many precious gems, yerei Shamayim with extraordinary middos, are offered and rejected out of hand as prospective sons- and daughters-in-law only because the family is not "chashuv," distinguished, enough? Even when it is clear that the young man or woman is rare and exceptional, trivial issues can stand in the way.

One might wonder at this preoccupation with ancestors. In-laws are important, but in the end, the couple is not going to live with them but will build their own bayis ne'eman. Everyone admits this to be true, and yet most people are concerned about "what people will say."

A veteran shadchan tells of one father who was disinclined to consider an excellent boy only because people would say he was making a match with such an ordinary family. The shadchan suggested that if the only thing about the match that bothered him was what other people would say, he should make a small family engagement party and not tell the whole world about it. Where is it written that you are obligated to publish an engagement announcement in the newspaper?

"It is a great shame to pass up a good shidduch merely because you think it's not impressive enough to make those who read the engagements column stop and take notice," he said.

The shadchan went on to tell the man about the time he made a shidduch for one of his own children, and for some reason the other side did not want to publish an announcement in the paper. "Baruch Hashem," he said with a smile, "we have merited to see the couple living happily, and we shep untold nachas from their lovely children."

The girl's father finally agreed that the shidduch was probably a good one, but the part about the newspaper ad still nagged at him.

"If I don't make a formal announcement, shadchanim will continue to call me," he worried.

The shadchan agreed that this was true, but after a week or two they *would stop calling. The father asked how his extended family would know about it if they didn't see it in the paper. The shadchan laughingly assured him that this problem would be taken care of as soon as everyone received his wedding invitation.*

In spite of his great efforts to convince the father that he was worried about inessential things, he was unsuccessful. The worry about "what people will say" overrode the positive traits of the boy and the solid, if unexceptional, character of the family. What a pity.

A Timely Memory Lapse

SHIDDUCH STORIES generally have one of two themes. The first is, "Every delay is for the best," and the second is, "One must never become discouraged." At exactly the right moment, the right idea will come into the mind of the right person, even if one must undergo some heartache before that right moment comes along. People can truly see wonders in the way Hashem runs the world through shidduchim. If one keeps this in mind, it will be easier to exercise patience and *bitachon* while awaiting one's *bashert*.

Rav Rephael Rosenthal gives a class at our local shul. One of the regular participants is the rabbi's neighbor, Tanchum Lavan. Although Rav Rephael's acquaintance with Tanchum is slight, he sees him every evening at his class and occasionally in the stairwell of their apartment building.

Rav Rephael has a close friend, Elisha. Their friendship dates back to their days together in yeshiva and has stood the test of time. Elisha appreciates Rav Rephael's erudition, and often seeks his counsel on personal issues. The Rav's advice has always proven valuable, and Elisha has never regretted confiding in his good friend.

When Tanchum's daughter was proposed for Elisha's son, Elisha had no special reason to be enthusiastic about it. For one thing, his son was an excellent, top-notch *bachur*, and for another, he had never heard of the Lavan family — the name meant nothing to him. But when the shadchan told him that Rav Rephael was a close acquaintance of Tanchum's, Elisha's eyes lit up. If Rav Rephael knew Mr. Lavan, that was another story. He would be able to find out exactly what he needed to know.

As soon as Rav Rephael came home from giving his class, the phone rang. Although he was exhausted, when he heard Elisha's voice on the other end of the line he found new strength. He was always happy to help his dear friend.

After hearing Elisha's query, Rav Rephael paused a moment or two and stifled a yawn. "Tanchum Lavan? Umm, sure I know the name. Of course I know it. But right this minute I can't remember who he is. Ribbono shel Olam, where do I know that name from? Lavan, Lavan. I don't know what to tell you, Elisha. I keep drawing a blank."

"They told me that you know Tanchum Lavan very well," Elisha prodded, trying to jog Rav Rephael's memory.

"Of course I know him," Rav Rephael said. "I just can't remember from where."

There was silence on the other end of the line. Elisha was somewhat uncomfortable, and didn't want to pressure his friend.

"Listen," Rav Rephael said finally, "I'm very tired right now. For some reason I just can't place the man. I guess I'm not getting any younger," he chuckled. "As soon as it comes to me I'll get in touch with you. What's the name again? Lavan? Strange. It's on the tip of my tongue, but I just can't remember at the moment."

Elisha, not wanting to end the conversation on an unpleasant note, tactfully led the conversation to other topics before wishing the Rav a good night.

Rav Rephael put down the receiver and went to fix himself a cup of coffee. Suddenly the name Lavan struck a bell. "Of course! What came over me?" he said out loud. "Tanchum Lavan, my downstairs neighbor! I saw him earlier tonight at class. How can I have forgotten him? How could I *not* know him?"

The Lavan family had lived in the same building as the Rav for several years. The plaster walls were not thick enough to muffle the shouting in the stairwell. Shouting and slammed doors were daily occurrences. They were, to put it mildly, a dysfunctional family. Tanchum generally was a quiet, introverted man who never raised his voice except on Friday afternoons when the pre-Shabbos preparations were at their height. At those times, well, he was far from quiet.

Rav Rephael was panic-stricken. How could he have blanked out like that? Now he found himself in a singularly unpleasant position. Elisha would check out the family and would hear about the family's problems. He would come to the obvious conclusion that he, Rav Rephael, had purposely pretended not to remember his own neighbor, one of the participants in his class, because he did not want to tell Elisha the truth.

Yet Rav Rephael felt it was his duty to prevent this shidduch from going through at all costs. He did not think it would be a good match. No, the families were not at all compatible. Elisha's son did not deserve to fall in with such an irascible family. The Rav hurried to the phone and, with a sinking feeling inside at the prospect of the unpleasant task awaiting him, he dialed Elisha's number. He would have to tell him that his memory had returned and that, unfortunately, he knew that the family had problems and he would have to advise them to seek another match.

The line was busy and remained so for a long time. Rav Rephael felt it was important that he speak with Elisha as soon as possible, but he just could not get through. He knew Elisha did not have another line, a cellphone, a fax, or a pager. There was no way to reach him other than via his one phone line, and that was continually busy.

Throughout the evening, Rav Rephael dialed Elisha's number to no avail. He began to worry that the shidduch with the Lavans' daughter might even then be moving forward. If it were to go through, he would never again be able to look Elisha in the face. Eventually, however, Rav Rephael's fatigue caught up with him, and he decided to pursue the matter the following day.

The next day Rav Rephael had a hundred and one matters that demanded his attention from early morning until late at night. Immediately after giving the class, he rushed home to change clothes and hurried to a friend's son's wedding. Seeing Tanchum Lavan at the class had reminded him of his obligation to call Elisha, but he was the *mesader kiddushin*, so he had to reach the hall on time. After that, he still had to drop by and say "Mazal tov" at a neighbor's son's bar mitzvah. At that affair, an old acquaintance pulled him aside to ask his advice on a certain urgent matter. By the time Rav Rephael arrived home it was after midnight.

The next morning Rav Rephael awoke a bit later than usual, and during the course of the day the shidduch between Elisha and Tanchum Lavan was all but forgotten. However, when he saw Tanchum again at class, the whole issue came to the forefront of his mind, and he decided that as soon as he arrived home he would phone Elisha — come what may. Who knew if the shidduch had not already gone through?

The moment Rav Rephael walked into his apartment, the phone rang. It was Elisha. The commotion he heard on the other end of the line sent a chill up Rav Rephael's spine. Indeed, his worst fears were realized. "Mazal tov!" Elisha shouted into the telephone. "Rav Rephael, we've made a shidduch! We're in your building! Come down to the Lavan apartment and drink a *L'chaim* with us!"

Rav Rephael froze and could not utter a sound. In his imagination, he could hear the screams and the sound of dishes being shattered from the Lavan household. The shidduch had gone through. Elisha was such a good friend. How could he have let this happen?

Yet Rav Rephael was not one to question Hashem's will. With a heavy heart, he went down the flight of stairs to bless his friend and his neighbor that they *shep nachas* from their children and see them build a *binyan adei ad*. These were not empty words of congratulation; it was a heartfelt plea that indeed everything should go well for the young couple.

One day a few months after the wedding, while he was talking to Elisha, the subject of shidduchim came up. Rav Rephael tried to change the subject, but Elisha had something on his mind. "Do you remember when I asked you about the shidduch with Tanchum Lavan's daughter? I always wanted to tell you that..."

Rav Rephael started to shake. He felt cold, then hot. It had finally arrived — the moment he had feared for so long.

"...we soon found out that the Lavan family had some problems."

Rav Rephael felt faint. Elisha continued. "But my daughter-in-law? What can I tell you? She's a jewel. My son is so happy. They have a wonderful life together. After all, he doesn't live with his father-in-law, and in his own home peace and contentment reign.

"I have often thought of what my son would have missed if I had heard about the Lavan family's problems beforehand and dropped the shidduch. You were so wise, Rav Rephael, to have suddenly "forgotten" that you knew Tanchum Lavan. Thanks to your memory lapse, we were able to take our diamond and place her in the proper setting."

At that moment Rav Rephael Rosenthal felt a heavy weight lifted from his heart as the words of the Rambam resonated in his mind: "Blessed is He Who has mercy on His creatures. Blessed is He Who removes darkness and brings light. Blessed is He before Whom there is no injustice or forgetfulness" (*Hilchos Tefillah*, end of *Seder ha-Tefillos*).

Heavenly Messengers

WHO DIDN'T KNOW the Talisky family? Our moshav was small, and not only did everyone know everyone else, but they were all followers of the same Rebbe. Everybody's daughters went to the same school, and all the boys learned together in the same *cheder* and studied together in the same *yeshiva ketanah* and *yeshiva gedolah*. Most of the young people settled down there after they got married. Most of the residents seemed happy enough to continue living there; they did not seem to aspire to a more urban lifestyle.

The Taliskys, however, always seemed to be having problems. Their teenage children preferred to visit friends, neighbors, and relatives as often as possible, sleeping over whenever they could, rather than be at home. The family was not a happy one, and everyone on the moshav knew it.

Areleh was the oldest child, a remarkable young man. One could not detect any sign that he came from a dysfunctional home. Blessed with many fine character traits, he was a genuine *ben Torah* who devoted himself to learning. Throughout his childhood years, Areleh's teachers had recognized his outstanding qualities, and had made an extra effort to give him the warmth and encouragement they knew he was lacking at home. By the time Areleh was a young man, his teachers could say with satisfaction that they had succeeded in helping him fulfill his potential and had set him on the right path.

When Areleh was ready to enter yeshiva, his rebbes decided it was in his best interest to study far away from home. They therefore chose for him an excellent yeshiva known for its exacting standards. They even arranged for some young married men studying there to keep an eye on Areleh and report back to them. His mentors were pleased with his progress and diligence, and delighted to hear that he was popular with his peers and rabbis alike.

When the time came to arrange a shidduch for him, it seemed to have been decreed on High that Areleh marry into a happy, stable family. This made up for the lack of parental attention he had suffered in his childhood. And there wasn't a warmer or friendlier home on the whole moshav than that of Bunim Dushinsky.

The shadchan first discussed his idea with Bunim's brother and brother-in-law. They all agreed that Areleh was a first-class *bachur*. But when they proposed the shidduch to Bunim himself, he was reluctant to consider the match. He had never heard a word said against Areleh, whom he rememberd well. Bunim's daughter was a fine girl with all the wonderful character traits that distinguish a true Jewish daughter, and he knew that she could make an excellent match with a good boy from a good family. Why should Bunim settle for less?

When the shadchan saw Bunim hesitating, he asked Areleh's rosh yeshiva to talk to Bunim. The rosh yeshiva could not praise Areleh enough, and stated unequivocally that he was the best boy in the whole yeshiva. Bunim Dushinsky was impressed with the rosh yeshiva's enthusiasm, and he certainly did not doubt his sincerity, but still he did not feel 100 percent confident in going ahead with the match. He told the shadchan he would think about it. As a result, the whole thing dragged on and almost came to a standstill.

One Shabbos, three bachurim visited the moshav, curious about rural life. They had arranged to sleep in the home of a moshavnik who was spending Shabbos elsewhere. After *Ma'ariv* on Friday night, Bunim Dushinsky noticed that no one had invited them home for the Shabbos meal, and declared that they would be his guests.

During the meal, the *bachurim* asked many questions about the community. They asked if the boys generally went away to yeshiva after bar mitzvah, as some do in the cities. Bunim told them that only a few boys went away; most stayed at home and learned in the local *yeshiva ketanah* and *yeshiva gedolah*. If a boy went away to yeshiva, he said, it was generally an indication that he needed special attention or help.

The three *bachurim* said as one, "But the best boy in our yeshiva is an out-of-town boy, and he actually comes from this moshav."

"Who is that?" asked Bunim.

"Aharon Talisky," they answered. "He's a really fine *bachur*." They spoke of Areleh with such enthusiasm that Bunim began to have second thoughts about the proposed shidduch. More than anything, he was taken aback at the *hashgachah pratis* that had brought these *bachurim* to the moshav. He finally decided to go ahead with the shidduch.

Later that month Bunim's daughter became engaged to Areleh Talisky, and to this day Reb Bunim Dushinsky has never regretted his decision.

An Unexpected Phone Call

W E ALL BELIEVE with perfect faith that Hashem rewards every good deed, but since we live in a time of *hester panim*, the system behind reward and punishment is also hidden from us. Every so often, however, Hashem allows us a glimpse into this system. These glimpses should be treasured and stored in our hearts to strengthen us during the hidden moments.

Every shidduch is a story of *hashgachah pratis*, but I believe mine has an added dimension to it. When my son turned twenty-one, my husband and I realized that the time had come to start looking for a shidduch for him. Although my son possesses many good qualities and is highly intelligent, he was simply unable to sit and learn day and night, and we braced ourselves for a long search. Unfortunately, many families will not even consider the good qualities of a boy who is not the outstanding *masmid* of his yeshiva.

One evening soon after we had set the wheels in motion, the telephone rang. A woman we knew only slightly called to suggest a shidduch for our son. We immediately began to look into it and, to make a short story even shorter, we found all the details eminently satisfactory. Things went smoothly, the parents liked each other and came to an amicable agreement about all the details, and we arranged for the couple to meet. *Baruch Hashem,* there also things went well, and before long our son became engaged to a truly wonderful girl.

For weeks afterward, both sides, including all the close relatives, were bombarded with good wishes and complimentary remarks about the wonderfully suitable shidduch. We ourselves were awed at the speed and smoothness of events — this was the first time either of the pair had met a prospective candidate!

One evening, as my husband and I were discussing this wonderful blessing for the hundredth time, he suddenly said, "Wait a minute! I just remembered something.

"Do you remember when our son was a child of about five or six, there was a young man in his teens who used to come to daven in our shul in a wheelchair? The poor boy had lost a leg from cancer, and our son, who was always a tremendous *ba'al chessed*, decided to appoint himself as that young man's helper. He used to stand and daven right next to him during the whole service in order to be at his beck and call."

Indeed I remembered. The young man passed away some time later, and we moved to a different neighborhood. The whole incident was forgotten. But my husband suddenly realized that our *shadchante* was none other than that young man's mother!

I cannot help but imagine that that young man had been waiting all those years in *Shamayim* to repay his little helper.

Tzviki

BEREL LOOKED LONG and lovingly at his newborn son lying in his bassinet. It was his ninth child. The familiar, warm, fatherly feeling rose in his heart, and he felt attached to every line in his son's asymmetrical face. Tzviki had also been born with a breathing problem, and he had already undergone a complicated operation which left him with a strange, loud whistle with every breath he took. Yet Tzviki was a greater treasure, Berel felt, than all the money in the world.

In his infancy, Tzviki's breathing problems were a terrible burden for his dedicated parents. The family suffered through awful nights with inhalators and oxygen masks. The neighbors pitied them and acquaintances looked the other way, disturbed by the peculiar-looking face that peeped out of the baby blankets, but Berel's heart was deeply attached to Tzviki. He was thirty-five when Tzviki was born, but he didn't feel too old to tussle and play with his beloved son just as he had with his older children.

That is how it is: Hashem decrees — and fulfills. When He issues a decree against a person, He infuses him with powerful abilities to withstand it. The love Berel felt for Tzviki infected the entire family. Tzviki grew up like any normal baby. His brothers and sisters loved him just as they loved their brother who had been born two years earlier and their sister who was born a year and a half later. To his parents' joy, Tzviki's development was natural and normal. Physically he was healthy and emotionally he was a delight, *baruch Hashem*.

Everything was fine except for his overly loud breathing and his somewhat frightening appearance. When his parents brought him to preschool for the first time, the teacher turned white as a sheet. Her assistant quickly found some corner of a toy shelf that suddenly needed urgent dusting. Berel noticed their reaction and explained that Tzviki was a perfectly normal child in all respects. In two days, he promised, everyone would get used to his looks.

Although the teachers got used to him, the children kept their distance. One of the older children decided to pick on him, and the other children followed. One day Berel himself saw one of the smaller children grab a toy from Tzviki. Berel was upset and yelled at the boy.

"Why? Why did you do that?" The child was frightened and started to cry. That set Tzviki crying too, and even Berel's eyes suddenly became moist.

Tzviki became inured to this type of incident as he grew up. Since he was endowed with normal abilities and intelligence, he went to an ordinary *cheder* with other children his age. They, however, thought nothing of the blessing of being able to breathe normally and had never felt the pain of having people grimace as they did whenever they looked at Tzviki's face.

The years passed, and even when Tzviki learned to accept his lot, Berel was infuriated anew by each insult. It took Berel years to understand that the rest of the world did not appreciate the worth of his treasure and had no notion of Tzviki's diamond character. Berel finally learned to make peace with the situation and accept it with love rather than anger. Berel came to a firm conclusion: it was enough for him that Tzviki was Tzviki, and that he and ha-Kadosh Baruch Hu knew it. He no longer needed Tzviki's acceptance by the rest of the world.

This resolution strengthened Berel twenty-five years later when Tzviki was the only boy from his entire class who was not yet engaged. "You know," Berel once told his brother, "I really don't understand it. My Tzviki is pure gold. Pure gold! I have no other words to describe him. How can it be that his looks stand in his way?"

"It's not only that," his brother said, trying to lower Berel's expectations. "People say he is naive and a bit withdrawn, immature."

Berel was furious. "What else would you expect? Life hasn't been too good to him. Of course he's withdrawn. Of course he's a bit different. So what? Tzviki needs a warm, understanding family to marry into, and they in turn would receive a pure, untainted soul.

"It's true that I see only his good side," Berel added. "But Tzviki really is a wonderful boy."

Berel knew he was right, but he nevertheless had to constantly repeat to himself this refrain: It's enough that Tzviki is Tzviki. Hashem and I know it and I don't need the whole world to know it too.

"Leave it to ha-Kadosh Baruch Hu to manage things," Berel reassured Tzviki. "He knows your virtues, and He knows that your disability shouldn't force you into a life with people who are not worthy of you. We will wait patiently and Hashem will help."

And so they waited. And waited. Berel was already in his sixties, but he was not impatient. He was sure it was only a matter of time, and in the end Tzviki would be married like everyone else, establish himself, and raise a wonderful family, b'ezras Hashem. It wasn't easy, but when you know something is for the best, you can live with it. Happiness doesn't necessarily walk hand in hand with an easy life.

It is said that finding a shidduch is like splitting the Red Sea. For Tzviki salvation came from a completely unexpected direction, as it so often does in the case of shidduchim.

One searing afternoon in Elul, Berel and Tzviki were walking toward the grave of the holy Ari in Tzefas. The heat of the beating sun dried up everything, and they sat down to rest a bit. They had come to pray at various graves of tzaddikim in preparation for the Days of Awe. They took another sip of their drinks and were just about to start walking again when a black car stopped next to them. A chassid opened the window and asked them in Yiddish how to get to the cemetery. Berel told him they were also going there and suggested that if he gave them a lift they would all get there faster.

Tzviki sat next to the driver and Berel sat in the back. The car drove along the quiet road, with only Tzviki's breathing whistling in the air. As they left the car, the three walked down the long hill toward the cemetery. For some reason, the chassid stayed with them the whole time, from the grave of the Ari to the grave of Rabbi Pinchas ben Ya'ir. The man, who had come from abroad and did not know the area, suggested that they continue traveling together to Meron. Again Tzviki sat in front next to the driver, while the three marveled at the *hashgachah pratis* that had arranged such convenient transportation for Berel and Tzviki and such good guides for the visitor from afar.

In Meron, while Tzviki was davening in front of the holy grave site, the chassid called Berel aside. In a low voice, the man asked Berel about Tzviki; his name, his general situation, and the reason for his noisy breathing. Berel told him everything, for Meron opens hearts. In a whisper, the visitor told Berel about his sister, a wonderful girl of nineteen, who had also undergone a difficult operation at birth, which had scarred her face and affected her breathing. "She has every virtue," he said in a trembling voice, "but the world doesn't recognize it."

"It's enough that Hashem knows it," Berel repeated his motto, and he stood amazed while the Red Sea opened up at his feet.

...And the Study of Torah Is Equal to Everything

(Mishnah Peah, Chapter 1)

Learning Cannot Be Compromised

ABOUT FIFTEEN YEARS AGO, a friend of mine, the director of an organization that runs a network of educational and charitable institutions in Eretz Yisrael, called me and offered me a temporary job.

"For the survival of our institutions," he said, "I think we must have a large fundraising event. We would like to organize a gala dinner, and we will set up a special office for this purpose. We will need someone to run it for the few months it will take to plan and set up the dinner, and to attend to all the preparations down to the last detail. We have a large staff all over Israel with whom the preparations must be coordinated. I think you could do a good job for us, particularly since you are self-employed and have flexible hours and workdays."

He was right. *Be-siyata diShmaya*, I felt truly suited to the task, and I felt that I would be working for a good cause. The main work would need about three weeks of my time, about five or six hours a day, and they would provide all the office help I would need. Last but not least, they were willing to pay me an excellent salary.

The job turned out to be more complicated than I had expected, but, *baruch Hashem*, I was able to cope with its demands. I was responsible for every last thing from A to Z: from arranging the participation of the communications company that was going to back the event, to deciding which fruit the caterer would put in the fruit cup; from designing the invitations, to editing the journal that would be given out at the dinner.

The event was a great success, and the funds we raised went a long way toward maintaining the institutions for the next few years. Heaven helped me arrange a successful affair that fueled the growing reputation of the institutions and made the directors very happy. My salary was paid in full and on time, and I was satisfied.

A few years went by, and the organization's director decided to hold another dinner. He asked me to head the organizing committee again. After several weeks of great effort and hard work, and with God's help, the event was a success. In the years following, I was asked to organize a dinner for the third and fourth time, each time with resounding success, and the extra income helped me out of many family emergencies.

Last year I read in the newspaper that the institutions were planning to hold yet another gala dinner on Rosh Chodesh Adar, and I knew that I would be asked to fill the position for the fifth time. Although I knew they were pleased with my work and were anxious to take advantage of the experience I had acquired during the previous fifteen years — and though the extra income would certainly be most welcome — this time I did not look forward so eagerly to accepting the expected offer. This time I had to take something else into account.

For two years I had been giving a Gemara *shiur* to about twenty young married men. The class was given every evening, and I knew I would not be able to devote myself unreservedly to organizing the dinner if I continued teaching.

You see, one of the principal emphases of my class was the value that *kevius itim*, learning regularly at a fixed time, added to the value of the learning itself. We had often discussed the importance of not only learning Torah, but of acquiring the habit of regular learning times and not allowing anything to interfere with them. We built our faithfulness to the *shiur* out of the firm persistence and innumerable sacrifices of the participants. We were determined that, come what may, the class came before everything — for our own sakes, for the sake of our children's education, for this world, and for the World of Reward.

In light of this, I did not see how I could sever this connection to eternal life — even for a few weeks — for a job in the temporal world, no matter how important or even necessary it might be. There were, after all, others who could organize the dinner, and no doubt many candidates would apply. Moreover, the class, to a certain degree, rested mainly on me.

On the other hand, I thought, perhaps I could find someone to take my place to ensure that the class would continue while I organized the dinner. What a bitter taste I would have in my mouth, though, when I announced to the men that I would be leaving the class for three weeks. It might result in others skipping a *shiur* here or there to take care of pressing matters. Our firm discipline would be shattered, and then what would happen to learning Torah?

I deliberated. I wavered back and forth. On one side was the dedication to Torah of twenty young men and the gravity of breaking our *kevius*. On the other side lay the temptation to do something I knew so well how to do, something that was meaningful to me and served a noble purpose. Not only that, but I was about to publish a new set of Shas in an innovative small format. The Shas would ensure many added hours of learning Torah by virtue of its size, and would be a tremendous service to many. To publish it, however, I needed a great deal of money, and the temporary job would just about cover my expenses.

Still, I thought, the eternal daily sustenance of a Jew is based on fixed times for Torah study, on a commitment to learning that is like an immovable stake planted firmly in the ground. As the *maggid shiur*, I had to be a model and example of such faithfulness. I did not know what to do. I tried to understand what ha-Kadosh Baruch Hu wanted me to do just then, but it was hard to see which thoughts came from the *yetzer ha-tov*...and which were from the other side.

Finally, I decided that I would not call them; I would wait and see if they called me. If they called and offered me the job, I would take it as a sign that I should look for a substitute *maggid shiur* and I would accept.

The phone call was not long in coming, and the invitation was firm. "We really need your expertise this year. Our financial situation is precarious, and the prevailing economic situation has made it difficult to continue. The institutions are in danger of collapse, and their future is in the balance. The rabbis with whom we have consulted have instructed us to do everything to maintain our educational and charitable work, and even to expand our efforts," the director told me.

When I explained my problem to him he answered, "This is

ratzon Hashem; it is a matter of *kevod Shamayim.* With your help, we can continue to maintain Torah for thousands of young children, yeshiva students, and *kollel* men. You will have the merit of being a partner in all this. Besides," the director continued persuasively, his spiritual motivation apparent in his words, "what is being asked, after all? Only three weeks. On Rosh Chodesh Adar, it will all be over."

I gave him a halfhearted agreement. "All right," I said, but my heart wasn't in it, and I was not at peace with myself. I heard the other side of the story, the *shiur* and its twenty members calling me in the same language: "You must come. This is not the time for excuses. The *shiur* is in danger; its future lies in the balance. All are called to be faithful to it, and no one is exempt. This is the *ratzon Hashem,* a matter of *kevod Shamayim.*"

I had found a replacement to give the class, but I was still uncertain. If a *maggid* shiur leaves for money, no matter how holy his cause, then why shouldn't one of his students who sees covering his debts a goal no less holy than publishing a book, do the same? After all, I would be the one who had proved that dedicating hours to Torah is a flexible thing and that anything could be done at its expense.

One morning, I opened the paper and saw a notice put out by the organization I was supposed to begin working for. It was addressed to all the activists in the country, and gave a list of the representatives in every region and the names of the coordinators. A quick glance showed that my name and phone number appeared large and clear. It was a sort of final seal, ending my deliberations on the matter.

That evening, after class, I told the men about the situation and my doubts. I explained that although in principle there was no doubt that learning Torah was above all else, there were still times when a person had to get up in order to perform a mitzvah. Just as a person can stop his learning to take care of his basic needs, so it is sometimes necessary to close one's Gemara for the needs of the hour. But I also explained that it had not been this principle alone that had convinced me to take the job. The main thing was the large amount of money I still needed to publish the Shas I had told them so much about.

I made it clear that though I felt far from wholehearted about it, once my name had been printed and published, I no longer had a choice. I told my students that I would leave them with a substitute for the next three weeks until Hashem in His greatness would bring the great mission of supporting a network of dozens of Torah institutions to its happy conclusion.

The members of the *shiur* were understandably shocked. What I was doing completely opposed the firm policy of faithfulness to learning by which the class was run. And I had even admitted openly that it was not the holy work that had spoken to me, and that it was not that there weren't many other talented people who could do the job — but that I was doing it for the money. I would not have left the *shiur* before this to find funding for publishing the Shas, so why was I leaving everything behind me for three weeks for this dinner?

One of the men said, "This is a question for a Torah authority. Why haven't you asked a Rav what you should do?" He was right, of course.

The next day found me standing before one of the *gedolei ha-dor*. I explained my quandary and apologized for having come to him after the fact, after I had already been appointed to do the job.

"The class will be fine with a substitute," the Rebbe said after a while. "The publication of the Shas will be assured, but for you personally, it is not worth it. You personally have committed yourself to a bad deal. To leave a Torah *shiur* for one day? To miss participating in a Torah class? It is not a simple matter."

I corrected the false impression I had given the Rebbe. "I meant to leave the class for three weeks, not just for the day of the dinner."

"Three weeks, not one day?" repeated the Rebbe. "There is no question about three weeks. Of course you should not do it. It's not worth it. Not at all worth it."

"And what about the large sum I need so badly?" I asked hesitantly. "I don't get such an opportunity every day, especially for so noble a cause."

"Money?" asked the Rebbe in surprise. "Money is something to talk about? Are these people the ones who give money? Ha-Kadosh Baruch Hu can send you money from some other source, but a Torah *shiur* one doesn't miss."

The Rebbe added one more thing. "Even when I thought you meant one day only, I felt that it was not worth it to you, for it reminded me of something that happened in the time of the Chazon Ish. A Jew from Bnei Brak, who gave a regular class in Ramat Gan, once came to the Chazon Ish on a very stormy, wet winter day. He asked the Chazon Ish if he had to make the effort to go to Ramat Gan in such weather. Public transportation wasn't running, he explained, and probably no more than one person would show up for the class. Was it worth the effort?

"The Chazon Ish told him, 'For one Yid it is worth *walking* from Bnei Brak to Ramat Gan is such heavy rain.' I remembered this story when you told me of your dilemma," the Rebbe told me, "and based on that, I decided that for the sake of only one man in the class, just one, it would be worth it to give up the job and all the money. But when it turns out that it would be for three weeks, then there is no question. It is inconceivable. It is not worth it to you. It's a bad deal."

Our Sages say, "What does one who sees sages of Israel say? *Baruch she-chalak me-chochmaso li-yereiav,* 'Blessed is He Who gave of His wisdom to those who fear Him.' " We, small human beings that we are, have no notion of the holiness of the Torah. We don't have the faintest shadow of a concept of the worth of one word of Torah study, which is why I was able to put money for a holy cause and working for a holy cause on a higher footing than a regular Torah *shiur*. Only those wise in Torah can prevent us from throwing away a treasure with our own hands.

There was once a resident of Chelm who wanted to roast potatoes over a fire. He looked for some tinder with which to start his fire, and found a sackfull of rustling hundred-dollar bills. Being a simple wagon driver, he had no idea what dollars were. He hoisted the sack of money onto his shoulders, ran out to an empty field, set fire to the sack, and began roasting his potatoes in great good humor. As the flames began to consume the bills, the wagon driver sat back to wait for a veritable feast. He had found superb tinder today, he thought, with none of that sooty smell of burnt wood to spoil his potatoes.

A man passed by, saw what the wagon driver was doing, and began to shout. He fell upon the wagon driver and beat him about the shoulders, crying, "Put out the fire! Oh, what a fool you are! With the stuff in that sack you could have bought acres of potato fields! What is more, you could have had servants serving you roasted potatoes from morning till night!"

The wagon driver defended himself, saying, "But just think of the delicious supper I will have."

The man furiously shouted, "Forget about the supper you're going to have. With your own hands, you have destroyed enough money to support you for the rest of your life!"

Lehavdil a million *havdalos*, a Torah shiur is worth much more to me than a sackfull of hundred-dollar bills. But I wanted, in my ignorance, to burn my sack so I could prepare a rich, tasty meal of a few thousand shekels, in order to publish a set of *sefarim* — to lose a fortune in order to find a short-term solution to a problem.

"Money?" the Rebbe had said. "Money is something to talk about? Are these people the ones who give money? Ha-Kadosh Baruch Hu can send you money from some other source, but a Torah *shiur* one doesn't miss."

With Hashem's great mercy, my sack had not yet been burnt. I still had the merit of saving my great treasure, my regular *shiur*. With an uneasy heart, I canceled the delicious meal I had expected to have.

"I sincerely wanted to help," I told the worthy director, "but my Rebbe judged that the class comes before everything else."

The director made one last attempt. "Did you tell him both sides? Did you say your talents are very important to the crucial campaign ahead of us?"

"I told him everything, in detail, but his ruling was that one does not give up a Torah class."

From there I went straight to the main office of the organization, gave back the briefcase full of material and the beeper they had given me, and called my substitute to cancel. I arrived at the class that evening with peace of mind. The group could not believe their eyes. "I had a hard time with it," I told them. "I asked *da'as Torah* and the answer was clear."

Since I would not be able to fall back on the ample earnings from the dinner to finance my Shas, I figured I had better do my bit of *hishtadlus*. I had accumulated a short list of people I thought might be willing and able to help me financially. It would probably take me a long time to raise as much as I might have earned working those three weeks on the dinner, but I began to make a few telephone calls nevertheless. The first person I called was a man who a year ago had said he was definitely interested in the project, but at the time I had first contacted him, he was unable to help me. When I called this time, he asked me to come see him on Rosh Chodesh Adar.

At the appointed time, I visited him in his office and explained the various advantages of the small-size Shas I had prepared for publication. Each tractate was to be printed separately in a small, inexpensive format that could easily be carried in one's pocket. He agreed with me that it would be a boon to students and working men alike. The affable gentlemen withdrew a checkbook from his pocket and wrote out a check for me on the spot.

To my utter astonishment, the amount written on the check was almost exactly the same amount I would have received at the dinner, to be held that evening on Rosh Chodesh Adar.

Setting Aside Time for Learning

 ORDCHA, A YOUNG MAN from Ashdod, faithfully attends a *shiur* every evening that ends at 8:00 P.M. This year on the night of his grandfather's yahrtzeit, his family had arranged to gather for a *seudah* in Bnei Brak. In order for

Mordcha to participate, he would have to leave the central bus station in Ashdod on the 8:00 P.M. bus and no later. The next bus left at 9:30.

Initially he considered making an exception and leaving the class a few minutes earlier. His conscience, however, did not permit this. It told him in no uncertain terms that even a few precious minutes of Torah study takes precedence over everything else. He then thought that since the bus takes about fifteen minutes to do its round of stops in Ashdod, he might just be able to take a taxi to the last bus stop in town and still get to the *seudah* in time.

It would cost him more that way, but he concluded that it was worth it for him to lose out monetarily for the sake of the mitzvah's reward, for in the end, nothing costs more dearly than *bitul Torah*.

The class ended at the regular time and Mordcha went outside to look for a taxi. The street was a main thoroughfare, and ordinarily taxis were easy to find. That evening, however, for some mysterious reason, there were no taxis in sight. He began to walk toward a taxi station nearby but when he got there, no taxis were waiting there either.

Now this was very strange. It was already 8:30, and Mordcha was certain the bus for Bnei Brak had already left the city. Resignedly, he turned around and set out for his home. He was consoled by the thought that at least he had not lost a single moment of Torah learning, and thought that perhaps it would be a merit for his grandfather's memory on the day of his yahrtzeit.

As he walked past one of the last stops on the bus route, he was pleasantly surprised to see the eight o'clock bus to Bnei Brak pull up. Naturally he boarded the bus, and the driver told him that they had been delayed for half an hour in the terminal because of a bomb scare.

Mordcha quietly thanked Hashem for having worked things out so well. He had saved the expense of a taxi and still caught the right bus. He would be able to join his family at the yahrtzeit gathering, and he was particularly grateful that he had not wasted a precious moment of his learning. He felt it was a clear sign from Above that it does not pay to make concessions on spiritual matters, however small they may seem.

As it happened, Mordcha had to apply this principle again soon thereafter when the yahrtzeit of his grandmother came around. Once again the family planned to gather together at a *seudah* in her memory, once again in Bnei Brak. This time Mordcha spent no time at all worrying how he would get to Bnei Brak on time. Obviously, he would go to his *shiur* and leave at the appointed time. His trip to Bnei Brak would take place somehow — or not at all.

Mordcha managed to find a taxi when he left the class, but because of a traffic jam, he arrived at the last bus stop too late. He waited a few minutes at the stop in the faint hope that someone would pass by in a car on the way to Bnei Brak and take him along, although it wasn't likely that a passing driver would expect to see anyone at the bus stop at that hour and thus slow down.

To his astonishment, however, a driver did stop and offer him a lift. It turned out to be a friend who had recognized him, and he offered to take Mordcha to Bnei Brak. Once again, Mordcha experienced *hashgachah pratis* and the satisfaction of knowing that he had not neglected the smallest part of his duty to learn.

Signs from Above

NOT LONG AGO, I heard about the grave of Rav Avdimi d'min Haifa. It is situated just at the entrance to the present-day city of Haifa. Those who prayed at his grave, especially on *erev Rosh Chodesh*, were said to have merited having their prayers answered. This *segulah* was said to be particularly effective if you came to pray three consecutive times on *erev Rosh Chodesh*.

Hashem surely listens to everyone's prayers, whenever and wherever they are offered. Nevertheless, this does not take away from our belief in the famous words of the Ran, that just as there are certain auspicious times in which our prayers are more readily received, so are there certain places that in the merit of their inherent holiness and the holiness of the *tzaddik* resting there, they cause our prayers to be more easily heard and accepted. In the words of the Ran, "It is praiseworthy to visit the graves of *tzaddikim* and to pray there because prayer in such places is extremely desirable [to Hashem]."

It just happened that I was in need of a *yeshuah* in a certain matter when I heard about this *segulah*. The following *erev Rosh Chodesh*, I traveled north from Jerusalem to pray at Rav Avdimi's grave. A few days later I could already see a marked improvement in the matter I had prayed about at the grave, and I gave heartfelt thanks to Hashem for his salvation, and for the *tzaddikim* whose strength is often greater after their deaths than during their lives. Hundreds of years after their lifetimes, *tzaddikim* continue to assist, defend, and bring deliverance as they elevate *tefillos* and act as advocates for us on High.

I devote a specific hour every day to learn with a certain *bachur* at his yeshiva. No matter what happens, I make a special effort never to miss this learning session. When the next *erev Rosh Chodesh* approached following my first visit to Rav Avdimi's grave, I told the *bachur* of my plans and that I would be happy to take him with me in my car to Haifa. I was anxious to return and pray once again next to Rav Avdimi's grave, but I didn't want to miss our learning either. I suggested that he ask permission from his rosh yeshiva to accompany me.

The rosh yeshiva answered that he knew that the Rebbe of the chassidic circle to which the yeshiva, as well as the *bachur* and I, belong, opposed traveling, and always counseled his chassidim to travel as little as possible. The rosh yeshiva did not specify the reason for the Rebbe's objection — whether it was due to spiritual or physical dangers on the road.

After hearing the rosh yeshiva's decision, I decided that I, too, would forgo the trip. If the Rebbe opposed traveling, then I, as a loyal chassid, was willing to forfeit all *segulos* and remedies, exalted as they might be, and submit to the Rebbe's will. I told the *bachur*, who was somewhat disappointed, that a person never loses out by listening to his Rebbe.

Even though I had decided not to travel to Haifa to visit his grave, I still felt a special connection with Rav Avdimi. On the morning of that *erev Rosh Chodesh*, I lit a candle in his memory, and thought that even if I was not at his grave personally, I would still be there in spirit. Before I began learning with the *bachur* I said to him, "Everything that we learn and every mitzvah that we perform today will be for the merit of Rav Avdimi of Haifa."

I was certain that if we filled the day with mitzvos for the merit of Rav Avdimi, we would benefit from it and have our prayers answered even if we were prevented from going to the actual grave site. Complying with the wishes of the Rebbe was a mitzvah in itself.

In this spirit we decided to extend our regular learning session by an hour. The learning seemed to flow, and we both derived great satisfaction from it. During the extra hour that we had taken upon ourselves, we suddenly came upon a *memrah*, a saying, of Rav Avdimi d'min Haifa.

"I can't believe this!" the *bachur* exclaimed. I could hardly believe it myself. I felt my heart skip a beat from excitement. It was as if Rav Avdimi himself had come to learn with us.

What was incredible about this is that it is very unusual to come across a saying of Rav Avdimi in the Babylonian Talmud. In the whole Gemara there are only five such sayings in his name! It was really an extraordinary occurrence to come upon one precisely when we were learning in his memory, during the extra hour that we had added in his honor. This reminded me of something I have heard pertaining to those who are unable to go to Meron on Lag ba-Omer. *Chazal* say, "Rabbi Shimon can be found in the Gemara." We had found our way to Rav Avdimi.

We repeated the words several times, and we were all the more amazed to see that this halachah was especially significant for us under the circumstances. "Rav Avdimi of Haifa said, 'Ever since the destruction of the *Beis ha-Mikdash*, although prophecy was taken from the prophets, it was not taken from the scholars.'"

We continued to learn with even greater enthusiasm, feeling that this was Divine confirmation that we had made the correct decision in obeying the Rebbe and not canceling our learning session. We were even more astonished a short while later when we came across another saying of Rav Avdimi in tractate *Bava Basra* (12b). I thought I was dreaming. Two out of five within one hour! I could not have felt more in touch with Rav Avdimi even had I made the trip all the way to his grave.

It is impossible to fathom the full metaphysical and eternal significance of even one Torah learning session. Nor can we fathom the depths of the wisdom of our *gedolim*. We must never belittle either of these two foundations of *Yiddishkeit*, not even for matters that we may think are more important. I was guided by Heaven to obey the Rebbe and cancel my trip; as a result, I was with Rav Avdimi in spirit and had the privilege to learn two *halachos* in his name, thus causing "his lips to murmur Torah in his grave."

When even the most ordinary person performs a spiritual act with enthusiasm, his act will be sanctioned in Heaven and he will receive Divine assistance.

He Has Because He Gives

A WORTHY *TALMID CHACHAM* in Jerusalem decided to strengthen Torah study by founding *yeshivos bein ha-zemanim* (yeshivas that operate during vacation), to be located in various shuls throughout Eretz Yisrael. He appointed a young man in each shul to be his representative. Each of these young men had to organize classes and special Torah lectures for the boys who participated. Each representative was to inform the boys of the learning times and record their attendance. Afterward, he was to send this list to the *talmid chacham,* who intended to buy a gift for each boy who attended regularly.

This was an expensive undertaking, for there was a large number of participants. The founder did not have the means to support such a large-scale project. He was not wealthy; on the contrary, he was the father of a large family and had many debts to pay.

Why did he do this? Only because he was a man willing to take upon himself an additional debt of tens of thousands of shekels every year so long as Torah was not neglected. Just as he counted on Hashem's help to marry off his children, he felt certain that Hashem would help him find the means to carry out this project as well. The Creator would certainly help him shoulder an added load that was only initiated to honor Him and glorify His Torah.

Torah was studied by dozens and dozens of boys before Pesach and Sukkos, on *chol ha-mo'ed* and *isru chag*, and the day before *Yom Tov* as well as *Yom Tov* afternoons. Many of the parents of these boys were aware of the greatness of this project, and were eager to offer their monetary assistance. Some even made donations without being asked. Some of the founder's friends and acquaintances also wanted to partake in this privilege. There was no lack of money. All this only proved to the initiator that Heaven was constantly helping him. If a person does only a little bit, Hashem will do the rest.

Everything was going smoothly. The representatives did their jobs, large groups formed in many places, and pages of Gemara were learned for hours.

During the 1999 Pesach break, a friend of the *talmid chacham's*, an ardent admirer of this project, handed him an envelope containing five thousand shekels. This man, one of Hashem's many messengers, was a regular donor who had once even gone into debt for this cause. The *talmid chacham* was filled with joy. He thanked the donor for everything, but the man shrugged it off, honestly feeling as if he should thank his friend for the privilege of helping.

The next day, Heaven rewarded them both. The founder's friend was notified that he had won a large amount of money in the national lotto: five thousand shekels! He hurried to his friend once again, to show him who really had to thank Whom.

As the Jewish saying goes, "He does not give because he has; he has because he gives."

Glossary

The following glossary provides a partial explanation of some of the Hebrew, Yiddish (Y.), and Aramaic (A.) words and phrases used in this book. The spellings and explanations reflect the way the specific word is used herein. Often, there are alternate spellings and meanings for the words.

ABBA: father.
A"H: a Hebrew acronym for *aleiha ha-shalom,* "May she rest in peace."
ADAM HA-RISHON: Adam, the first man.
AKDAMUS: a special liturgical poem recited on the Festival of SHAVUOS.
AL HA-NISSIM: a prayer of thanks for miracles, added to the prayer service and the Grace after Meals on Chanukah and Purim.
ALIYAH: lit., ascent; the honor of being called up to say the blessings over the Torah; a section of the Torah read in synagogue.
ALTER BACHUR: (Y.) lit., "older boy"; an unmarried man above the usual matrimony age.
AMORA: (A.) a Sage whose opinions are included in the GEMARA.
ARONO BA: lit., "his coffin is arriving"; the usual opening line of the obituary notice of someone being brought to Eretz Yisrael for burial.
AV BEIS DIN: the head of a Jewish court of law.
AVODAS HASHEM: service of God.
AVRAHAM AVINU: our forefather Abraham.

BA'ALAS CHESSED: a woman distinguished by her many acts of kindness.
BA'AL TESHUVAH: a penitent; a formerly non-observant Jew who returns to the Torah.
BACHUR: a boy, a young man.
BARUCH HA-MEICHIN MITZ'ADEI GAVER: "Blessed is He Who prepares the steps of man."
BARUCH HASHEM: "Thank God!"

BASHERT: (Y.) meant to be, destined.
BAYIS NE'EMAN/BATIM NE'EMANIM BE'YISRAEL: everlasting Jewish home(s).
BEIN HA-ZEMANIM: YESHIVA intersession.
BEIS DIN: a Jewish court of law.
BEIS HA-MIKDASH: the Holy Temple in Jerusalem.
BEIS MIDRASH: a "house of study"; the study hall of a YESHIVA.
BEIS TEFILLIN: the box holding the TEFILLIN.
BEN TORAH: one who is devoted to Torah.
BESAMIM: the spices used in the HAVDALAH ceremony.
B'EZRAS HASHEM: "With God's help"; "God willing."
BIKUR CHOLIM: the MITZVAH of visiting the sick.
BINYAN ADEI AD: an eternal edifice.
BITACHON: trust and faith in God.
BITUL TORAH: the misuse of one's time in non-Torah pursuits.
B'LI AYIN HA-RA: "barring the evil eye"; said to ward off possible misfortune.
B'LI NEDER: lit., "without a vow"; a phrase that changes a firm promise into an intention.
BRIS: the circumcision ceremony.
BUBBIE: (Y.) grandma.

CHALLAH/CHALLOS: special braided loaves eaten on the Sabbath and Festivals.
CHAMEITZ: leavened foods that are prohibited on Passover.
CHAREIDIM: ultra-Orthodox Jews.
CHASHUV: important, distinguished.
CHASSIDISHE: (Y.) chassidic.
CHAS VE-SHALOM: "Heaven forbid!"
CHAVRUSA: (A.) a partner in Torah study.
CHAZAL: a Hebrew acronym for *Chachameinu zichronam liverachah*, "Our Sages of blessed memory."
CHEDER: (Y. colloq.) lit., room; a religious primary school for boys.
CHESSED: lovingkindness.
CHESSED SHEL EMES: lit., "true kindness"; a kindness that cannot be reciprocated, such as that done for a deceased person.
CHEVRAH: a group of friends.
CHEVRAH KADDISHA: (A.) a burial society.
CHILLUL HASHEM: the desecration of God's Name.
CHOL HA-MO'ED: the intermediate days of the Festivals of SUKKOS and Passover.
CHUMASH: (one of) the Five Books of Moses.
CHUPPAH: lit., the wedding canopy; a wedding ceremony.

DA'AS TORAH: the accepted, Torah-based opinion of a rabbinic authority.

DAF YOMI: lit., "a daily page"; a program of learning a page of TALMUD a day.

DALET AMOS: four cubits; about six feet.

DAVEN: (Y.) pray.

DAYAN/DAYANIM: Jewish judge(s).

D'VAR TORAH: lit., a word of Torah; a Torah discourse.

EISHES CHAYIL: lit., "a woman of valor"; chapter 31 of the Book of *Mishlei*, which extols the Jewish woman.

EMUNAH: faith in God.

EMUNAS CHACHAMIM: faith in the words of the Sages.

ERETZ HA-KODESH: the Land of Holiness, i.e. the Land of Israel.

EREV ROSH CHODESH: the eve of the new Hebrew month.

EREV SHABBOS: the day preceding the Sabbath, i.e. Friday.

ESROG/ESROGIM: citron fruit(s), one of the Four Species used on the Festival of SUKKOS.

GABBAI: the secretary or treasurer of a synagogue or TZEDAKAH organization.

GAN EDEN: the Garden of Eden.

GANTZE FABRIK: (Y. colloq.) a whole big enterprise.

GAON: a genius in Torah learning.

GEDOLEI HA-DOR: the great Torah sages and leaders of the generation.

GEMACH: a free-loan fund.

GEMARA: commentary on the MISHNAH (together they comprise the TALMUD); a volume of the TALMUD.

GENIZAH: a repository for unwanted or damaged holy books and objects.

HACHNASAS ORCHIM: hospitality.

HA-KADOSH BARUCH HU: the Holy One, Blessed is He, i.e. God.

HALACHAH/HALACHOS: Jewish law(s).

HASHEM ELOKAI: the Lord, my God.

HASHGACHAH: supervision.

HASHGACHAH PRATIS: Divine supervision; Providence.

HAVDALAH: the blessing recited at the conclusion of the Sabbath and Festivals, separating the holy day from the rest of the week.

HEIMISHE: (Y.) lit., homey; simple, warm, unpretentious.

HESTER PANIM: the concealment of Divine compassion.

HISHTADLUS: effort.

HISTAPKUS: being satisfied, making do with little.

HOSHANA RABBAH: the seventh day of the Festival of SUKKOS.
HY"D: a Hebrew acronym for *Hashem yikom damo*, "May God avenge his blood," said when mentioning a Jewish martyr.

IGROS: lit., "letters"; responsa.
IMA: mother.
IMENU: our mother.
INVEI HA-GEFEN BE'INVEI HA-GEFEN: an expression for the perfect marriage; well-matched.
ISRU CHAG: the day after a Jewish Festival.

KASHRUS: the Jewish dietary laws.
KEIN YIRBU: lit., "May they multiply"; said after mentioning one's children or grandchildren.
KEVER RACHEL: the tomb of our matriarch Rachel.
KEVIUS ITIM: setting aside fixed times (for Torah study).
KEVOD HA-RAV: "Your honor"; used when speaking to a great rabbi.
KEVOD HA-TORAH: the honor of the Torah.
KEVOD SHAMAYIM: the honor of Heaven.
KIBBUD AV: honoring one's father.
KIDDUSH: the sanctification blessing of the Sabbath and Festivals, usually recited over a cup of wine or grape juice.
KIDDUSH HASHEM: the sanctification of the Divine Name; martyrdom.
KIPPAH: a skullcap.
KOL NIDRE: the opening prayer of the Yom Kippur service.
KOLLEL: a center for advanced Torah study for adult students, mostly married men.
KOSEL: the Western Wall in Jerusalem.

LAG BA-OMER: the thirty-third of the forty-nine days of the Counting of the Omer between Passover and SHAVUOS, which is a semi-holiday.
LASHON HA-RA: malicious gossip; speaking badly of another person.
LASHON KODESH: lit., "the holy tongue," i.e. Hebrew.
L'CHAIM: "To life!"; a toast made to celebrate a happy occasion.
LEHAVDIL: lit., to distinguish; used when mentioning holy and non-holy matters in one breath.
LICHVOD SHABBOS: in honor of the Sabbath.
LO ALEINU: "It shouldn't happen to us!"
LULAV/LULAVIM: palm branch(es), one of the Four Species used on the Festival of SUKKOS.

MA'ARIV: the evening prayer service.

MAGGID SHIUR: a rabbi who gives a Torah class.
MAROR: bitter herbs used in the Passover SEDER.
MASHGIACH: the spiritual guide, counselor and/or advisor of a YESHIVA.
MASMID: a diligent student.
MECHAYEH: (Y. colloq.) "a pleasure."
MECHUTAN: one's children's in-laws.
MENACHEM AVEL: to comfort a mourner.
MESADER KIDDUSHIN: the person who performs a Jewish wedding.
MESIVTA: (A.) a YESHIVA high school.
MEZUZAH: a rolled parchment containing the prayer SHEMA YISRAEL, placed on the doorposts of Jewish homes.
MIDDAH/MIDDOS: character trait(s); quality(-ies) or attribute(s).
MIKVEH: an immersion pool for ritual purification.
MINCHAH: the afternoon prayer service.
MIN HA-SHAMAYIM: from Heaven.
MINYAN: a prayer quorum of ten adult males.
MI SHEBEIRACH: a prayer for one's welfare or recovery.
MISHNAH: the codified Oral Law redacted by Rabbi Yehudah ha-Nasi; a specific paragraph of the Oral Law.
MITZVAH/MITZVOS: Torah commandment(s).
MOSER: an informer.
MOTZA'EI SHABBOS: lit., "the departure of the Sabbath," i.e. Saturday night.
MOTZA'EI SHAVUOS: the evening after the Festival of SHAVUOS ends.
MUSSAR: Torah ethics and values.

NACHAS: pride; pleasure.
NISAN: the Hebrew month corresponding to March/April.

PARASHAH: the weekly Torah portion.
PARASHIYOS: sections of the Torah contained in the TEFILLIN.
PARNASAH: livelihood.
PASKEN: (Y.) to render a decision regarding Jewish law.
PEYOS: sidelocks.
PINTELE YID: (Y.) the spark of YIDDISHKEIT found in every Jew.

RACHMANUS: compassion, mercy.
RATZON HASHEM: the will of God.
REFUAH SHELEIMAH: "Have a complete recovery."
RIBBONO SHEL OLAM: Master of the Universe.
ROSH CHODESH: the first day of a new Hebrew month.
ROSH MESIVTA: the dean of a MESIVTA.
RUACH HA-KODESH: Divine inspiration.

SABA: grandfather; grandpa.

SEDER: lit., "order"; the Passover night ceremony recounting the Exodus from Egypt and the liberation from bondage.

SEFER: a book; a holy book.

SEFER TORAH: a Torah scroll.

SEGULAH/SEGULOS: useful (often kabbalistic) endeavor(s).

SEUDAH: a festive meal.

SEUDAH SHELISHIS: the third Sabbath meal.

SHABBOS: the Sabbath.

SHABBOS KODESH: the holy Sabbath.

SHACHARIS: the morning prayer service.

SHADCHAN/SHADCHANTE (Y.): a matchmaker.

SHADAI: one of the Names of God.

SHALOM ALEICHEM: "May peace be with you," a traditional Jewish greeting.

SHAMAYIM: Heaven.

SHAS: a Hebrew acronym for *shishah sedarim*, referring to the entire Babylonian TALMUD.

SHAVUOS: the Festival of Weeks, celebrated seven weeks after Passover and commemorating the giving of the Torah at Mount Sinai.

SHECHINAH: the Divine Presence of God.

SHE'EILAH: a question arising in Jewish law.

SHEIRUT: lit., "service"; a shared cab.

SHELOSHIM: lit., thirty; the (end of the) thirty-day mourning period for a close relative.

SHEMA YISRAEL: lit., "Hear, O Israel"; the opening words of the fundamental Jewish prayer which proclaims the Unity of God, recited in daily prayers and at bedtime.

SHEMIRAS HA-LASHON: guarding one's tongue from LASHON HA-RA.

SHEMONEH ESREH: lit., "eighteen"; the eighteen blessings of the *Amidah* prayer.

SHEP NACHAS: (Y.) to reap pride.

SHEVA BERACHOS: lit., "seven blessings"; one of the festive meals given for newlyweds during the first week after their wedding.

SHEVAT: the Hebrew month corresponding to January/February.

SHIDDUCH: a marital match.

SHIUR: a Torah class.

SHIVAH: lit., seven; the seven-day mourning period for a close relative.

SHLEP: (Y.) drag.

SHLITA: a Hebrew acronym for *she-yichiyeh l'orech yamim tovim, amen*, "May he live long."

SHUK: the marketplace.
SHULCHAN ARUCH: the code of Jewish law, authored by Rabbi Yosef Karo and completed in 1555.
SIDDUR: a prayer book.
SIMCHAH: happiness; a joyous occasion.
SIYATA DISHMAYA: (A.) Heavenly assistance.
SIYUM: a celebration upon completing the study of a tractate of MISHNAH or TALMUD.
SUGYA: (A.) a topic in GEMARA.
SUKKOS: the Festival of Tabernacles.

TAHARAH: the ritual purification of a dead body before burial.
TALLIS: a prayer shawl.
TALMID CHACHAM: a Torah scholar.
TALMUD: the basic corpus of Jewish law (200 B.C.E. to 500 C.E.), consisting of the MISHNAH and the GEMARA.
TALMUD BAVLI: the Babylonian TALMUD.
TALMUD TORAH: a Torah primary school.
TAMMUZ: the Hebrew month corresponding to June/July.
TANACH: an acronym for the Bible, i.e. the Torah, the Prophets, and the Writings.
TATTIE: (Y.) father; daddy.
TECHIYAS HA-MEISIM: the ressurection of the dead.
TEFILLAH/TEFILLOS: prayer(s).
TEFILLAS HA-DERECH: a traveler's prayer for safety.
TEFILLIN: phylacteries.
TEFILLIN SHEL ROSH: the head TEFILLIN.
TEFILLIN SHEL YAD: the hand TEFILLIN.
TEHILLIM: (the Book of) Psalms.
TESHUVAH: repentance, return.
TISHAH B'AV: the ninth day of the Hebrew month of Av, commemorating the destruction of the First and Second Temples.
TUR: the code of Jewish law predating the SHULCHAN ARUCH, authored by Rabbeinu Yaakov, the son of the Rosh.
TZADDIK/TZADDEKES: a righteous, pious man/woman.
TZAROS: troubles; anguish.
TZEDAKAH: charity.
TZENTER: (Y.) lit., "the tenth"; the tenth man needed to complete a MINYAN.
TZITZIS: ritual fringes worn by men on a four-cornered garment.
TZIYUN: tombstone, monument.

VASIKIN: the earliest morning prayer service, whose participants recite the SHEMONEH ESREH prayer at sunrise.

VIDUY: the confessional prayer.

YAHRTZEIT: (Y.) the anniversary of someone's death.

YATKE: (Y.) store.

YERUSHALMI: a Jew who lives in Jerusalem.

YESHIVA: an academy of Torah study.

YESHIVA GEDOLAH: a YESHIVA of higher learning, usually for boys after the age of 18.

YESHIVA KETANAH: a YESHIVA secondary school.

YESHUAH/YESHUOS: salvation.

YETZER HA-RA: the evil inclination.

YETZER HA-TOV: the good inclination.

YIDDISHE YINGEL: (Y.) a little Jewish boy.

YIDDISHKEIT: (Y.) Judaism.

YIRAS/YIREI SHAMAYIM: fear of/one who fears Heaven.

YISBARACH: May He be blessed (refers to God).

YISGADAL VE-YISKADASH SHEMEI RABBA: (A.) the first four words of the Kaddish prayer.

YM"SH: an acronym for *yemach shemam*, "May their name be erased."

YOM TOV: a Jewish Festival.

ZECHUS: merit (n.); privilege.

Z"L: an acronym for *zichrono liverachah*, "May his memory be for a blessing."

ZOCHEH: merit (v.).

ZT"L: an acronym for *zecher l'tzaddik liverachah*, "May the memory of a righteous person be for a blessing."

ZY"A: an acronym for *zechuso yagen aleinu*, "May his merit protect us."

ZYA"A: an acronym for *zechuso yagen aleinu, amen*, "May his merit protect us, amen."